SEX WORK

Writings by Women in the Sex Industry

Edited by Frédérique Delacoste
and Priscilla Alexander

Published in the United States by Cleis Press, P.O. Box 8933, Pittsburgh, Pennsylvania 15221, and P.O. Box 14684, San Francisco, California 94114. First Edition. 10 9 8 7 6 5 4 3 2

Cover Design: Pete Ivey
Typeset: Will Miner & his Wild Bats/CalGraphics

Printed in the United States.
ISBN: 0-939416-10-7 24.95 cloth ISBN: 0-939416-11-5 10.95 paper
Library of Congress Catalog Card Number: 86-72847

"she hated the rain" and "New York City Tonight" were first published in *Azalea*, Vol. I, No. 2, Spring 1978. Copyright 1977 by Sapphire.
"Lesbians & Prostitutes: A Historical Sisterhood" by Joan Nestle is excerpted from *A Restricted Country* (Firebrand 1987).
"Girls, Girls, Girls" by M.M. Chateauvert was first published in *Common Lives, Lesbian Lives*.
This book is available on tape to disabled women from the Womyn's Braille Press, P.O. Box 8475, Minneapolis, Minnesota 55408.

SEX WORK

Writings by Women in the Sex Industry

Acknowledgments

Our heartfelt thanks to all the people who helped create this book:
To the women whose words are the lifeblood of *Sex Work*; to
Margo St. James who made prostitutes' rights an issue in the United
States; to Sue Campbell and Felice Newman who cared for this
project and did a superb editing job;

To the Friends of Cleis Press — Marcie Barent, Paulette Balogh,
Cheri Kindler, Mary Ann Krupa, Rhonda Lazarus, Anita Mallinger,
Mike Powers and Anne Pride — who trusted this book before it even
existed, and who raised money to send it to the printer; and to the
Pittsburgh community, especially Leanna and Richard Day for their
enlightened support;

To Carole, Gina, Eva, Veronica Vera, Pieke Bierman, Bruce Tyler,
and the *Oldest Profession Times*, Helen McNamee for sharing
valuable information, and especially Judith Cohen for her help in
understanding AIDS;

To Brigitte Gluba, foreign correspondent and close supporter.

To Felice
>for her work
>her complexity
>her humor
>her unfailing honesty

and

To all the women who have ever worked

TABLE
OF CONTENTS

PART II: CONNECTIONS

PART III: UNITED WE STAND, DIVIDED WE DIE: SEX WORKERS ORGANIZED

INTRODUCTION

'Les Putes Sont En Grève...'

It was in 1975, on the 8:00 news, that I first heard prostitutes speak for themselves. A few brief sentences, from the St. Nivier church in Lyon, soon interrupted by the newsman: "And now, back to you in Paris." His smile was understood by millions. *"Les putes sont en grève..."* (*"The hookers are on strike."*) That was a good one. Chuckles at the dinner table, pass me some bread please, pour me some wine.

I had seen the *putes* many times before. As a child, with my father on our Sunday morning strolls in the streets of Paris, rue Blanche, rue Pigalle, La Madeleine...Years later, on my moped, my freedom, I discovered rue St. Denis: women in mini skirts walking nonchalantly, groups of three rapping over cigarettes; one had tall black leather boots, and a whip at her side. After I passed her on my *mobylette*, I wanted to turn back, but was afraid to be rude. I went back several times but never saw her again.

And then once, while waiting for my turntable to get fixed, I had an espresso in a small cafe, and I saw them, gathered around two small tables, slowly sipping their coffee, rubbing their hands — for it was a cold winter that year — talking like they knew each other well. I was sitting at the bar. *La patronne* was washing glasses and I could see her, them, me in the large mirror behind the counter. It was my first experience of a "women only" space.

Twenty years later, I feel as though I've turned the bar stool around and we are finally face to face.

When I first thought of this book, I looked for a sex worker or former sex worker to edit it. Our intent at Cleis Press is to publish books that document women's resistance on issues that have previously been either invisible or distorted by sexist ideology. We look for women editors and writers who are directly affected by these issues. "Understanding comes from listening to those who know how it feels," said a reviewer of one of our books.

And so, for two years, I contacted potential editors for *Sex Work*. No one came through, and I decided to edit the book myself. Gathering the writings for *Sex Work* has been an extraordinary process.

Calls for manuscripts first went out to city newspapers, feminist newspapers and magazines; to the WHISPER newsletter, U.S. PROS and other prostitutes' rights organizations; to individuals and to massage parlors. Priscilla Alexander, who was not yet co-editor, sent a personal letter along with our call for articles to many women on the COYOTE mailing list.

My intent was to provide space for women to write about their lives. I tended not to trust those who labeled *all* sex workers as victims, but I was open to all points of view as long as they came from working women themselves. A woman who works in the abolitionist movement in France said, "You will never get the real stories. The articles you receive will be written by cops and pimps." But I never doubted for a moment. You cannot make an ass drink if it is not thirsty (*On ne fait pas boire un ane qui n'a pas soif*), says an old French proverb. I hope this book brings the source closer to the many people who believe that sex workers cannot speak for themselves.

Most of the women who called to ask about the book, perhaps a bit nervous about what a feminist press might do with their writing, ended up sending articles. For many women, Priscilla Alexander's name was enough to inspire complete trust. Some just called to tell me how supportive they felt of the project. Their words may not appear here, but they all helped make this book.

During the project, Priscilla and I became friends. She shared her knowledge of prostitution; I shared some of my Sephardic recipes, and progressively *the* book became *our* book. We chose articles reflecting a diversity in the work and experience of the working women. It is with this in mind that we arranged the articles. In December 1986, Gail Pheterson came to San Francisco and helped us contact the women of the Red Thread and the Pink Thread who then submitted their articles. Because their work embodies a course for change, we feel that the example of the women in Holland is particularly useful. *Sex Work* will hopefully be a bridge between sex workers and the rest of the women's movement.

The book you are holding is made of trust. For some, it marks the beginning, for others the continuation of a potentially mighty alliance between all women.

The words are out. Who will listen?

Frédérique Delacoste
San Francisco, March 1987

Why This Book?

People often ask how I got involved in the prostitutes' rights movement, although they never ask how I got involved in the women's rights movement, or why I became a lesbian. I often think the question is euphemistic for "What's a nice girl like you doing here?" asked so often of women who work as prostitutes. Perhaps the question is an oblique way of asking if I am — or ever was — a prostitute. In any case, I never have literally worked as a prostitute — i.e., I never asked for, or received, money in direct exchange for sexual services — although I was stigmatized as a whore, at one time.

The first time I remember thinking about prostitution is when I was thirteen or fourteen years old. I read an article in the *New York Times Sunday Magazine* on New York's "revolving door" policy of arresting, booking, and fining prostitutes, and then letting them go. The author discussed the option of decriminalization. It made perfect sense to me then, and I have never seen any reason to change my mind.

I don't know if I thought of it much again until I entered Bennington College, at that time the only residential college in the United States without a curfew for women. (Bennington, primarily a women's college, was progressive and was intended to be a bastion of intellectual thought.) We could stay out all night if we wanted to, any night, as long as we "signed out" at the gate, stating where we were going, and giving phone numbers where we could be reached. Some evenings, we would dress in our best clothes and sit in the living room of our dormitory, playing four-way solitaire, and waiting for the fraternity brothers from nearby men's colleges to descend on our campus. If we were studying in our rooms, they would yell down the halls and up the stairs, "Anyone want a date?" And we would traipse down the stairs hoping to be selected.

Later, when I told anyone where I had gone to college, the questioner would respond in a knowing, leering way. After all, we were known as the "whores of the Northeast." When I moved to California, where no one knew about Bennington — or knew only that it was a liberal arts college — I heaved a sigh of relief. The subject did not come up again until 1970 when I was working as a teacher. A parent — male, of course — who was a member of our school's board of directors, asked me where I had gone to college. I told him, and he immediately responded, "What did you major in, fucking?"

All that sat in my brain, festering, until 1976. I had blossomed under the women's movement's light, reading everything I could get my hands on. I had read *Against Our Will*, in which Susan Brownmiller intimates that prostitution perpetuated the sexual objectification of women. I accepted it without much thought, although still I did not think prostitution should be a crime. In November, I met Margo St. James of COYOTE. The organization had some money, the proceeds from a Hookers' Ball, and she offered me a job as her secretary. Immediately, all of my experiences at Bennington began to come out of the fog where I had hidden them. I began to meet prostitutes, and by listening to them, I recognized a power that had seemed out of reach before. By the time the money ran out, six months later, I was committed to the struggle for prostitutes' rights, for my rights as a sexual being, and I have worked on this issue ever since.

My ideas about prostitution have changed in the years since then, largely as the result of talking with so many prostitutes. Early on, I remember being most impressed by the victimization of prostitutes. At times I have been overwhelmed by the relationship between childhood abuse and the lives of prostitutes, and have seen prostitution as a negative result of that abuse. After all, according to the traditional psychoanalytic point of view, prostitutes are labeled as masochists who see their bodies as commodities. But I began to see other ways of looking at it after many women told me that the first time they felt powerful was the first time they turned a trick.

I have come to see that prostitution is many things, and cannot be viewed from only one point of view. In that way, it is much like marriage. At one time, both were economic institutions; the only difference between a wife and a prostitute was that the prostitute was paid by many men and the wife by one. However, as "love" has come to dominate at least the decision to marry, and as serial monogamy has become the norm, money has become the main factor that distinguishes prostitution from marriage. In any case, prostitution, by definition, is the exchange of sexual services for money. Some prostitution is forced, and forced prostitution is clearly rape combined with kidnaping and perhaps brainwashing. At the other end of the spectrum, there are women who make a clear decision to work as prostitutes, a few because they enjoy sex and have no qualms about enjoying sex as work. Most women who work as prostitutes, I think, do so out of economic motives — the hourly pay is better than that paid for most of the work women are allowed to do. Some get to like the work as they become skilled at it. Other women hate it from the beginning to the end. And still others like some aspects of the job while hating parts of it.

There are terrible problems with prostitution, particularly when it is illegal. I have spoken to women who work for massage parlors and escort services who have been conned out their earnings. And they have no recourse — if they want to continue to work — because if they were to file a complaint, the business would be raided by the police. They could, I suppose, blackmail the dishonest employer, by filing pimping and pandering charges, which are felonies in this country. However, if they are illegal immigrants, for example, their employers could get them deported. If the prostitution laws were repealed and prostitution was recognized as legitimate work, prostitutes who are so victimized would be able to sue for the missing income.

Which brings me to the reason for this book. Prostitution will remain a crime in this country, and in other countries which criminalize it, so long as there is no identifiable voting bloc that clamors for changes in the law. As it stands now, horrible police abuses can be reported in the newspapers and be just as quickly forgotten. Prostitutes get scapegoated for AIDS and few people cry out. Prostitutes are murdered and the police tell no one until ten or more have been killed by one person. And even then, there is little outcry in the square world.

None of this will change, it seems to me, until prostitutes speak out in all of their varied voices. In this country, there are three main organizations that work specifically on prostitutes' rights. There are some significant differences between them. COYOTE (Call Off Your Old Tired Ethics), and its parent organizations, the National Task Force on Prostitution (NTFP) and the International Committee for Prostitutes' Rights (ICPR), work from the perspective that women have the right to determine, for themselves, how they will use their bodies, whether the issue is prostitution, abortion/reproductive rights, lesbian rights, or the right to be celibate and/or asexual. We believe that most of the problems associated with prostitution are directly related to the prohibition and the related stigma associated with sex and especially with sex work. While we consider the economic status of women to be a major factor in the amount of prostitution in the world, we do not think that economics is the only factor, nor do we believe that prostitution would disappear altogether if classism, and the closely related caste system of racism, disappeared. The overwhelming majority of COYOTE's active members and its sister organizations are prostitutes and ex-prostitutes, many of whom have made the decision to come out publicly in order to break down the stereotypes and myths which surround them. The NTFP sponsors an annual meeting in the United States where policies and strategies are discussed and voted on, and the ICPR holds similar meetings of women internationally.

The U.S. Prostitutes' Collective, and its related organization, the English Collective of Prostitutes, is affiliated with the international Wages for Housework Campaign. They see prostitution as primarily a class issue. They believe that poverty forces poor women to work in the sex industry. I read as a subtext in most of their writings a belief that prostitution should disappear, but only when women can earn enough to support themselves and their families without it. The active members of U.S. PROS and the English Collective of Prostitutes include prostitutes and non-prostitutes, although organizational policy asks that individuals not declare their status because of the potential risk of arrest and/or deportation.

WHISPER (Women Hurt In Systems of Prostitution Engaged in Revolt) believes that all prostitutes are victims, that no woman ever chooses to work as a prostitute, and that prostitution can only be understood as an institution created by patriarchy to control and abuse women. I believe that all the women who speak for WHISPER have actually worked as prostitutes, and many of them use pseudonyms to protect themselves.

All three organizations want the laws against prostitution *per se* repealed, although they disagree about how society should address the industry that surrounds prostitution, in particular, pimping and pandering or procuring.

The pieces in this book are in many different voices — voices of pain, voices of power, voices of hard work. The women who have contributed their spirits to this book write in poetry, in prose and in fiction. Some are members of COYOTE and its sister organizations; others are members of U.S. PROS and its sister organizations. And some are allied with WHISPER. Almost all of us worked in the industry at some time in our lives; a few of us have never literally done sexual work, although our lives were filled with allusions to it. All of us are united in wanting an end to the pain in women's lives, an end to abuse, an end to violence.

I hope this book helps the struggle along.

Priscilla Alexander
San Francisco, February 1987

Part I: IN THE LIFE

Telling a Woman/ Driving at Night

Carol Leigh

I tell a woman
what work I do for money
Don't you ever feel afraid?
She asks, staring into the headlights
through a curtain of long, brown hair
which obscures half her face
like Veronica Lake
Yes, I'm afraid
Sometimes I try not to feel afraid
Four months ago I was raped
I was afraid of being tortured or killed
I answer, driving my dark green Vega
wearing a turquoise angora sweater
dark red lipstick, new hairdo, good pants
I'm stronger, won't quit
and they're not going to stop me
She laughs and pushes the hair behind her ear
Bars of light drift upward, over our eyes

Living on the Edge

Peggy Morgan

Exotic dancer. A poised, well-dressed woman with the body of a fashion model, she exudes the kind of sexiness that has men dropping at her feet. She's somehow different from the rest of us, gracefully dancing her way through intricately choreographed shows to sultry bluesy music in glittery costumes. She drives fancy cars, wears expensive clothes, and off-hours, she hobnobs with smooth-mannered, wealthy underworld types.

Is this what you see when you think of a stripper? Take those surprised, quizzical looks I get when I tell people what I do: who, this short, chubby dyke, a *stripper*? Is she hiding some "exceptional" body under those faded jeans and old sweatshirts? What does she *do* with all her money? She lives in a dump and doesn't own a car — or even a television.

I've been stripping in Boston's Combat Zone for five and a half years, and I can tell you, it's not quite what you'd expect. Despite my college degree, and aspects of the job I find unpalatable, I'm quite comfortable with it and am in no great rush to change.

So, what is it like? For the most part, I've worked the 1:00 to 8:00 afternoon shift. The money's better at night, but the staff is rougher, customers drunker, and you're required to lay out a considerable amount of money for costumes. "Costumes" on the day shift are, for the most part, bargain basement lingerie or stripped-down street clothes: many dancers do their shows in just a blouse and underwear. "Show" is more euphemism than description. We do four sets (more or less, depending on how many dancers are working) of three songs each, which just involve walking back and forth along the rutted wooden runway with an occasional calculated wiggle or shimmy here and there.

But, then, dancing isn't the point of this business. In between shows, we are required to hustle seven dollar "ladies' drinks," for which we are paid a one dollar commission if we make or exceed the daily quota of twelve. Another dollar goes to the bartender, and five to the house.

Then, there's "dirty mixing." In the past, that included being able to hide away in a dark corner with a customer and turning a regular trick, but in the last year or two the vice squad has paid us frequent and unwelcome visits in an attempt to close down the Combat Zone, so we're pretty limited to hand jobs. Not that we can't get picked up on prostitution charges for that — it *has* happened — but it's easier to hide and cut off what we're doing if an undercover cop (most of whom we know by face, if not name) shows up.

The usual price (we call it a "tip") for a hand job is ten to twenty dollars, though sometimes we're paid more, above and beyond what the customer has spent on drinks. Naturally, the house doesn't want to lose out on the customer's money, so we're required to get a "bottle" if we're to "fool around." "Bottles" start at twenty-one dollars for a regular 12-oz. beer (three dollar commission for us) and thirty-five or fifty dollars for large mixed drinks (five- and seven-dollar commissions respectively).

Customers run the gamut — we get our share of weirdos, but most are perfectly normal guys. The differences between them lie in how they see and treat *us*. The best of them come into the bar knowing what it is they want — to get off — and what we want — money — and can pull the transaction off smoothly, making pleasant conversation and treating us with respect. In exchange for their money, they get a willing ear to listen to them, or in the case of hand jobs, a witness to the potency of their pricks, a reassurance that they are still powerful, real men.

But the macho, insecure types need more. On some level they know what a great equalizer prostitution is, and they aren't satisfied with a simple business transaction. Not only do we have to work at getting them off and making them feel good, but we have to put up with their clumsy, grubby hands pawing our bodies — *and* pretend to enjoy it. It's not that these customers really want to please a woman — most of the time these are the same ones who'll argue about money or make a fuss about having to pay up front. They simply want to feel power over the whore, who is by implication of her class and gender someone beneath them.

All told, I make about four hundred dollars a week between dancing, commissions and "tips." There are no benefits, no sick pay, vacation pay, overtime or insurance. Extra money can be made by meeting customers outside the bar on our own time for "dates" (tricks), but if you miss a day, you miss your pay.

Doesn't seem like the kind of job you'd find a politically aware lesbian in, does it? I was out of the closet as a lesbian and an ardent feminist for three years before a large debt in the middle of my senior year in college brought me into the Combat Zone. Stripping three days a week was the only way I could make ends meet, pay for school, pay off my debt and still continue my studies.

In those days, I remained carefully closeted at work, and outside, confused by both the cultural stigma of sex work and the apparently immutable feminist party-line that such work was degrading and oppressive to women, I kept my mouth shut.

Sure, some of it was difficult. The first time I did a hand job, I was paid forty dollars, went in the bathroom and threw up. I had never been shy about being naked, but since I've always been "overweight" by most people's standards, I was very sensitive to the occasional comment or jeer about my weight from a customer, and was convinced that anyone who declined to buy me a drink was refusing because I was too fat.

When I first started, I was afraid of most of the other dancers. They seemed very tough and street-wise, prone to fighting at the least provocation. Either they've gotten less tough over the years, or I am more used to it. Now I'm one of the oldest and have the most seniority, so I rarely run into any trouble — and then only if the other dancer is very drunk or high and I've unwittingly pushed one of her buttons.

Most know that I'm gay. I don't hide the fact, but I don't mention it often. The few women I can speak openly to about my life have either had relationships with women at one time or another, or have gay (usually male) friends outside. Still, they see no connection between telling queer jokes or insulting a customer by calling him a "faggot" and how I might feel about this. As far as they're concerned, I'm gay because I'm disgusted with men — which they can identify with — rather than because I prefer women.

There have been times when I've had to deal with one of the dancers going around telling my regular customers that I am a lesbian in an effort to take their business away from me. This infuriates me, and it's one of the reasons I don't talk about my private life at work very much. Some customers have refused to sit with me again, especially since a lot of hysterical misinformation about AIDS has found its way into the daily newspapers. On the other hand, I find it even more repulsive when customers are titillated by the distorted notions they have about my lifestyle.

There seems to be a myth on the outside that a disproportionate number of lesbians work in this business — which is pure bunk. In all the years I've been there, I've known only three other lesbians (one of whom I got the job for) and a handful of bisexual women who worked at the bar. There is no unity among us either; they seem very uncomfortable when I try to acknowledge our common ground. So I only offer occasional polite questions about their lovers or whether they've been to any of the gay bars lately.

Once in a while, I'll have a dancer come on to me — with the expectation that simply because I'm a lesbian I'm dying to jump her bones. Inevitably she's surprised and even insulted when I politely refuse her advances.

It's not worth trying to raise anybody's consciousness — I'm there to work and with all the booze and drugs flowing through the place, rhetoric will just go in one ear and out the other. The best I can do is just be myself and let my co-workers draw their own conclusions and hope they'll be positive.

Most of the dancers are straight, in their early twenties, and from poor or working class backgrounds. Some graduated from working the streets; a few still work for pimps. Many are single mothers working to supplement their meager welfare checks. Beyond meeting the basic necessities for food, clothing and shelter, working in the Combat Zone is the only way they can afford the symbols of success that society has dangled in front of them all of their lives: nice clothes, jewelry, cocaine, eating out in fancy restaurants. Compared to the alternatives — slinging hamburgers for minimum wage, assembly-line drudgery, or trying to subsist on paltry government subsidies — putting up with the groping hands of a few drunk men looks pretty good.

Ah yes. But *I'm* different: I come from a middle- class family, and I have a college degree. How often I hear: "You really could do better — why don't you find a *real* job?" What do people *really* mean when they set out to save me from this sordid business?

There are the assumptions that women who go into sex work are uncontrollably sexual, that it's something intrinsic to their nature, like a disease; and that poor and working class women are innately morally inferior and more sexual than the happy upper classes, who can "control themselves." Therefore it's okay for *them* to do this, but I really should be "above all that."

Well, let me tell you, the bottom line in this business is money.

Nobody — not myself, not the other women — enjoys being pawed, poked, prodded and fucked by men we wouldn't give the time of day if we met them elsewhere. The fact is, women still only make sixty-seven cents to every dollar men earn, and have to do twice as well to be thought half as good.

In my own experience with "square" jobs, I've put up with condescension and sexual harassment that either would take compli-cated grievance procedures to redress — with no guarantees — or was too "subtle" to confront without arousing accusations of oversensitiv-ity and craziness. Besides, I had to worry about being fired if it was discovered that I'm gay — all this for a wage I could not live on. I'm not stupid or lazy, but I never managed to hold down any other job for longer than six months. The fact is, there's a livable wage to be made in the sex business, and *we* decide when, where and with whom we'll do what. Money talks, bullshit walks, and we don't have to put up with anything we don't want.

Yes, we are more comfortable with our bodies and sexuality than most people. Taking our clothes off in public, we realize there is nothing sacred or secret about our bodies. We don't have "private parts," dismembered from the rest; they are parts of the whole. Having a customer fondle a breast, for instance, may not be pleasant, especially if he's rough, but it doesn't feel like being violated. It's part of a job, and really no different than if he touched an elbow. It's not sexual; it's *work*. Using our whole bodies to earn a living makes it clear how much sexual feelings really come from our minds: a lover may touch the same way a customer does, but produce an entirely different feeling.

Over the past two years, I've cautiously come out in the women's community as a stripper. This was made easier by the fact that some women had begun to talk and write about sexuality openly and honestly. Not surprisingly, the debates over pornography, butch/femme and s/m have erupted into roaring controversies, with those on the exploring-sexuality side denounced as being brainwashed and as oppressing other women. We are split into good girls and bad girls — just like society's Good Women and Whores. Only this time the fears of moral inferiority and uncontrollable sexuality are couched in feminist political language.

Confusing autonomous sexual explorations (like s/m and butch/femme *playing*) with acts of real violence, and limiting, prescribed male/female roles is like confusing the prostitute with prostitution. A prostitute can't very well tell a trick the truth: "I really just want your money — I don't want to touch you or have you touch me," if she's to have any business. But she also knows that what she does for money is not an expression of her own sexuality. It may look like sex but it sure doesn't feel like anything she does with lovers. In the same way, for example, the whips, chains and role-playing of s/m don't mean a desire to hurt anyone, but rather a desire to explore intense feelings of power, trust and vulnerability in a sexual context.

Society decrees sex a moral issue — especially for women. Beneath this facade, we find that this is really a political tool, designed to maintain the social order. We're immediately put into the "loose," immoral camp if we admit to a desire for women, or an interest in multiple sexual partners, playing with physical restraint, costumes or gender roles — in short, anything that strays too far from the notion that women don't want sex for any reason other than to please and serve men.

Conversely, a desire for celibacy is laughed off as "frigidity" rather than respected as a choice; lesbians are ridiculed as weird creatures unable to "get a man." It's no accident that the number one male fantasy is of a woman dying to suck his cock. The penis is man's symbol of his power and superiority, the one proof that he is different from woman, and his justification for dominating her.

But he's insecure about this supposedly God-given superiority; he knows he *needs* women, at very least, for the survival of the species. In order to survive this conflict, he splits women into two kinds: Good Women, who don't desire sex for themselves, who, at the extreme, only submit to his desires when absolutely necessary for procreation; and Bad Girls, whores, whose function is to reassure him, through worshipping his penis, that he really *is* superior.

This may seem like an extreme description of male-female relations in this day and age. We may argue that we have nice, comfortable, equal relationships with our men, or that, by virtue of being lesbian, we've escaped those dynamics entirely. But think of the way successful women are accused of "sleeping their way to the top"; or how independent women are branded either "loose" or "man-hating dykes." We've so internalized these messages that we still see the body as a sacred temple, untouchable and pure and divorced from the mind; and the flip side, seeing strippers and prostitutes as out of control of their sexuality, mere yardsticks to measure our own normalcy against. Thus we still *live* the Good Woman/Bad Girl split.

We're really out of control of our sexuality when we see our desires as dirty and troublesome, keeping them hidden and separate from the rest of our lives. This leaves us open to being controlled from the outside — letting others (especially men) convince us that we really want what they want us to want.

In January of 1986, I helped produce and performed in a lesbian-only strip show in Boston. For me, that was the culmination of several months of openly playing with sexuality: wearing leather or lacy, revealing clothes to parties, sleeping with a number of different women — and a couple of men (friends, not tricks!) — and exploring butch/femme roles. There were consequences. Some women couldn't get past seeing me as The Stripper or the blonde bombshell. Others projected their own ambivalences about sexuality onto me, intimating that I was carrying this too far.

The night of the strip show, a lot of issues that had been on my mind for years came together. Women of all different sizes, from quite small to quite large, performed. Rather than having the acts restricted to the high-heels-and-make-up monotony of straight male porn, the shows included everything from tough leather butch to wholesome body-building poses to lacy feminine cross-dressing. Above all, while we were performing and *playing* with parts of our sexualities, we were still being ourselves. We were there for one reason only: to have fun, sexy fun, on our own terms, and so was the audience. Unlike the Combat Zone, where men come primarily to reassure themselves that they are still men, rulers of the universe, the women in the audience were warm and supportive, and really got into it, without losing sight of the fact that we were whole people and not just bodies on display. Even feminism has told us to be wary and not trust images that turn us on, so it was wonderful to take stripping, or at least what I like about it, out of the context of work and do it in a safe, friendly atmosphere where I could be myself.

That night I got a sense of what it would be like if we all really had the freedom to be sexual as we chose, unhampered by proscriptions, expectations, or the economic need to pretend other than what we feel.

Peggy Morgan is not my real name. I don't have the luxury of using my real name, given the source of my livelihood for the past five and a half years. I'm not so naive as to think that I wouldn't have future troubles with jobs, housing, or if I chose to have children. There are enough closed-minded zealots, threatened by my existence, who'd be only too glad to use it against me.

I am not ashamed of who I am and what I do — lesbian and stripper — and can't wait until the day when it will be safe to use my real name. In the words of the tune I've adopted as my theme song at work, the theme from *La Cage aux Folles*, "I am what I am":

"I am what I am, and what I am needs no excuses,
I deal my own deck, sometimes the ace, sometimes the
   deuces
It's one life and there's no return and no deposit
One life so it's time to open up the closet
Life's not worth a damn till you can shout out
'I am what I am.' "

Out in the Cold

Jean Johnston

It is cold, a bare barren cold. The street is empty except for the fire and us "girls." We are the women waiting for work on the fringe of the park. Waiting near the fire which we built. Waiting for the warmth of a car, or maybe half an hour in a hotel room. Arctic air slices through my tight jeans and burns. I want to reach down and touch my legs so I can feel them, but it's too cold to take my gloved hands from my pockets.

Cherry is standing close by, staring at the fire. I put my arm in hers and pull her closer to the fire and to me. I don't have to worry that her man will see. He's sitting on the other side of the park in his green Cadillac. His car is probably turned on to keep him warm. Cherry once told me she met Tredwell when she was sixteen. "He had a yellow Cadillac then. And he had on a yellow suit with matching shoes." She comes from a small town in Ohio and when she looked out the window and saw Tredwell for the first time she said, "Mama, a movie star. There's a movie star downstairs!" Well, her mama knew all about Tredwell, but that didn't stop her baby from running off with him. Another time Cherry told me that she asked him what he was going to do when she got too old to work. He said he'd buy her a candy store or something like that. Maybe in Queens, that's where they live.

The fire starts to die down. Kim and Desi go into the park looking for some firewood. Cherry and I cross the street as winds whip into our flesh, through to the bone. On top of some garbage cans we find the Sunday News. I hear a clanging sound and we grab the paper fast, running to the other side of the street. Behind us I hear rats scatter, but tell myself it's only the wind.

Desi runs down the street toward us, pavement hitting high heels. She has a table leg and throws it into the fire. I feel my face burning.

"Where's Kim?"

"She gotta date."

From under a brown suede cowboy hat Desi stares into the rising flames. Desi doesn't have a man. She's thinking about Lana, her woman. Desi doesn't want Lana working out here. One time Lana got stabbed by a trick on 12th Avenue. He stabbed her all over her arms and chest, then left her by the Hudson River to die. She almost did. So, now Desi works here to support Lana's kid who lives with her aunt in Brooklyn.

She throws more paper into the fire and I push it with a broomstick. The winds are blowing the fire toward her. She moves closer to Cherry and me.

A car turns the corner and Kim gets out of a tan Toyota. She's five months pregnant, but it doesn't show yet.

"How'd ya do?"

"Shit. There ain't no money out here tonight baby. It's too cold."

"Yeah, only ho's and fools out tonight."

Kim is nineteen. Her mother turned her out, five years ago, when she was fourteen. Her mother used to work out here, too, until she O.D.'ed on junk last year. They had the same man, Ronnie. He has an after hours club uptown. I go there sometimes after a good night, blow some coke and dance.

Another car is coming down the street. It slows up when it reaches the spot where we're standing.

"Wanna date honey?"

"You goin' out?"

Without even opening his window to answer, the guy in the black Impala nods and motions for me. I get in the car and he pulls off. He doesn't want to spring for a hotel, and parks under the Manhattan Bridge. The radio is playing. It's 4:00 a.m. The wind chill is 30 degrees below zero. This guy's going to get his money's worth because I'm not in any hurry to get back outside.

He comes.

Back on the street Cherry is alone crying by the spot where the fire has been.

"What's the matter, honey?"

"I'm freezing and Tredwell says I can't go home until I get a hundred dollars more."

"You wanna come home with me?" Wiping away her tears she shakes her head.

I took her home with me once, but Tredwell came looking for her. He told me, "You think you's a man, bitch. Running off with my ho like this." Then he took Cherry home and gave her a beating.

"Cherry, honey, I'm gonna go. You sure you won't come with me?" She shakes her head again.

Downstairs, the subway platform is as barren as the street above, but it's warmer. I think about Cherry, still out there in the cold. I feel helpless. The feeling fades as I count the money from under my wig. I put fifty dollars into my pocket and slip the rest back under my wig.

I ride the F train for two stops, reaching the street as dawn is breaking. I meet my man — the only man I really have — he's selling little cellophane bags of white powder fastened with red tape. I hand him fifty bucks for five bags, and tucking them into my glove, I walk away.

The Continuing Saga
of Scarlot Harlot I

Carol Leigh

Are you one of the insatiable millions — those who are curious about most aspects of the prostitute's existence: our loves, our traumas, our sexual habits and our finances?

Perhaps you've imagined yourself a sex professional, offering the most exotic pleasures to a wealthy, mysterious and sex-starved clientele. Have you envisioned dinners atop the Saint Francis, or in the dungeons of L'Etoile, dressed in a sexy elegance fit for the Academy Awards? Well, that describes my life.

(Just kidding.)

Perhaps you've envisioned yourself poised tough in the Tenderloin amidst needles and panties, a fate you strive to avoid by paying your rent on time, and your telephone bill, and by moderate use of the plastic. The abuse of plastic credit cards has been the ruin of many a poor girl. God, I know.

And you, sir?

Unloved and unlaid in weeks, months, even years? You may have imagined yourself "taking a walk and buying some," or procuring the services of an elegant courtesan, fresh off the pages of *Hustler*.

"But how will I get her phone number?" you ask. Will she lay like a lump, give me a disease? Will she steal my money? Will she fake it?

Wonder and worry no more! Here it is! All the information you probably want about the *fille de joie*, snuggling up to your eyeballs in the persona of Scarlot Harlot. That's me. Of course, I am a prostitute.

If you've been following my saga, you know that, though I strive to divorce myself from the stereotype of the Sorry Slut, that image insinuates itself into my life like a commercial for my oppression.

***

When last we left Scarlot, she was recuperating from a short affair with a poet/actor who stole her savings, then began threatening her on the telephone, demanding more money and sex.

"He wanted to be my pimp," she explained. "My girlfriends said they'd beat me up and never talk to me again if I went along with him. Of course, I told him where to shove it and in what position. And I know plenty of them because of my experience."

"Prostitution is a crash course in assertiveness training," says A. I'm learning, and A, the toughest of the prostitutes, is a fine teacher.

Memories of rape. Fear of rape. Frightened and haunted, Scarlot raved, "How can we protect ourselves from the pimps and rapists when we're so busy protecting ourselves from the police? I give up. I hate this fate."

Scarlot withdrew. Agoraphobia, fear of the marketplace, possessed her.

She vowed to remain in her luxurious cell, depending only on her telephone for business and companionship. No more personal lovers. Clients must present solid references. Scarlot became one of the vast number of ivory tower prostitutes; these serious women who pass their time painting, writing, watching television, reading best-sellers and pop psychology and waiting, waiting, waiting for the phone to ring...

Brrrring...Brrrring...Brrrring...

This better be money.

"Hi, Scarlot. Listen, I need your help." It was N, a friend and member of Scarlot's sex workers' support group. Her voice was plaintive.

N was only twenty-four. She'd worked as a prostitute for several years. Recently, she decided to go straight. Now she's a secretary. She plans to get married and pregnant. "I'm entering the Big Beautiful Women Beauty Contest. They want me to send in a list of my accomplishments. What can I say? I'm an expert in fellatio? I worked the streets and now I.."

"You worked the streets? I didn't know you worked the streets." I was impressed. And, yes, this did sound like a job for Scarlot Harlot.

"Yeah, well, I only did it a couple times. Last time was when me and T went down to the 'Loin. It was T's first time. 'Ya gotta get in the car with the guy,' I told her. 'How else are ya gonna do it?' But T was too stupid. This dude pointed her out, but she ran away. So I climbed in his van. I don't think he was into it. I had to force him. He got off okay. After that, I had it with the streets. It was too rugged. I moved my ass back into a massage parlor."

"That was an accomplishment," I said, trying to be helpful.

"Yeah, but not for a beauty contest," she moaned.

"I guess not, but you were a great whore."

"Thanks, Scarlot."

"Well, it isn't fair! We should be proud! No one understands or respects us. I hate this secrecy and isolation."

"That's the way it blows, honey. Hey, I'll just say I'm a social worker."

"Or an actress. We need status as actresses!"

"Thanks, Scarlot."

Not Huarachas in Paris

Phyllis Luman Metal

I met him under the Eiffel tower at noon. We had planned it that way. He was tall, high yellow, a great jazz musician with a somber intensity about him. I had helped him escape to Paris to re-do his life, find appreciation for his music, and forget the insults America had heaped upon him and his people. I was in love with him, so much so that I had left my family behind — feeling guilty, knowing I would return, but grabbing these few delicious moments in Paris. It was June. I was a middle aged hippy wearing huarachas, a long Indian skirt and an embroidered Mexican blouse. "Not huarachas in Paris!" he had exclaimed when he saw me. "Couldn't you just glance at a *Vogue* to see what was *a la mode*?" We laughed. "How much money did you bring?" I said three hundred dollars. "Oh my God. That is what we have to live on in the most expensive city in the world, and I will die on these cobblestones before I go back to America."

It had taken all my money to get us both there. I was a potter, and I had sold every pot I had. We both sat down and laughed.

Needless to say the three hundred went very fast, even living on the top floor of a hotel where all the young backpackers visiting Europe stayed. I started going to the Krishna temple to eat and to bring food home for him. We moved to a less expensive hotel in the Arab quarter. On the street were the "girls," still as statues wearing minis up to their crotches. And then at last we had no money to pay the concierge. She said, ". . .*argent? argent?*" as we ducked past her. My love went every night to sit with the French jazz musicians at the River Bop. I went along to hear him play. But finally we knew the day had come. Something had to be done or we would be walking the streets and sleeping by the Seine.

Every afternoon when I came out of the Krishna temple off Avenue Foche, cars would pull along side me and stop and I would quickly walk on. It finally dawned on me what the well-dressed women on the corners and strolling up and down Avenue Foch were doing. When the limousines pulled alongside they climbed in and were driven away. And so, on an afternoon when the concierge had threatened to call the police, I decided. I would enter one of those limousines and take my chances. And I did. The driver spoke no English but my French had come back to me by now...

I explained to Monsieur that I was an American. He looked amused. He was bald and I was fifty-five. I was still wearing my Indian skirt, peasant blouse and huarachas. I looked like no other hooker he had ever seen. He drove to a small building with an inconspicuous sign in front, *hotel*. He assisted me out of the car and we entered. A madame was seated behind a Dutch door. She asked, *"Pour la nuit or pour un moment?"* And it was for a moment. Monsieur paid her, and a maid in uniform led us upstairs. She opened a door and ushered us into a room with a red carpet and mirrors on all the walls and ceiling and a crystal chandelier. She turned down the bed, checked the bathroom to be sure there was mouthwash, deodorant and cologne. Monsieur tipped her and she left. He opened his briefcase, which I assumed was filled with important papers. Instead, he pulled out a black lacy garter belt, black silk stockings and a black bra. "For me?" I asked. He shook his head. He undressed and put them on. "Don't laugh," he said. "Oh, no, I think you look adorable," I said. He handed me a French porno comic book and told me to read, and then he ate me up, and fucked me. We had a very good time. We played like two children. Finally, he checked his watch and said it was time to go home for dinner and a romp with the children. He laid three hundred francs on the bureau and said he would look for me next week. I found out the girls at Saint Denis in the Arab quarter only made twenty-five francs per trick.

I was working where all the millionaires looked for girls. I took the money back to the City Hotel on Rue Meslay where my love was practicing. I told him what had happened. He said, "Oh my God, you didn't!" But I did, I said. "Well I was a pimp once upon a time so I will educate you." And he did. "We have gone full circle," he said, "from friends to lovers, to now whore and pimp. We have done it all." And the next afternoon found me on the stroll on Avenue Foch in front of Onassis' mansion, and another monsieur opened his limousine door for me. From then on I had a regular job. My love went down beside the River Seine to practice his jazz flute and I went to Avenue Foch to find a gentleman with a limousine who would take me to a *maison de rendezvous*, as the little buildings discreetly marked *hotel* were called.

Triple Treat

Rev. Kellie Everts

Samara is twenty-six years old, and a veteran of live sex shows. Rev. Kellie Everts interviewed Samara about her life in the business.

I started in this business at eighteen. I worked in a whorehouse, but not as a whore. I worked in the front office over on Forty-fifth Street, across from the Peppermint Lounge. I used to make five hundred dollars a week, but I got fired because of this lady who worked there and became jealous of me. I made a lot of money, but didn't save any.

After that I became a waitress, making seventy-five dollars every two weeks. But the welfare found out I had a job and took my money away. I simply could not support myself, my mother and my baby. This girl told me, "I know a job you can do, but you got to take off your clothes." I've never had a hang up about my body, so I said, "Let's go." We both went. They hired us on the spot, at Peepland.

I've worked in a lot of clubs. Once, I went to a bar to dance and the owner said he couldn't give me a job unless I gave him a blow job once a week. I told him I was just there to work, and so he said he couldn't use me. Some clubs did not want to hire me because I was black or because I looked young; I look like a baby, like I'm sixteen or seventeen. Some like black girls, but black girls who have either big tits or light skin, who tend to look more like Puerto Ricans.

Then somebody told me about the Triple Treat, and the guy who auditioned me suggested simulated sex shows. My boyfriend didn't like it, but I told him, "You're not giving me any money; I'm going to do what I have to do." I tried to keep a relationship with him because he was the baby's father. I danced for a year and did lesbian shows. I worked with men, too, but I got busted three times. And we were only simulating. I got sick and tired of getting busted.

I went to Show World and built up a pretty good name for myself. I had my name up there in lights. I did acts with black girls, white girls. People started to think I was a lesbian, but I wasn't. Working with the girls is easier because you go up on stage and play. Some people go up there and do the real thing, but to me it is a game. Play with one tit, play with the other tit. She does the same thing to you. You can both dance, or take turns dancing. If you're really into it, I guess you eat each other out.

Working with men is a strain because you've got to get them hard, even if you don't do the real thing. Nobody wants to sit there and see a man and a woman fumbling, because that's what they do at home. They want to get ideas, go home and try new things. They think we're getting quality money, but we're only getting three hundred or four hundred dollars a week for forty-two shows, six shows a day, seven days a week.

This business has been good to me. I have learned a lot since I was eighteen, and I've met a lot of nice people, all kinds of gay people, transsexuals, transvestites, and I look at everybody as normal. We're all doing the same thing and we shouldn't look down on one another.

The only danger is getting into drugs. One of my girlfriends got into drugs. She was so beautiful, black, light skinned, big tits. She started to shoot up. I took her aside and talked to her, got her some help. I was the only person who tried to help her.

I've never been raped though I've been around a lot alone since I was eighteen. I mean those places, like way out in Connecticut where if you don't catch your train or bus you sit alone on a bench all night. I've been scared and carried mace and knives, but no one has ever bothered me.

I've only had two boyfriends and I could never come with just their cock in me. The men climax almost every time. My first partner used to hold back at the beginning, but after a while he didn't care. The one I go with now tries to hold back and tries to make me come. You know that thing about, "Are you coming, are you coming?" It gets to be a real strain. Me, I like to be kissed more, to be hugged. I like to be affectionate all day, kiss, hug, almost every minute. This to me is better than coming.

At work, I don't let myself get emotionally involved. I know that if I let myself get involved, I will have problems. I just do the job, get dressed and go home.

When I go out there, I'm putting on an act. I'm not getting no rocks off, believe me. In all my years of working, I've never come on stage, with a girl, with a guy, or with myself. When I go out there, it's just like putting on a business suit and going downtown to work.

What Happens When You Are Arrested

Gloria Lockett

When I was working on the street in Hollywood, the Los Angeles Police Department would round up a group of prostitutes. Before they would put us in the police car, they would take our purses, dump them on the ground, and make us pick the things out of the gutter. When they decided who was going to jail, looks were a big factor. The police would take the hands of the women who were not going to jail, and they would burn them on the hood of the engine. The women who were going to jail were piled in the back seat, usually six, seven or eight women. The police would drive us around for an hour or so, handcuffed, with people sitting on us. One time, the car was so crowded, one officer made me sit on his lap, handcuffed.

In Hollywood, the police arrested me for "obstructing justice" when I warned another prostitute of his presence. Both of my arms were almost broken when he picked me up by the handcuffs and threw me into the back of a pickup truck, which was the vehicle he and his partner used when trying to arrest prostitutes.

The first time Deborah got arrested, she was handcuffed behind. The officer was drunk and tried to kiss her and fondled her breast and body in the elevator of the hotel.

In San Jose, the police drive you around and leave you off in dark areas.

In Las Vegas, the police almost broke Deborah's arm when they arrested her.

In Berkeley, when the police used to drive us around in their cars for hours, one officer pulled into a very dark alley and demanded a blow job.

In Hollywood, a police officer who had responded to an ad in the paper (by that time we had stopped working on the street) came to our house in a car without a license plate. He pulled out his handcuffs so he could handcuff me to the bed and have intercourse with me. Luckily, I ran away.

I have been arrested thirty or forty times, who's keeping count? I've never done any time, but I have had to take cases all the way to jury trial at least nine times. In California, there is a mandatory thirty-day sentence for the second arrest, forty-five days for the third. The police make you think you will lose if you go to trial, so most women plead guilty and do the time.

The Continuing Saga
of Scarlot Harlot II

Carol Leigh

I provide sexual service to a handful of clients, most of whom I've
known for at least a year. I trust these married businessmen. I know
their real names and I have their phone numbers at work. They tell
me they love me or like me so much. They pay what I ask and they
leave when their time is up. I trust them. I need to trust them.

"You're crazy, girl! Don't let your guard down. Men have a bad
attitude towards women. Especially working girls. Fucking us over is
a game for them. Why do you think they call 'em tricks?"

"No, no, no! I can't be that suspicious!"

But it's worth it. I only have to work a couple hours a week. The
rest of my time I spend at the typewriter, complaining and bragging
about my life. I stay home a lot. I entertain myself. At night I pick up
my guitar and sing:

"My life was so boring, Til I started whoring..."

Pretty funny, huh? Oh, forget it! I'm being facetious, sarcastic,
sardonic. I'm miserable. I hate this fate. I made those changes in my
life, but I can't go on living in fear and isolation. I can't. If only...If
only the streets were safe...If only women were not haunted by
submissive images. I remain home and depend on my telephone.

And what of telephones? Oh, those twisted umbilical cords! I have
three obscene phone callers — two of whom don't seem to know that
I'm a prostitute because they don't mention it. Many women are
plagued by this phenomenon. We restrict ourselves to listing first
initials in the phone book rather than our full names, because there is
an army of men out there who use the telephone book as a map. They
choose their targets, call and attack.

If only we weren't haunted by these invasions...If only we could protect ourselves. If only we could choose to be sexual whenever and with whomever we want...if only...

...I give up. Wait a minute...what a great idea! Yes, I will stay home. So far I have rearranged my life to protect myself from the evils of this world. What I should do is formulate a plan to rearrange the world and make it safe and fair. Perfect! I can't wait. This useful endeavor will certainly keep me occupied as I pass the time in my luxurious cell.

The Birth of Scarlot Harlotism

I will begin by reorganizing our nation's economic structure.

1. Prostitution is too rampant. Most of us are forced by economic need to share this deep intimacy. About half the prostitutes I know are mothers who support their families. My solution: Ronald Reagan and Congress will arrange to pay mothers decent salaries for child-raising. This will eliminate about half the prostitution. The remaining prostitutes will make more money. Everyone will be happy.

2. In general, all the boring, dangerous and unpopular jobs will pay more than the interesting, popular jobs. That will improve most people's lives.

I have a lot of ideas. I'll write them down and organize a comprehensive plan. And when I've completed this manifesto, then I will...

Hong Kong Massage

Emma Marcus

A well dressed Frenchman in his fifties came in. He wore a hand tailored linen suit and sported a handkerchief in his lapel. He said he was a physician so I thought he was going to be worth a lot, but after paying the twenty he had only fifty dollars left. I offered him a hand job and then a blow job, but he insisted that he only wanted sex, which meant fucking. It was getting late in the day and fifty was better than nothing. He counted out the money and had four extra dollars, so I took that, too.

I undressed and he grabbed my breasts and kissed me. Our lips locked, his hands were working away and we knelt down on the mattress. I offered him a rubber, but he brushed it away in contempt.

"Are you clean?" he asked.

"Yes, are you?"

"Of course," he replied indignantly.

I lay back and he pulled my ankles up. He lifted one of my legs over his shoulder and put it in. He stroked a few times, rotating his hips in little circles.

"Lick me here," he demanded, gesturing under his arm.

"Under your arm?" I asked incredulously.

"My nipple," he said crossly. "Bite it. Hard. Harder!"

I bit his nipple as hard as I could and as he came he let out a little cry.

"Did you come?" he asked.

"No, of course not. Women don't come like that." I got up and began to dress.

"What's this?" he asked. He was staring at his cock with alarm.

"Probably blood. I'm menstruating."

"But you shouldn't have! How could you? I'll get a disease," he shrieked.

"What? No, it's just menstrual blood. Listen," I said, getting angry, "you were the one who didn't want to use a rubber."

He was holding his cock away from his body as though it were a bomb that might explode. "The microbes, they travel through the blood," he said. "I must wash immediately. Where's the bathroom?"

"Down the hall on the right. Really, it's nothing."

He was still holding his cock away from his body. With his free hand he grabbed a towel and held it in front of himself like a shield. I opened the door for him and he ran absurdly down the hall.

I finished dressing and hoped that he wasn't going to make a scene when he came back. I didn't want the other women to know that I'd fucked him without a rubber. "You must never do that again," he announced as he stepped back into the room. "Never, never! I'm going back to the hotel now. I have some penicillin ointment in my suitcase and I'll put it on immediately. I'm a physician and I know about these things, so I'm sure it will be all right. But you must never do that again," he said. "Never, never. Do you understand?"

"Okay, yes," I agreed, to pacify him.

"It's very dangerous."

I doubted it, but I wasn't going to argue with this relic of archaic science. "I hope you don't get too bad a case of it," I said, pulling the sheet off the mattress. "The penicillin will probably take care of it if you put it on soon. Just make sure you put a lot of it on." His eyes, registering alarm, suddenly disappeared behind the hugely billowing white sheet I had snapped into the air.

**

Candy and I were playing Scrabble on Friday morning while Lili and Susie watched television. Kim was with one of her regulars, who'd brought her two dozen pink roses, as well as paying her, I imagined, a good tip. "How does Kim do it?" I asked. "They're all crazy about her."

"It's because she hates sex," Candy answered. "It turns them on." Kim was always complaining about how this one was too big for her or that one took too long.

"She does have beautiful breasts, though," I said.

"She had an operation on them," Susie said. "I did a guy who said her boobs were hard, like a shoe. A facelift, too. You know she's thirty-nine years old and all that stuff about just doing this to make money for her mother. . .it's bullshit. She's been doing it for years, since she was a teenager in Korea."

It was Candy's turn to answer the door and the guy, a heavy set man with a cruel face, said he wanted her, but she wouldn't do him. She was sick of the work, she'd told me. And she'd been refusing to do anybody she didn't like. Consequently, she wasn't making very much money. And what she did make she'd spend immediately after work, buying clothes that she'd later discover didn't fit right. I'd gone shopping with her one day after work and she'd bought an expensive and beautiful Chinese lamp for her bedroom and then had accidentally left it on the bus going home. It seemed like a symptom of something.

The man didn't look so bad to me so I smiled a big one at him. "Would you like a massage today," I cooed.

"Well, I'd like her," he said, gesturing at Candy.

"I'm busy," she said, not looking up from the letters she was rearranging.

"I'll give you a real nice massage," I told him.

"Okay, I'll take you," he said, pointing at me. I asked him for the twenty and he went to take a shower.

"I don't like him," Lili said.

"Why not? What's wrong with him?" I asked.

"He'll want you to talk dirty," Candy said, still not looking up from her letters.

"Oh, that sounds all right. Sort of interesting. Lili, what do I say?" I asked.

"Cunt, pussy, dick, cock."

"Fuck me with your huge dick," Susie sighed and pretended to swoon.

"I want that hot throbbing dick in my mouth," Candy said, laughing a little hysterically.

"He pay good though," Lili said.

"How much?"

"Eighty. And then he'll want someone else. He always does. He want two girls."

"Do a bad job," Susie said. "He'll want you to suck his cock, but just jerk him off. 'Oh, yeah, in a minute, in a minute,' you say, 'I'll suck it real good for you.' But just do this," she said, gesturing like a bartender shaking a drink. "You'll have your eighty anyway. Just make sure you get the money first."

"Yeah, I always do," I told her. Susie was known for being a good hustler, which meant that she could get a lot of money out of them without giving them very much sex. Carol had done a double with her once and described to me how Susie had put on a performance like she was really hot for the guy, but insisted, "Oh, sweetheart, if you want to see my other breast it's got to be thirty dollars more." Hustling wasn't my style, though. I liked it when they appreciated the good job I did for them.

He was sitting naked on the massage table when I walked in. His chest was covered in dark, fur-like hair and he was swinging his legs back and forth. "I want a real light massage," he told me, "like something crawling on me."

I tickled him back and front and he arched his back in excitement and slid his buttocks back and forth. He reached his hand around my head and pulled it towards him to kiss me, but I turned my head so he caught me on the ear. He let go of my head. "Do you suck cock?" he sneered at me.

"Well, we have some business to take care of first."

"Okay, how much?"

"Eighty."

"I want to come in your mouth."

"Not for eighty."

"How much then?"

"Forty more."

"I'll give you forty more. I don't care about the money. But after I come in your mouth, I'm going to kiss you and drink it."

"Okay," I said. He drew several bills out of his pocket and I noticed that one of his hands was deformed, a paw with only two stubby fingers and a thumb. With it he handed me six twenties, spread out like a small green fan.

"Do you like to talk dirty?"

"Sure," I ventured. "But I don't know what to say."

"You like to suck cock?"

"Uh, yeah."

"You make love with women?"

"I've done that."

"You like it?"

"Yes."

"You come?"

"Yes."

"Use a dildo?"

"No."

"What then?"

"Tongue."

"Like this?" he asked, grabbing me at the waist and going for my crotch.

46

"No, no." I pushed him away. I didn't want him to touch me. "No, here, I'll do you. Let me suck that delicious cock for you," my embarrassment finally dropped in favor of saving myself something worse than his dismal, probing questions.

He had a little, curved doggie cock and small, tight balls. I pushed him back onto the table and licked his erection. "Umm, what a luscious prick," I said, circling the head with my tongue.

"Suck it, baby, suck that big mother. Oh yeah, you must have sucked a lot of cock to have learned to suck a man's cock like that. Go on, baby. Lick that dick."

I pulled my head up and began masturbating him with my hand.

"You must have sucked a lot of cock to get so good. You suck a lot of cock?"

"Yeah, I've sucked some," I said, without much enthusiasm. "Look, why don't you jerk yourself off a little and then I'll suck you at the end," I proposed. He agreed, asking me to lie on the mattress so he could stand over me. His big belly obstructed any view of his face. I sucked him off at the end and he kissed me afterwards like we'd arranged and I spit the stuff back into his mouth.

I hadn't liked the guy, but he seemed like an easy hundred and twenty. I smoked a cigarette while he finished dressing. He was an accountant, he said. His wife had died in a "tragic accident" six years ago. That's why he came here, he said.

Candy said that he came back later in the day and she'd agreed to do him. He'd wanted to come in her mouth and had insulted her when she wouldn't let him. "I could have fourteen year old girls in Mexico do it for five dollars," he'd said. Susie was mad at me, saying he'd given Candy trouble because of me. "It's disgusting to take it in your mouth," she'd complained to me. "It spoils them if you let them do things like that and it's no good for the rest of us. Ugh, how can you let them spew that stuff into your mouth. . .you'll get sick."

"I didn't swallow it," I answered, apologetically.

I wondered later on if it was true about his wife. It happened a lot lately, not knowing if people were telling the truth. Like Lili's description of Kim; was it true she had worked in Korea? She seemed very professional, as if she were experienced, but she had been nice to me and I didn't want to think she was a liar.

First one of Kim's regulars came in. Susie got picked after that. Kim came back and showed us an opal and gold ring the man had given her. "I wonder how much it cost," I said. "He's so nice to me, a real gentleman," Kim said, proudly smoothing down an imaginary wrinkle on her skirt. I wished that some man would give me jewelry.

It was my turn next. Kim went to the door and let him in for me.

"He look nice," she told me. "He go take a shower. You go in room in five, ten minutes."

I went to the bathroom to get ready. When I came back the television was on. I lit a cigarette and watched an ad for a bath tile cleanser and then one for laundry soap. Lili had cradled herself crosswise into the green overstuffed chair, and was thumbing through the latest copy of *Vogue*. Holiday was folding sheets. For a moment, I thought of us as housewives. And this man taking a shower, I fantasized, is my husband. I'll go into our bedroom to wait for him, and he'll come in with a towel around his waist, still wet from the shower, and he'll lift me up in his arms and kiss me.

***

I got another one later in the day. He was about sixty-five, and a regular customer, so I knew he'd want sex and that he wasn't a cop. Most of the women liked the older men because they paid better and were easier, quicker and less demanding. But I was repelled by the pale flabbiness of his body, and when he started feeling me during the massage I pushed his hand away.

"How much for a hand job?" he asked.

"Sixty," I said, figuring I might get out of it by being expensive.

"Okay," he said, and reached for his pants. He pulled his wallet out and squinted over the bills, trying to read their denominations in the dim light. His fumbling aroused a rush of contempt and disgust in me.

I jerked him off for a while and then he started to talk.

"You really know how to please a man, don't you?"

I nodded assent. Talking dirty, I figured, was more than he'd paid for. It seemed the most compromising act of all, involving as it did my imagination as well as my body.

"You like to see a man come?"

"Uh huh."

"Why?" he asked.

Because then I know it's over, I thought to myself, and barely stifled a hostile laugh.

"It's exciting," I said.

"It excites you, eh, to see a man come?"

"Uh huh."

"I'd like to put it in, you know."

"Would you?" Greed and disgust wrestled within me.

"How much more would that be, to put it in?"

What price would discourage him, I wondered. "Sixty more," I said.

"Okay," he agreed, and struggled blindly with the bills again.

I undressed and we lay down onto the mattress. I turned my head to my side to he wouldn't try to kiss me. He pulled my legs over his shoulders and slid it in. My cunt contracted and rose up involuntarily. He stroked a few times, his pace matching my own rhythms. I felt myself involved, as if in a fantasy, of him my father, and me, sexy girl child, his good girl, bad girl, favorite.

"It's really good," he said.

"It's really hard now," I said, feeling crazily lewd. "You can really fuck, can't you?"

"Oh, sweetheart," he moaned, and clasped his mouth onto one of my breasts.

The fantasy was gone as quickly as it had come over me. I was left, however, with a measure of affection for his having stirred something in me. As he dressed I noticed that the softness of his body was pleasing, his shoulders were white, powdery and gracefully shaped.

As I let him out the front door he thanked me profusely and I let him kiss me on the cheek.

Pain, Pleasure and Poetry

Mistress Lilith Lash

About eleven years ago, I found myself with a young daughter to raise, and a lot of sexual frustration. To work off some of my sexual needs, without bringing them home, I began to answer ads in the underground newspapers. I was older and sexually experienced at the time, so I tended toward straight forward approaches like, "Want your pussy eaten for hours? Call. . ." I found this a friendly, direct way to get orgasms I needed. What an improvement on picking up unknowns from barstools who usually passed out cold upon contact with a bed and then expected me to provide breakfast for the wonderful time they assumed we'd had.

The men and women (I never ask a tongue's gender if it licks me the right way) I met through the ads were sober, experienced, experimental, and, like me, wanted the comes without the contracts. They were also a great deal of fun. Through several people contacted in this manner, I found out about more advanced adult toys and games.

The first time I tied up a man, whipped him raw, and fucked him with a dildo, I learned something I had forgotten about myself. I liked it and it really turned me on. Though the first time I did it for a guy in trade for hours of expert muff diving, I soon was looking actively for slightly kinkier ads.

About this time I realized I wouldn't be able to become a stenotypist, as I had planned, because I hated the machine, and I discovered I'd have to start as a court reporter. I'm allergic to structured and authoritative environments and institutions.

In addition to going to school from 8:00 to 5:00, and leading an active, promiscuous and imaginative sex life, I was averaging about four nights a week on the open poetry stage. I was having fun, but my poems weren't edible.

I lucked out and discovered a B&D club that was hiring. When asked if I was a dominant or submissive, I hired on as the former, figuring it was a business in which it is better to give than receive. Besides, when I was in New York at nineteen, and broke, my girlfriend had turned me on to a guy who had paid me to tie him with his neckties and throw oranges at his balls from across the room at ten bucks a hit. Even nearsighted it was an easy and well paying gig. He was lucky I had been such a bad pitcher in high school or I probably would have liberated his life's savings.

Remembering that interesting experience, I decided to combine business and pleasure. I was able to come a lot at work and therefore take better care of my mother and daughter at home. I'm a dominant, not a sadist. I only hurt men who think it's kind to be cruel; I couldn't turn myself on with unwilling "victims." You don't think I get paid for real pain, do you? No matter how far out or excruciating the session is, I can tell by the erection (or lack of it) what the real response is.

A dominant has responsibility. If a man says "no lasting marks" he is put through a gradual build-up of increasingly painful procedures. But, though it may seem impossible from the intensity of stimulation engendered, there are really no welts or bruises. The red hot I induce disappears in about half an hour though a tingling reminder may still be with him when he drives to the office the next day.

Sometimes a man will want "markings" to jog his fantasies if he travels or lives alone. These I inflict with care to last no longer than two weeks. The only exception I've made to this rule is piercing and placing a permanent stud in the foreskin of a loyal slave who begged for it for years.

There are strict rules to B&D. If the "victims" want to yell stop but mean go, there is always a code word or key that really means they've had enough. This is usually "mercy," or "uncle," or even "key." No professional top pushes the limits of a bottom much beyond this point. The word is always simple and never changed so it can be remembered under times of stress.

To a point the bottom is in control, and the top doesn't carry things too far for fear of losing fun bottoms to play with. But, I still say a top is top, because if someone is restrained and totally helpless one could conceivably do anything to him. That is part of the turn on — I know I really have complete power over the bottom's body. The other part of the turn on is the trust established on the submissive's side as he surrenders totally, knowing the dominant has the power to decide how far to take it.

I encouraged many oral slaves in the beginning and still like to get off plenty on the job. But, of course, given these precarious times, I have to be very meticulous about sterilization. I prefer for the men I fuck to bring their own dildoes. If I use mine, I use latex rubbers and nonoxynol-9. The spankings are like specific and advanced massage. They can be deliciously built up to what seems like hard corporal punishment, if that was their purpose rather than erotic stimulation. Beginning lightly and briskly to bring the blood to the surface of the skin, which helps prevent later bruising, using furs and feathers to tease when the pain seems to outweigh the pleasure, and eventually wailing away to a crescendo that often produces spontaneous orgasm. If the pain is too great for a climax, the afterglow will bring one on quickly in response to a hand or vibrator.

The reason pain and pleasure can be merged by an experienced hand is because both reactions come from the same place in the brain. When excited (sexually, painfully, or through fear or exertion) endorphins are released. This is a natural opiate the body provides. The trick with s/m is to apply enough pain and/or fear to bring out the endorphins without inflicting unnecessary damage. I don't hurt men because I hate them; I hurt them because I love them. The greatest sexual turn on is a turned on partner, and imagination is endlessly entertaining.

If you restrict your sexual life, even it will become boring. All people of whatever age need to play. With B&D you can act out pre-arranged skits, or make it up as you go along. It constantly tests your creativity and ingenuity. A hardware store will never look the same to you again. It's better to provide amusing games and diversions that make lives worth living. A man who's just been fucked up the ass while wearing false eyelashes and crotchless pink panties is very unlikely to rape or kill.

Needless to say, I'm happy with my life. I get paid for writing by a variety of sources. I have written pornography, worked for a feminist publication, plotted horror stories, science fiction, speculative fantasy and mainstream. If I can imagine it (and I usually can) I can put it into words. I have given lectures to college audiences on sexual variations. I have also written, produced, directed and edited films and videos. I get paid for some creative acts and do others gratis or just for myself. I bloom constantly in my environment.

Humphrey Bogart said sex was the most fun you can have without laughing. I think it's even more fun when you can laugh. Creative sexuality, involving props and role playing, is a safe and cathartic means to satisfaction in the disease-plagued eighties. I like to fuck and suck as well as anyone, but I want to live a very long life. I see my regulars, a clientele built up over many years in the game. And they have become valued friends.

52

Interview with Nell

Priscilla Alexander

Priscilla: Tell me about your work.

Nell: I think there are class divisions in prostitution. It breaks down around race, but also class background. I am in an elite position because some friends who had worked for years on the street built up a different kind of clientele, business men. When they stopped working, they passed their clientele on to me. That's the only reason I got into this position. When I thought about hooking before, I always thought I'd go to go-go places, massages parlors, and street walking. I thought those were the avenues open to me.

I identify more with women on the streets, because we share the same background.

When people talk about hookers and whores, they don't mind the women who are on call, you know, the women who have clientele, it's the women on the streets they nab on. They're the ones who get so much shit. When they attack them, they're attacking me. I grew up in projects, and when people start talking about black people and women on the streets, it gets into a whole lot of racism, and sexism, shit they don't understand. It makes me angry. That's why I defend all whores and all women on the streets.

Some women make a point of saying, "Well, there's a difference between me and hookers on the street, there's a difference between hookers." There's the upper class, you know, there's ladies. I've heard really classist statements coming from women I worked with. They felt they were better than other hookers.

Priscilla: Have you always worked through referrals?

Nell: Yeah, I worked with a woman who called me.

Priscilla: Did she work too or was she just a go-between?

Nell: She worked. We worked together as a group. If she had a guy who wanted more than one woman, she would just call me up and say, "Show up." It was easy, convenient, security was good.

Priscilla: So you always worked with other women?

Nell: Yeah. The only time I was ever alone was when I traveled. It's interesting that even women who work on the streets usually work in groups. They go to a hotel, then they come back, and they check in with each other. If one doesn't come back, they know. They watch out for each other.

The women I worked with were all lesbians. It made the circumstances very supportive. The rest of the lesbian community offered little support. There are tons of lesbians who don't like heterosexual women, or women who are involved with men, and they can't stand prostitutes. They don't ever identify lesbians as being prostitutes, the two are like extremes to them. There's never any meeting.

Priscilla: Little do they know.

Nell: How little they know is true. Once, at a party, a lesbian I knew took me apart and told me, "Don't talk about it." "Talk about what?" "About hooking." I mean, could you walk up to somebody and say, "Please, don't come out of the closet." It's the same kind of thing.

Priscilla: Maybe she wanted to protect you.

Nell: Protect me from what? There is nothing wrong with it. What is there to protect? I had long discussions with P about Women Against Violence, before marching on Broadway, about what that says to women who are working inside, how it alienates the women inside, how they get heckled if they support the marchers. I knew she never talked to any of the women in these places. It's typical, though; in all movements the people "to be saved" rarely have a voice, or get to be leaders.

I know my value, you see, I know my worth. When you're making money for yourself, there's an immediate value on you, you're selling yourself, your personality, your charms, your appearance, your ability to persuade, your ability to sell. It takes skill, definite skill, and a lot of strength. I've come to appreciate those qualities in myself.

I figured out that by the time I was twenty, I had gone to bed with a hundred guys and never gotten paid for one of those tricks, right? Not one. I could have made a fortune when I was young, getting screwed by all those assholes. Now I think differently. It's not because I get taken out to dinner or treated nicely that I'm going home with someone and go to bed with her. I don't sell myself short for anybody, under any circumstance. I know my value, and I know my worth. I know what I can do with my body — it's not for free and it's not for pay. So it has been good for me to get that sense of possession, of worth about my body, being able to use it for something, knowing what I can do with it.

I've talked to a guy who considers himself somewhat of a whore, but not in a professional way, he just goes to bed with people, you know, like that, meets guys in alleyways, meets guys in the bathroom, meets guys everywhere. One time he was really short of money and I said, "Well, go turn some tricks. God, you turn tricks every day, every day you come home and tell me about all these tricks you picked up, go turn a trick for money." He couldn't do it. He could *not* do it. I mean, I walked him downtown, on the streets. I said, "I'll be around the corner, I'll wait for you, you know, I'll be right by you." He came back to me and he goes, "There's no choice. I can't pick the trick and it just turns me off, I can't do it." "But you do it all the time, you're not selective anyway, I can't believe this." He could not break that barrier of actually doing it for money, you know, of saying, "I sold myself."

To me this was insane. I just never realized how difficult it was for people to make that transition. It was a case of getting money when you needed money. I did not think then that I had taken such a big step. I had considered myself a whore from the time I had become sexually active, even before I became sexually active. From that time on, I had thought of myself as a whore and it was like, well, I'm gonna make money at it, and, sure, try to get paid for it.

she hated the rain

Sapphire

She hated the rain. Never could figure out what people be talkin' 'bout when they be talkin' 'bout gentle, refreshing, spring rains bathing the earth's surface! This nasty ass, cold greyness pouring down combining with shit in the street sho' wadn't sweet. Her wig was wet. Hairspray and rainwater mingled with perspiration and ran down her neck. Her feet were like blocks of ice. "Muthafuck this shit," she mumbled, "I'm turnin' in for the nite."

As she strolled past the likker store, she looked down the street at the elementary school she usta go to wondering what her mother would say. Well, she thot, least I ain't on welfare. The street was deserted. At 3:00 in the mornin' Webster and Grove looked like something out of a movie. She shivered and quickened her pace. Some putty faced pig in a blue chevy slowed down and while cruising along side her leered, "Pssst! Wanna date? Huh honey? How 'bout it?" She almost ran; she couldn't have taken another feebly dick, pink, hairy son of a bitch if he'd been shittin' fifty dollar bills. She walked over to Hayes Street, lo and behold, a bus, a rare occurence at 3:00 in the mornin'. She hopped on the bus, sauntered to the back hopin' Willie wouldn't be upset 'bout her not gettin' no whole lot of money. Shit! Wet as it was the muthafucker oughtta be glad she got what she got. She jumped off the bus and motored down the street hopin' there was some brownies left 'cause all nite she'd been wanting somethin' sweet. She started up the stairs, slid up to the door and laid on the bell. No one answered. She wondered what was takin' so long. Shit! Even if no one else was in Jackie be in. She was always the first one in! Sometimes she thot that bitch had a stash 'cause can't nobody come up wid that much cash every nite! "Hell," she muttered, "What's wrong wid these fools?" She laid on the bell again. Willie usually be home about this time, too. Finally she heard footsteps approaching the door. They musta been fuckin'. Still that son of a bitch didn't have to take till Christmas to answer the door. She heard him on the other side of the door, his footsteps, his breathing.

Willie opened the peephole and said, "What cha want?"

"Nigger r u crazy," she said, "What u think I want! Lemme in!"

"How much cash u got?"

"Bout seventy-five."

"U trifling bitch, u mean u been out all nite and ain't got but seventy-five dollars? You musta been jivin' roun' smokin' weed wid the other bitches!"

"Willie u know better than that. I ain' lazy. It's jus' been slow. Come on daddy," she wheedled, "open the doe."

He opened the door, grabbed her arm, yanked her around and placed a well aimed patent leathered foot in her ass and said, "Bitch u get in when u got my money."

Enraged and scared she sobbed, "Bu..but Willie it's rainin'!"

Willie slammed the door, opened the peephole and tole her, "Walk between the raindrops baby, walk between the raindrops."

Police as Pimps

Karen

In 1975, I had run away from home. I met a man who was nice to me and later on turned out to be a pimp. At the time, I was fifteen years old. I was from North Carolina, and very naive to the ways of the world. He told me he was going to take me to California to be a model. What I found out when I arrived was that instead of being a model, I was to be a prostitute. He put me on the streets of San Francisco.

One week later, I met Vince. He was a vice officer. He started coming around where I worked and buying me cigarettes. And when it was cold, he would bring me doughnuts and cocoa. He said he wanted to be my friend. I didn't know anyone in California, and I was very lonely and scared, so I believed him. He finally got me to tell him everything that had happened. My pimp, my age, my parents, how much money I was making. This went on for about a month. Then he told me he wanted me to make love to him. He said if I did, he would make sure I never got busted by vice. So I did. He saw some bruises on my body that had been inflicted by my pimp. He told me that I did not have to be abused anymore by my pimp, and that he would take care of me. He even said I would not have to give him all of my prostitution earnings, just half. I told him I would have to think about it because I was scared of what my pimp would do to me. Vince told me not to worry about it, he would take care of it.

I left my pimp and contacted Vince. I told him I still wanted to work the streets. He said I could as long as I continued to have sex with him and gave him some of my money. He would be my pimp. He would bring all of the vice officers by, where I was working, one at a time, so I could see them, and so they wouldn't arrest me. This went on for a few months until I had saved enough money so I could go home to my parents.

The Continuing Saga of Scarlot Harlot III

Carol Leigh

No wonder I'm all stressed out. This work is weird. This stigma is weird. I'm weird. Everyone I know is a weirdo. It usually takes about an hour to wind down after an encounter. What should I do now, while I'm waiting, waiting for the next phone call?

I can always read *The Mamie Papers*, a collection of letters written by a brave and guilty whore at the turn of the century. The book depresses me. I cringe as she calls herself unclean and immoral. There is no repose.

I'd rather be contemporary, anyway. I think I'll watch television. I check out the Guide. Oh, no! I can't believe it. Margo St. James on a talk show, and just in time, I tune her in.

Ah, there she is, chronically courageous, impenetrably brave, grinning out from the commercial in her stylish pink sweater dress and thick, neat farm-girl hair. I admire her ease, yet I worry through the patter of the talk show host, posed carefully seductive in his loveless sports suit. I relax as I observe his good-natured interrogation.

"So, you're retired now?" He seems disappointed.

"Not tired. Just retired," Margo replies in her alto drawl as she stretches comfortably on her couch. The audience chuckles. The host mugs a pout.

"Would you be inclined to kiss and tell?" he asks, squirming in his seat.

"Oh, we don't kiss. Too many germs," she replies and sits, erect. "By the way, why are you rubbing your thigh?"

A whore speaks! Not quite the revolution I had hoped for, but she certainly is afforded respect. The audience gasps, titters and applauds this heroine. They seem to care.

Margo and the host continue to serve and swat their double entendre until flutes signal a commercial interruption.

"Thank you very much, Margo St. James..."

But Margo interrupts. The cameras are stuck. The music stops.

"Wait a minute. I have an announcement to make. COYOTE is having a Hookers' Convention during the Democratic Convention. We're inviting the delegates to stay in our homes, the female delegates, of course. That's informal. I'll put up a few in my lobby," she belts as the music ascends, her voice fading behind the horns.

"Thanks," he says, quite rushed, "And now a word from..."

Just my luck. And just as I was beginning to relax in my nest of cash and condoms, I witness a call to duty on my television set. Well, I suppose I was asking for it.

I just knew, when I decided not to join the Cats and Candlelight Womenpower Commune, that I had opted to confront my oppression on a daily basis. Rather than excusing myself from the men's world, I chose to challenge the enemy, my boyfriend at the time. He never quite agreed with me, and finally I grew to smother my bitterness, complaining to my sisters in angry whispers.

"I despise men's tacit acceptance of our oppression. It's a conspiracy!"

As the years rolled by, I grew inwardly understanding and outwardly calm. A flick of fate made me a prostitute. I was poor and alone when I first moved to this open city. It seemed like the logical thing to do. In these last years I have developed a caring for the men in my bed. Individually and close-up they seem innocent and vulnerable. Besides, they are my clients, my lovers, my wards, my employers, my intimates. Eventually, the word patriarchy began to slip from my vocabulary.

I learned that women led the movement to make prostitution illegal. The Suffragists. My foremothers.

And now, I consider the challenge and call for a new tally. We are the whores. Who are our friends?

I must descend from my icy abode and attend those bagel brunches, contriving platforms amidst feminist hunches. Together we will make prostitution an issue along with the other issues such as abortion rights, equal pay, lesbian rights and rape. We will organize and speak, and they will be staring at us.

That's right, I'm afraid. Our potential astounds me. The fact that prostitution is illegal shocks me, almost paralyzes me. Am I allowed to help organize a Hookers' Convention?

I don't think I'm allowed to talk to another prostitute. That's conspiracy. Suppose I was describing a new sexy dress I had purchased in order to make my fortune? It's illegal to talk about business.

I don't think I'm allowed a personal lover. He would be suspected of being my pimp and may be called in for associating with me.

Theoretically, I'm not allowed to talk to anyone. I have very few rights, except the right to a trial and certainly not one by my peers.

Priscilla Alexander, friend and activist, once said:

The right to be a prostitute is as important as the right not to be one. It is the right to set the terms of one's own sexuality, plus the right to earn a good living.

So, descend I must. And luckily during my retreat, I wrote a song about our struggle. Perhaps I'll play it over coffee and croissants to an audience of whores, friends and activists.

> We're doing prostitution
> Although it's no solution
> It's just a substitution
> We make a contribution
> We've found a resolution
> To our destitution
> We don't want persecution
>
> We're doing prostitution
> It's an age-old institution
> Ya know, it's not pollution
> We need some absolution
> Perhaps a revolution
> A brand-new constitution
> To end this persecution
>
> Yeah, yeah, c'mon yeah!

In the Massage Parlor

Judy Edelstein

The customer looks like the all-American football player type. He's young, middle-aged, blonde, broad-shouldered, and muscular. It turns out he's an executive for a lumber company. He's the guy who's supposed to represent the company's concern for ecology.

While I work on him, he talks at me. He claims that his company really cares about the environment. They're planting new trees, etc., the whole spiel. "And what are you going to do," he asks, "if the average American housewife wants colored toilet paper? We try to sell her on white, but we have to give the housewife what she wants."

After I've thumped and kneaded him all over, I start oiling his all-American-sized prick. He clamps one of his muscular arms around me and pulls me closer to him.

Pretty soon he leaves behind his lumber company personality. "Let me eat you," he begs, "just for a little bit."

"I don't do that," I say. I keep on stroking up and down on his prick.

But he keeps on asking me, and finally I can't take it anymore. I'm ready to do just about anything to get him off. "Okay," I say, "just for a minute."

So I take off my skirt and underpants and lie down on the table. He stands against the table, leaning over me, and starts to lick me. He's moaning and growling and biting me a little, being too rough. I think about stopping him, but instead I lay back and try to relax. All of a sudden I come.

I stop him from eating me and just lay there for a minute. He's still standing over me, and after a little bit, he starts to put his prick inside of me. I move away from him. "Lay back down on the table and I'll finish you off," I say.

So he gets back on the table, and I jerk him off some more, and finally he comes.

Afterwards I'm sitting in one of the empty massage rooms with the muzak turned off, feeling kind of shaky. I just can't believe that I had an orgasm with that jerk. I try to forget him, to think about making love with Laura, the woman I'm with right now. But all I can see is the customer's all-American face.

***

No customers have come in yet this evening, so I'm sitting in the turned-off sauna, just thinking.

When I first started working here, I knew I'd have to jack off the guys. But I thought I could deal with that. As my friend Kate, who works in another massage parlor, puts it, "It's just like pulling a toe." And pretty good pay for that. A hell of a lot better than typing or waitressing. Plus, I would have a chance to learn to do massage.

So I started working here, pretty naive. The first time a guy tried to feel up my breasts, I got really angry and wouldn't let him. So he got angry, too, and never came back.

Another time a repulsive old guy wanted to eat me. He kept offering more and more money, finally offered me two hundred bucks, but I still wouldn't let him. I even told him that money couldn't buy everything. He must have thought I was nuts.

Pretty soon I wised up. I figured I wasn't working here for my health. So the next time a guy tried to feel me up, I let him. That way he left me a nice tip and asked for me again.

Now I let most customers feel me up some. I've learned not to be there when they touch me. When they touch my breasts, I tell myself they're not really touching me.

For another five or ten bucks I sometimes do the massage topless or bottomless. What the hell, I figure, I might as well. But I can't bring myself to do blow jobs or let them screw me. Even though I'd make more money, I just don't want to do that. It turns my stomach too much.

Mostly the job is okay. I try not to let the guys get to me. And I go home afterwards and try to forget about it all. But sometimes I get scared. I think of the guy's hands all over me. I think about some stranger sucking on my breasts. And sometimes I wonder how I can let the men do that. I wonder what there is left for me. I wonder where *I* am.

***

We keep a card file on all our customers, with their name, description, maybe a few comments, and how often they've been in. That way we can keep track of which are regular customers, and not likely to be cops. Of course, lots of the guys don't give us their real names, so we have a lot of Smiths and Joneses in our card file.

Tonight I'm massaging a John Smith. He's a young guy, slender, the quiet type. He lies face down on the table and doesn't say a word while I work on his back and his legs. After I turn him over, I give him a face massage, working my fingertips into the shallow wrinkles on his forehead. His eyes are closed and he still lies quietly.

When I start to rub oil on his penis, he finally opens his eyes. "Let me put my arm around you," he says in a soft voice.

I move closer to him and let him put his arm around my waist. For some reason, I don't mind his touching me.

I hold his penis cupped between my hands and stroke slowly up and down, then a little harder and faster. His arm tightens around my waist and I feel his hand stroking my side.

As he approaches his climax, he begins to murmur. "Honey, sweetheart," he says, "you're so sweet, you're so good, you're so gentle. Honey, sweetheart, you're so beautiful." On and on. I notice that his eyes are closed again.

One of my hands makes oily circles on his chest, the other moves up and down on his prick. I start to feel sadder and sadder. It's not me he's talking to, not me he wants. It's someone who really loves him that he's wanting.

Finally he comes. Afterwards I stand there quietly for a moment, still holding his penis in my right hand, my left hand resting on his chest. Then I reach for a prick rag (my own name for the stacks of little towels) and wipe him off.

He opens his eyes and looks at me. "Thanks. That felt great."

"I'm glad," I say, smiling at him.

When I clean up his room afterwards, I discover that he's left me a ten dollar tip. Of course, I'm glad to get it. But somehow his ten dollar bill makes me feel sad too.

***

It's mid-evening, a pretty busy time, and I'm working on a new customer. We don't have him listed in our card file, and none of the other massage parlors I call know him either. So I'm being cautious with him, trying to size him up, trying to decide whether he might be a cop.

We talk for a while. I ask him what he does, is he married, all the standard questions. He says he's single and he works for United Grocers. It all sounds good, but I'm just not sure about this guy. So I figure I won't give him the hand finish.

I ask him to turn over. When he's lying on his back, I see that he's got a huge erection. It's pretty hard to ignore, but I try to.

I work very slowly on his face, then on his chest and stomach. "C'mon," he says, "aren't you going to give me the hand finish?"

"Well," I say, "we don't usually do that."

"Look," he says, "I'm not a cop." He even shows me his United Grocer's I.D.

I finally decide to take the risk, even though I'm still not sure he's okay. This job has got me so programmed that I feel I really *should* try to get him off. So I stroke up and down on his prick, around and over his balls, for what seems an interminable long time. His massage time is just about over when he finally comes.

He wipes himself off with the rag I give him. Then he sits up on the table and looks directly at me. "You know what?" he says.

"What?"

"I'm a cop," he says.

I just stare at him for moment. I can feel my stomach jerk in, my breathing stop. I picture myself in jail, my family's reaction if they ever found out.

He looks away from me. "I'm just kidding," he mutters.

It's hard to take it all in. "Jesus Christ!" I stammer. "That's no joke!"

"Sorry," he says. But I don't think he's really sorry at all.

***

The woman I work with most nights, who goes by the name of Pat, says the same crummy joke was played on her a few times. Both of us know, of course, that the joke could turn into a real trip to jail at any time. That's one of the risks of working here. I try not to think about it too much. I try not to imagine how I'd feel about being busted for prostitution.

Pat might not worry about this as much, because she used to be a hooker. Now she sticks to the massage parlors, and she has a lot of regular customers, so she must make almost as much money as before. I imagine it's a lot easier for her working here.

Pat's got straight reddish hair, is tall and thin, and is pretty nice. She always puts on a good show for the guys. A few nights ago she came in wearing a silver wig, false eyelashes, and lots of makeup. She looked so different I hardly recognized her.

Whenever her regular customers come in, Pat acts real glad to see them. She always greets them at the door, gets them a cup of our lousy instant coffee (which I usually don't bother with unless they ask), and acts real sexy with them. I don't know what she does in the rooms with the guys, but they always leave her good tips.

Sometimes I wonder whether Pat's hostess personality is all part of her act, or if she really likes the guys. Once I asked her if she liked her job, and she said she did. But I still wonder whether Pat thinks the show is real, that "sexy Pat" is really her. I don't know. Maybe she doesn't either.

***

I'm cleaning out the showers, during a break in our flow of customers, when Pat comes and tells me that Abe Fisher is waiting for me in room two. "Great," I say. Abe is an old Jewish guy who always leaves a good tip.

I get my bottles of oil and bring them into the room. As usual, Abe is sitting on the table with a towel wrapped around him, smoking a cigar. Already the air inside the room is thick with smoke.

"Hi sweetheart," Abe says in his faintly accented voice. "Are you ready for me now?"

"Sure am," I say, smiling at him.

Abe never wants a real massage. He wants me to "just tickle" him, as he puts it. So I spread some talcum powder on his skinny back and legs. Then I start stroking him with my fingertips, very lightly, all over his back and buttocks and upper legs. My hands move in rhythm to the soft muzak he likes to listen to.

He moans with pleasure sometimes, especially when I glide my fingertips across his buttocks. I watch his balls quiver and his prick get harder whenever my fingers brush against them.

At last he sighs and turns over. "Ah, sweetheart," he says, panting a little, "you make me feel so good." His prick is very hard by now, much harder than you'd think an old man's would be. I put a little oil on his prick and balls and stroke them gently.

Abe puts his arm around me, then starts feeling up my butt. "Why don't you take your pants, off, sweetheart?" he asks. "I'll give you a nice tip."

"Sure Abe," I say. I pull my pants and underpants down. Abe pats my butt, at first softly, then a little harder, while I keep on stroking his prick and balls. Then he makes his usual request. "Sweetheart," he says, "let me go between your legs."

I say "yes" as usual, so he gets off the table and stands facing me, his prick very full. My pants and underpants are down around my knees. I put a towel inside them, so his come doesn't soil them or god forbid grow another Abe Fisher inside me. Then he puts his arms around me and holds me against him. He holds me tighter and tighter as he thrusts with his prick, back and forth, back and forth between my thighs.

This doesn't really matter, I tell myself. It's worth it to get a good tip. But while Abe still presses and thrusts against me, I look over his shoulder. In the mirror facing us, I can see the grotesque sculpture that we make.

***

In every room in the massage parlor there's an oversized Barbie doll head which holds kleenex. You pull a kleenex out of the top of the doll's head.

The doll heads were the owner's idea, but Pat and I hate them. Pat says that pulling out a kleenex is like pulling a little bit of brains out of the doll's head. At the rate we use kleenex, I figure none of the dolls can have much gray matter left by now.

I think much the same about myself sometimes. I feel this job eating at me until I wonder if I'm all hollow inside.

***

It's later at night. The customer is an aging hippie from Los Angeles, with grayish-brown shoulder-length hair and a neatly trimmed mustache. He's wearing new-looking purple corduroy pants, tooled leather boots, and the classic suede leather jacket with fringe.

He takes a sauna first and then he's ready for his massage. "I like a good, hard massage," he tells me. So I work up a sweat kneading and pounding the large muscles on his back. "Hey," he says, "you're really good. I'm going to be a regular customer from now on." That sounds good to me, unless he's too much hassle. I could use a few more regular customers to keep the money coming in.

After he turns over, I give him a scalp massage. His hair is clean and silky, nice to touch. Meanwhile, he starts checking me out.

"Do you turn on?" he asks. "I've got some dynamite speed with me tonight. I could let you have some real cheap."

"No thanks," I say. "I'm not into speed."

"Too bad," he says. "This is really good stuff." He's silent for a moment, then he raises his head up and looks at me. "You know, with some people you never know where they're at. I'm glad you gave me an honest answer. I think honesty is real important."

"Yeah, so do I," I say. I start working on his chest, spreading oil over his chest muscles. He's quiet for a while again, and then as I move on to working on his stomach, he starts checking out the sexual merchandise.

"I really like head jobs," he says. "You do them, don't you?"

"Sorry," I say. "I don't."

He has a disappointed expression on his face. "Are you sure you won't do a head job? I was really hoping to get one."

"I'll give you fifteen bucks for doing one." He puts his arm around me and squeezes a little. He looks at me encouragingly.

What the hell, I think all of a sudden. Maybe I should try it. I could really use the fifteen bucks, and if I got into doing blow jobs here, I could make a lot more money.

"Okay," I say, "I'll do it."

"Great," he says.

I bend over him, ready to start his blow job right away and get it over with. "Hey," he says, looking offended, "I'm not ready yet. Make me hard with your hands first."

So I put some oil on his prick and start stroking up and down, holding it between my cupped hands like another customer showed me. "That feels good," he says. He unbuttons my blouse, pulls up my bra, and runs his hand over my breasts. Then he starts sucking on the nipples. I don't stop him. I figure this is part of the fifteen dollar deal.

Finally he says that he's ready for his blow job, so I bend over him and put his prick into my mouth. It tastes oily and too salty, but I try not to notice that.

As I'm sucking on his prick, he starts correcting my technique. First he moves my head so I'm right over his prick and turned toward his face. Then he shows me the correct motion. "Move your head up and down like a rabbit," he says. He demonstrates, moving his head up and down.

He looks so funny, nodding his head like that, that I have to keep myself from laughing. Jesus, I'm thinking, this guy is a great teacher.

I start moving my head as he showed me. "Hey," he says, sounding critical, "I can't feel you. Are you sucking?"

I start sucking on him harder. "That's pretty good," he says. "You don't mind doing this, do you?"

I take his prick out of my mouth for a moment to answer him. "It's okay," I say.

Then I go back to moving my head up and down and sucking. I'm starting to feel that I've really got the hang of this. Maybe I can stand to do blow jobs after all.

"That feels great," he says. "Just put a little bit more of it in your mouth."

So I bend over further and try to cram more of his prick into my mouth. It feels as if my whole mouth is full of his prick. I can almost feel it touching my throat.

He starts to moan and thrust his hips against me. All of a sudden I start to gag. It's too much! I want his prick out of my mouth right now!

I jerk up, letting go of his prick, backing away from his encircling arm. He opens his eyes. "What's happening?" he says, sounding irritated.

"I just don't want to do it anymore," I say.

We stare at each other for a minute. He's breathing heavily, looking really pissed. "Hey chick," he says, "are you going to charge me fifteen bucks for that?"

"I'm not gonna charge you anything," I say. My own voice is angry too. "I'll give you a hand finish instead," I say after a moment.

He lies back down, looking a little mollified. I put some more oil on his prick and start stroking up and down again. He grabs for my breasts and squeezes them hard. Then he slips his hands under the waist of my pants. His hand moves downward until he's pressing it between my legs. He starts to stick a finger inside of me.

I don't want him to touch me like that, so I move away a little. But his arm around me pulls me back and he keeps on rubbing his hand against my crotch. Mostly I figure it's not worth it to stop him. I just want to get him off and get him out of here.

Finally he comes, in a storm of heavy breathing. A moment later, he's polite again. "Thanks a lot. I really needed that."

"I'm glad it felt good," I say, handing him a prick rag. I try to sound sincere.

He lays a rap on me as gets dressed. "You know," he says, "I'm not a chauvinist. Some of my best buddies are chicks. I work on cars with them."

"Oh yeah," I say.

He buttons his silky, floral-print shirt. "And I know a lot of gay people too. It doesn't make any difference to me."

That's right, I think. I'm gay and it didn't matter to you at all.

He pulls on his pants. "Just so long as you do what feels good to you, that's the main thing." He slowly puts on his boots. "It's always a mistake to do anything you don't want to do," he says, "because you're prostituting yourself if you do that."

There's a taste in my mouth like vomit. Then I must be a whore, I think to myself. Because I didn't want to be with this guy at all. And I sure as hell didn't want him to touch me.

He hands me a five dollar tip. "I'll see you another time," he says. "The massage felt great."

"Thanks," I say. I try for a sexy smile, but I don't make it.

Speaking in Tongues

Jean Johnston

Bones crush
beneath hot breath
beer burps up out
onto my face
For weeks I think of nothing
but spit and pus and urine
shit clogs my colon
For weeks I feel
nothing but
salt waves soar
through my head
freezing behind my eyes
ice cracks
my skin
and hot blood blankets
my cold body
I am an alien.
to the men a pussy/ a cunt/ a bitch
a cocksucker
to the women a whore with lumps of semen
still sticking to my tongue
speaking another language
I am
learning to communicate

Girls, Girls, Girls

M. M. Chateauvert

Maluda stepped by nearly every night. Always in something different, usually around 10:30 or so — early, considering the street she was on. Sometimes she would look in the window as she passed; more often, she was too concerned with her own business and watched what the sidewalk had to offer instead. When she did look inside, her gaze first took in the neon signs and gaudy front with the old run-down hotel above it, and then her eyes rested on what the parlor's window displayed. Sometimes Maluda smiled when the doorman was rapping particularly well, and then she walked on down the sidewalk.

"Looking us over," someone inside would say.

She was alone most of the time; always walking single. If there was someone along, she was always a little ahead of him — for that meant things had already been arranged — or they were quietly rapping and strolling.

"Haven't seen her with an old man, have you?" one of the inside girls asked, and then they all started discussing Maluda.

"Never seen her riding with anyone, either, I bet," Jeri said.

"She good. She don't have to mix with the trash around here," Dawn put in.

"Maybe she don't have a sugar daddy," Chrissy said.

"Listen: none of you work downtown all night 'cept me and I've seen her with a man or two," Collette said.

"Probably just telling him to go back to L.A.," Sunny said.

"She don't come 'round here *all* the time, maybe needle's her old man," Jeri put in.

"Her old man's needle, Sugar," Collette said.

Maluda dressed differently too. Suit, pumps; umbrella and a rain-coat; or fine pants that tapered to her ankle. Unlike most of the rest, she looked like someone who was *supposed* to be going into a hotel. Not little-girl nice; most respectable, like a lady. Hotel security knew who and what she was, but because she looked like she couldn't be bothered, security let her pass by.

"Just who does she think she is anyway?" Anna asked no one in particular.

"She's just like anyone else out there: stupid," Candy said, putting on more lipstick.

In some ways she was, but Collette looked at the girls lounging around the lobby and knew different. Dawn: tall, half black, half white, who wore costumes often, fancy silk scarves wrapped around her waist and a camisole, with high heeled mules on her feet. Then there was Candy, who wore hot pants and white lipstick, her eyes heavy with false lashes. They all had their own style, creating the illusion that they were young and innocent or sophisticated and experienced. Each playing a part in a masquerade of desire.

Maluda watched all the signs of the street; eyes on the sidewalk's offerings, the doorways where street people hung out, the cars and their riders. She'd watch shoes — polished leather, cracked toes, shoes with rubber soles. Cars — finely waxed, low-riding, and plain, four doors. And pockets that were big with folded money, hands, or guns and badges.

Every night, Collette watched for her, checking to see if she was around. If she was out, it meant that business would be good, even though she was competition. The massage parlor always did its best when there were plenty of girls on the street, luring the men.

"Hey, hey sir, We-got-seven-girls-tonight. Come-on-in and pick out the one that's right-for-you! Or try a couple...Come on! Take one-back-to-your ho-tel tonight," the doorman barked out his call and grinned suggestively at passers-by. He saw Maluda and said, "Hey, hey pretty mama howsit for you this evening? Steppin' mighty fine as always. Street's hot, so're we, send 'em over your way in a bit." He tipped his non-existent hat as she went by.

Maluda kept walking. Hands holding a small bag by her side, her eyes ahead, Maluda went by the sign that said *The Sugar Shop*.

The juke box was loud inside; the beat of the disco music picked up the rhythm of the night street. The curtains swung with girls running in and out of the rooms, doors closed discreetly, money dropped in the safe. When the girls heard the outer door, they stopped to listen, waiting. If they didn't have to slip on their robes for Collette's call, they sighed and asked their customers for another quarter for the juke box. The mirrors blinked when the street lights shone through.

Collette was setting up the books for the night, arguing in her mind with the old man who owned the parlor. The day shift had been slow until around seven and then business had picked up. The old man would be angry if the house didn't clear at least a thousand tonight. But then, she had six good girls on, and a new one who had to be trained. There was a cop scare too, dammit. One idiot customer was all they needed to get busted these days. Still, there were a couple of conventions in town; the Hilton was full of doctors and Japanese businessmen, and around the corner at the Saint Francis were engineers from the midwest, she'd heard. Collette got up from the desk and looked in the mirror. She had on a new long skirt, her hair was freshly washed and hung like a shawl around her shoulders; she felt great. "We'll see," she said aloud and went out to the lobby.

"Hey, girl, where'd ya get those shoes? Can I try 'em on?" Jeri was asking Dawn.

"Chrissy's got glitter all around her eyes, look at her," came from Candy.

". . . and then I told that good-for-nothing nigger to get the fuck outa there. That asshole, you know what he did to me?" Sunny was talking about her man again with Anna.

"Everyone here meet Kathy?" Collette asked. Nods came from most of the girls. Collette turned to Kathy, "Old man get you a license yet?"

"Yeah," Kathy said and looked around again.

"Then you might as well come back to the office and I'll fill you in," Collette said as she turned and began to walk back. "These are the rooms, you might want this one since it isn't claimed." Collette pulled back a curtain, showing a small cubicle with three walls, the curtain making the fourth. The beanbag couch was made of a black, fuzzy material that looked dusty. A small plastic lamp on a plastic table, a box of kleenex, and a wall full of mirrors made up the rest.

Kathy said sure and looked at the carpeting.

"Here's the run-down and house rules," Collette continued, now seated in the office chair. "Always get him undressed first to make sure he isn't a cop. You only strip to your bra and pants — no farther — and you can't show anything. The law says you're not supposed to touch his parts either. I collect the money before he goes to a room, but you gotta get more from him, and that's gotta be turned in too. I'll write everything up and you get twenty-five percent commission off the top. There are no drugs and no booze. If you get into trouble, just yell and I'll come to the room." Collette listed it all off quickly, as she had done so often. "You got any questions?" she said, trying to be kind, and smiled at Kathy.

Kathy said no and looked at the pattern of Collette's skirt.

Anna yelled from the front, "Collette, we got customers — and they're cute." Collette checked out Kathy once more and went to the salesroom.

"Evening, gentlemen, I'm Collette, your hostess," she said, sitting down between the two suited men and looking them over. "This is the Sugar Shop and there are ladies here for you to spend some time with. We charge forty for the half-hour and seventy-five for about an hour. Whatever you do in the privacy of your room is between you and the lady you choose. What'll it be?" She smiled at them business-like and winked.

"Wall wadda ya say buddy? This here little lady is laying it on the line. Come on, I'll treat." He pulled out two one-hundred dollar bills. "Sounds good, bring 'em on in."

Collette held up the curtain and called off the girls' names as they came in. "This is Anna, Jeri, Candy, Kathy, Chrissy, Sunny, and this is Dawn."

The man holding the money got up, gave the two bills to Collette, then put his arm around Anna. "I'll take her." Anna, looking at the man, said to Collette, "And he's going to let me keep the change."

Buddy looked at Kathy, then said, "This one," pointing to Sunny. "Let's go then," Sunny said. Grabbing his hand, she led him to the back.

"Kathy, come with me," Collette said when they disappeared. "You take this change and receipt in to him and try to get him to take both of you," she continued, handing Kathy twenty-five dollars and a piece of paper.

As Collette was writing up the sale, Sunny came in to hang up her sweater. "I'm sending the new girl in with you, she's got his change."

"Okay, Collette." But Collette didn't see Sunny raise her hands and drop them, because she was busy with the books.

Collette lit up a cigarette and listened to the conversations in the rooms. Sunny was arguing half-heartedly with Buddy to let Kathy come in the session. Collette couldn't hear Kathy say anything, so she went to stand unseen by the room's curtain. "Well, give her a tip then. Let her keep five dollars, okay?"

Kathy came out of the room and Collette stopped her. "I'll write this up," she said taking the money from Kathy's hand.

In the lobby Collette directed Kathy to sit on the stool by the window. Kathy began smiling at everyone who walked by.

Duffy stuck his head in the door and looked at Kathy. "Hey pretty girl, want some foxy new clothes?" He walked in and opened his dress bag. "Tonight I got some pretty special stuff," and he pulled out a pantsuit of orange silk. The other girls looked up and few came close to see for themselves.

Collette let this go on for a minute and then interrupted, "We don't need any hot stuff in here, Duffy." Duffy looked at her and into his bag, then began to pull out a green blouse that matched Collette's skirt. Collette, still sitting in her chair, was amazed at his audacity. She had eighty-sixed him only last week. Duffy caught her look. "Okay, mama, I'll leave. Too bad though, I got some mighty fine trappings in here." He snapped his bag shut quickly, and turned to Kathy. "What's your name? You want to meet me later on?" he said smiling at her.

"No she doesn't. You trying to pimp on the side these days too?" Duffy spun around and looked at Collette. As she began to laugh at him, he turned and walked out the door, winking at Kathy in the window as he went up the street.

Collette shouted out to Doorman, "Keep that hustler outa here!"

"Yes ma'am. Hey, hey sirs, You oughta see what we got here for you. Come-on-in-and-take-a-look. There's-one-here-for-everybody!"

Collette was watching the street from where she sat doing her nails. Cars rolled by and the riders looked at the neon flashing *Girls Girls Girls*. Doorman watched the cars and if they stopped he walked out and gave a rap. He was also listening to the street whores who strutted, looked sharp, and called to men on the sidewalk. The girls were quick that night, leaving for only fifteen minutes at a time and then walking back down O'Farrell to Powell Street. On the sidewalk was the usual assortment of people who came out with the night: the dealers, the pimps, and other hustlers, all calling to one another and to their women. The Commodores wailed through the parlor doors and spilled onto the sidewalk, crashing with the honking taxis and screeching delivery trucks. The sound was electrifying to accustomed ears, overpowering to the uninitiated.

Collette remembered her first day on this street, searching for the door marked *Entertainment Industries*. She was surprised at the number of businesses on that block. The office door was next to the massage parlor and contrasted with the Arab-run corner grocery, the Greek coffee shop, and the antiques stores specializing in Oriental and European furniture. Farther down, there was a piano lounge, a four-star Italian restaurant, import shops catering to foreign tourists, a hot dog stand where young punks hung out at 3:00 in the morning, and a cigar and magazine shop with a shoeshine stand where the men stopped in the early evening to get hand-done shines. In the upper stories of the buildings were run-down rooming houses, dentists' offices, and better hotels. A few blocks up, this street turned into the outskirts of the Tenderloin, and a few blocks down began the richest stores: Saks Fifth Avenue, Brooks Brothers, and Gump's. This street was not the heart of the city, but merely one of many such arteries in a place where one couldn't go any farther west: San Francisco.

Collette sighed and blew on her nails. It was a long way from New York, the end of the Greyhound route, the end of Interstate 80. The bus took five days to get here, dropping her off at the station on Market Street, vulnerable to the men who wait in such places, looking for runaway girls like Collette was. She had escaped them; in fact, she hadn't known they existed until others had told her of them and told her the stories of girls who hadn't gotten away, who had ended up dead of heroin overdoses or beaten to death by the walking sticks of their pimps. She wondered where she would be if one of them had found her. Now though, because she had been able to turn the old man's head and through her own sheer luck, she sat arrogantly above those others. Collette yelled time to Sunny and Anna and lit a cigarette.

"Never-have-you-seen-so-many! *girls girls girls!* That's what the sign says, that's what we got. Yes, sir! Step-inside-and-try-one-out-for-size! You-can-have-her-here, you-can-have-her-there. So how about it gentlemen? Why not check it out?"

Collette watched Maluda walk down the street. A gang of sailor boys whistled at her, but Maluda looked back at the *Girls Girls Girls* sign. The boys picked up the hint and Doorman ushered them inside. Collette herded them all into the salesroom.

"Evenin'. Twenty dollars for fifteen minutes and fifty for the half-hour. Okay?" Collette brought in the girls who were playing older woman to their virgin male. "Which one's your pick?"

"Got myself a fifty," Dawn said, smiling at her boy.

"Come on son, give her the cash — I don't take no traveler's checks!" Sunny bossed her sailor.

Kathy smiled at her man and took his hand shyly.

Collette watched as all the girls were chosen. She counted their money as she walked back to the office. As she dropped the cash into the safe and started writing down the figures, she listened to bits of conversations. Anna came in and gave her twenty dollars more. "He wants to stay longer."

"Thanks, he and Anna? Listen in on Kathy, willya?" Collette said, giving Anna a quick kiss. Anna returned the kiss and went back to her sailor.

Collette walked slowly to the lobby, still listening to the murmurs in the rooms. When she sat in the window, Maluda came by, going toward the Hilton. A sheepish-looking man was following her. The juke box was silent so Collette yelled for more quarters. Everyone was showing good on the books, 'cept Kathy and she was so new so it didn't matter, unless, Collette thought suddenly, she was already stealing from the house. Damn, watch her. No one was fucked up yet either. No cops, good money, and a smooth-running house; it was going to be okay for once. Collette lit a cigarette and waved to some-one Doorman was trying to get in the door. No good. On the other side of the street, an engineer was picking up a whore. Collette cursed, then didn't care; he probably didn't have any money and was all trouble anyway. Let her deal with the drunk, she thought, looks like she needs the money for dope. Collette flicked her cigarette through the door. It arched over the sidewalk and landed in the gutter.

Collette's thoughts swung back to Maluda. She always wondered how anyone could stand pounding the pavement in high heels all night long. 'Course, Maluda wore good shoes, the kind you paid two hundred dollars for at Saks, that helped. Tonight Maluda had on a blouse of gold that glimmered against fine wool pants, all looking rich and tailored and somehow exotic at the same time. The gold reflected up onto her face making its tawny color even lighter. Her hair seemed to shine too — it wasn't nappy, nor did it look like it'd been processed, it looked like it was always just curly. Her face held eyes the color of the street when the neon went off. Maluda was classy, always stepping high.

A man stuck his head in the door and said, "I gotta wife, what do I need this place for?"

"Asshole," Collette said as he disappeared.

Sunny came out, running a pick through her hair.

"Why are you out here? I haven't called time yet."

"He's done, got no more money. He ain't mad, he's gettin' dressed. Hey Collette, why you sticking that new girl on me? You know I hate training the new ones, and this one is real dumb."

"'Cause you been around here longer than anyone else. And besides, if she's that dumb, you can make her do anything," Collette said, rising from the stool. "Sit here, willya? I wanna go hear what's going on in there."

A blue pin striped suit followed Maluda to the Hilton.

"Hey Mister Papa-san," Doorman called and moved his forefinger in and out of a circle of other fingers and thumb. "In here too, papa-san," he winked as the man walked on.

"Damn! That Jap's got money," he said to Sunny. "I been trying to get him in here all fucking night and there he goes with that bitch." Sunny nodded for she too had seen. "Nigger with a Jap and we got three blondes in here," Doorman continued to cuss.

"Who you talking nigger?" Sunny said. "Keep putting us in front, no wonder he never come in."

Doorman stepped inside quickly to talk with Sunny in private. "Hey babe, you want any ludes tonight? My man out there got some. He'll sell the whole script, or just a couple."

"You know I do. Collette stuck that new bitch on me tonight. She's so good she don't know a trick from a dick."

"You got it sugar," Doorman disappeared into the side alley.

When he came back, Sunny swallowed two and hid the rest with her stolen tips in her bra. Then she took a drink from the bottle she kept hidden away from Collette.

Collette hadn't told Kathy that the particular room she'd been assigned was the one closest to the office, where Collette could hear most everything from her desk.

"I don't believe it," Collette said to herself. "That girl is giving him her life story and he's eating it up. Guess you gotta believe those new ones'll do anything." Collette held her lighter to a Dunhill cigarette and blew the smoke toward the ceiling. Checking her watch and the time on the log sheet, she saw that there were only a couple of minutes left in the sessions. She closed her eyes and leaned back in the chair, shutting out the sounds around her. I need some coffee, she thought, or something. The phone rang; it was the old man asking to see how much they had in.

"Five thirty-five." The old man cursed her and went on about how it was almost midnight. "You damn well better get going down there, it's late and you ain't got half what you're supposed to by now!" He slammed the phone down. Collette told him to fuck off because she knew he couldn't hear her, and then yelled "Time!" as she went out to the lobby.

The sailor boys were getting dressed as the girls came into the lobby. Collette followed behind them.

"Bye y'all," Sunny called as her boy left.

"Stop in again next time," Dawn said to hers after she had kissed him good-bye.

"Hey, I can't go out with you. You ain't got no hotel room, honey.

Quit your rapping about it. I know you ain't got no more money either. I checked," Anna said to hers as he looked back at her hopefully.

"Hey Jack, give me a couple of quarters for the juke box before you leave — make me think about you," Chrissy said as her sailor put on his coat.

The sailor boys left smiling. Collette looked over the girls in various stages of renewing their make-up. The street was quiet now, except for a few of the less successful street girls. The juke box was playing slow hold-me-in-your-arms songs. Kathy was sitting in the window again; Sunny was standing near her, talking about the street. They watched Maluda pass by.

"She got those two street girls following her, too bad," Sunny was saying. As if hearing her, Maluda turned around and started walking back toward Powell Street. "See those two other girls? Bet they're new around here. They probably roll their tricks when they're asleep, and take anything they can fence down on Market Street."

"Why would they do that?" Kathy asked.

"Most likely their old man just put 'em out on the street and they being pushed to get the most they can," Sunny answered.

From where she sat, Collette could see the two. They were both brassy-looking, like they had just come over from Oakland. Their pimp was most likely hanging out in some doorway, watching to make sure his girls weren't keeping any money from him.

"Yeah, well, this place is a lot of shit too. Here all you do is clean them out of their money and then they get mad at you," Chrissy said, adjusting her Foxy Lady t-shirt.

"But out there you just got one price and you don't get anything more. They don't get mad either," Dawn said. "Besides, here you always got someone to back you up if you get in trouble. It's better here."

"Here it's all a game; you keep pretending you're going to give it to them and then you make them do it," Candy said, laughing at the joke of it all. "And you ain't got to be out there all night."

"Yeah, but you got to put up with that old man all the time," Jeri said. "Always comin' in here and putting his hands all over you, trying to make you fuck him in the back room. I swear to god, if he ever try to do that to me again, I'm going to knife that motherfucker."

"He get you yet Kathy?" Collette asked, knowing he had, because he never hired anyone until he'd fucked them once.

Kathy didn't answer. She was still trying to figure out what Candy had said earlier. "Then how come it don't work like that for me then?

You all got lots of money on the books and I hardly got any."

"Kathy, you heifer, you give it too easy. That crotch of yours is *gold*, you hear? And unless they pay gold, don't take no green!" Sunny said to her.

"It ain't much better out there either," Anna said. "Yeah, you got one price, and if they got it, they get it, or else they gotta walk on down."

"But sometimes you can play it, though you've got to know your trick. Shoes, pockets, and the look. Don't take them hungry ones or you won't make it back," Chrissy said.

"The cops'll bust you just the same, whether you're laying your rap on them in here or out there," Sunny said. "Them shoes is the clue: always look down before you look up."

"But not if you're like some of them out there," Collette put in. "Some of them know exactly how to do it. They ask just what they think the guy'll pay, and then hit 'em up for more before everything happens. Like Maluda. She's street-wise. Knows exactly how much and she can spot those rubber soles from a block away. She ain't gonna get her ass landed in jail, she'd just gonna keep walking these streets. I mean, like how you think she got so much anyway?"

"*Fuck* Maluda! Who give a damn 'bout her? She ain't nothin'. I been walking the streets since she was just a baby girl in Oakland. She think she so good," Sunny sucked her teeth and spat. "She fuck anything, no matter if they got money or they her mama."

Collette snapped back at Sunny, "What's the matter, gal? She steal your man one night?"

"Fuck off," Sunny said quietly. She flopped down on the couch and crossed her arms over her chest.

"Step right in here and the hostess will take care of you, sir," Doorman said as he opened the door and a man came in.

"Hold on! I know what this is, and no thank you!" The man turned to walk out.

"Wait a minute," Kathy said, grabbing the man's hand. "Whatcha leaving for? You don't know us, why not stick around a minute?"

The man started sweating. He wrenched his hand from Kathy's and raised it to strike her. Sunny jumped up and blocked the slap.

"Keep your hands off her, turkey tail!" she shouted.

The man straightened himself and readjusted his tie. Embarrassed and proud, he cursed Collette too, but seeing the doorman standing over him, he left, slamming the door behind him. Inside, the girls broke into fits of laughter.

It was the final rush before the bars closed. The conventioneers were ducking in and out of bars, looking for some final action. Taxis came down from Broadway, delivering customers to special places where hotel doormen had said there would be women and booze. The other inhabitants of the street were also coming back to life. Leather jackets and rubber soles walked by the parlor, glancing in quickly, then turning their eyes on the street ahead. A four-door followed them down to the corner.

Men started coming into the parlor, looking for girls to take back to their hotels. It was the best time of the night; money poured in. Men were willing to pay anything so they could go home to wherever they came from with tales of their exploits to tell at the corner bar. Collette knew what she was doing with this crowd; she could figure out exactly how much every man was willing to pay and asked them for it without blinking an eye. And if, when they pulled out their wallets, she saw that she had figured wrong, she told the girl, so both knew how much more they could expect.

Dawn and Candy had gone out on calls to the Hilton. In the back, Kathy and Chrissy had customers. The rest of the girls were sitting out front.

"What's that guy Kathy's with? Every time he's supposed to go, she brings me more money," Collette asked, puzzled. New girls weren't supposed to have such luck.

"Probably got him to fall in love with her," Anna said, taking the stool.

"Collette, let me go in there and see what's happening. I want some of that money," Jeri said, rubbing her hands together.

"Go ahead," Collette said. "But you tell her she'd better get done quick." One thing about Jeri, if there was money to be had, she would get it or throw the guy out.

Collette stepped outside to talk with Doorman and check out the street. "You hear anything about cops tonight?"

"Only seen some pass by here a while ago. Ain't heard nothin'. . . Hey, hey, sir, why not come in and check it out? This lady right here will tell you all about it."

Collette said hi. The man looked at her, and hitched up his pants to meet his waist.

"Right this way," Collette led the man. "In here." She glanced around the lobby. Sunny looked indifferent and Anna was putting on more mascara. As Collette was talking to the man, trying hard to get him to stay, Anna interrupted her. "Hold on," Collette said to the man, giving his knee a little squeeze, "I'll be right back."

Collette stepped into the lobby with Anna. "They got a squad car on the corner, they re rounding everyone up," Anna said, pressing her hands together.

"Fuck," Collette swore. Although they tried to talk quietly, the fear in their voices filtered through to the man in the salesroom. He came out fast, almost knocking them down.

"I'm getting out of here. I don't want my name in the papers," he said, seeing the police lights flash in the window. "No sir, no way."

Collette tried to stop him, to assure him that the police wouldn't come in the parlor, but then let him leave. No need to make things worse with an angry customer.

"Go turn down that juke box," Collette said to Anna, and then turned to yell time at the customers still left. The girls came out of their sessions confused and angry at being interrupted.

"Collette, what you mean calling us out? I was just getting some money from that tight-fisted bastard and then you go calling time like your life depended on it," Jeri yelled at her.

"Hold it Jeri, we got cops down there," Collette said.

"Cops? I thought places like this didn't get raided," the man who had been with Kathy said as he threw his tie around his neck. "Bye Sweetheart — I'd like to stay, but not like this."

The other man also came out partially undressed and said, "I knew it, that's all I need. I'll be back for my money later."

"Like hell you will," Chrissy said as he left.

Collette watched them go, then looked at the girls again. "None of you had better have anything on you or else you're gonna end up down at Bryant Street with 'em."

Sunny ran to the bathroom and the water started running. Collette, looking out the door, watched the street. At the end of the block, the police van's lights were going, and everyone on the street was watching. Most of the girls were going along peacefully enough, but some, to the excitement of the gathered pedestrians, screamed and ran the other way. Inside, the girls were tense, straightening their clothes and checking their lips. Usually if the vice squad was after street action, they'd leave those who worked inside alone. Doorman, standing by the side, quiet, let some doctors walk by. He looked at Collette and both knew it was too risky to try anything.

"Hey you all, come in for a real good time tonight! Hey you! With the money! Give me some of that!" Sunny's voice seemed to fill the street.

Everyone froze, while Sunny waved her hand at the doctors. The cops, running by after an escaped street girl, slowed down, hearing her. Collette knew they were itching to bust anything out of line tonight. Chief Gaines was getting rough since it was election time. Doorman stared at the darkened antiques store across the street. The cops, perhaps because they didn't want to lose the whore they were already chasing, ran on.

Collette jerked Sunny out of the door. "What the fuck do you think you're doing? Do you want to get us all busted? Well, we're doing just fine without your help. The cops were going to pass us by tonight and then you go shooting off your trap like everything's above-board and legal here, you bitch. What the fuck you on? Think you're so good no one's going to bust your ass? Or what? Answer me!" Collette slapped Sunny across the mouth. Her eyes glassy and her movements slow, Sunny fell to the floor sobbing.

"Fuck this shit," she said. "Get my ass busted once more and go up to the county for a time, don't care."

"And what? Get this place closed down and your license pulled, your ass back out on the street, like the whore out there. You been around here longer than most of us and you talking that shit? The old man wouldn't even hire you to work in his bar with that kind of record, whore. Get in back." Collette grabbed a cigarette and lit it, her hand shaking. She coughed when the smoke hit her throat.

Kathy, terrified by these events, followed Sunny to the back. She hated Collette for what she had done to Sunny. It wasn't fair. This place was no better than the home she was running away from. Coming back up front, Kathy grabbed her coat and ran out the door. The girls in front watched her go, shaking their heads.

"Girl, it's prime time tonight. Street's hot, tricks hot, and the tem-pers. . ." Jeri said.

"Collette, the cops are busy, they've gone on down to Bryant Street and it's too late for them to come back now," Anna said.

"Come on, it's 2:30, the bars are out and we got to make up this hour. We ain't moved much from the last time," Chrissy said.

"Yeah, the rush'll be over if we don't get to work," Anna continued, practical as always.

"Sunny didn't mean nothing, she's just fucked up. And that new girl's just a fool. It's hard, you know that," Jeri threw in.

"Oh yeah? How'd Sunny get it then? You letting in shit when I told you not to?" Collette turned on Doorman now.

"Hey, hey, not me. She asked for it, ran up the alley while you were in back," Doorman said.

"And what you doing letting her go out? You know you're not supposed to let her do that." Now all of Collette's anger was on Doorman, who turned coolly back to the street, to a man passing by.

Maluda had been able to escape the police because of Sunny's recklessness. She had slipped into the alley when the cops' attention was focused on the massage parlor, and eluded the round-up. When the man walked by, Maluda came out to the sidewalk. Safe, she looked at the doorman and then in the window. Collette stepped out and looked down the street, Maluda's eyes following hers. Another bunch of doctors got out of a taxi a little further down.

Maluda looked at Collette, at her waist-length hair and long skirt swirling in the night wind. Collette's eyes watched the convention-eers, figuring they'd come in, with their money. Maluda looked at Collette's strapped sandals and into her eyes. She had heard Collette lash out at Sunny, had heard the scorn in her voice when she'd ridiculed street girls; she'd also seen the new girl run out crying. They measured each other. Collette frowned, then turned on her heel and went inside.

"Hey, hey men. Seems like you need what we got. Step-on-inside and take-a-look . . . take-your-pick. This is what you came here for!" Doorman held the door open and ushered some men inside.

Maluda walked on down the street and turned into the parking lot. The men came out, not wanting what the parlor had to offer. One of them started toward Maluda, but stopped. The men turned the other way, back to their hotel.

Girls Girls Girls went off. The Sugar Shop's doors shut. Doorman watched Maluda drive off alone.

Bohemia Ho...Ho Ho Ho

Phyllis Luman Metal

The Bohemian Club in San Francisco is the most prestigious men's club in California. The summer encampment at the Bohemian Grove near Monte Rio on the Russian River is a two-week, three-weekend gathering of the internationally rich and famous. The private jets land in Santa Rosa and the limousines pour through the gates of the Grove mid-July each year. Approximately two thousand men, divided into different camps, such as Mandalay and Derelicts, gather on Friday with approximately two thousand employees to serve them. After dinner, the opening ceremony is held in a clearing surrounded by giant redwood trees. A flickering campfire creates the mood of an ancient Druid ritual. With great solemnity, "Dull Care" is abolished. The ordinary affairs of the world are then forgotten, and the festivities begin. For some it is a quiet, restful time of meeting old friends and listening to serious lectures. For others, it is a carousing time. And for George Crandall (pseudonym), it is a time to encounter the "girls" at the Hexagon bar just outside of Guerneville.

For nine years I was the mistress of George Crandall, Hillsborough resident, who married an heiress and inherited seventy-five million dollars. I had my I. Magnin charge account, my rent, telephone and utilities paid, a thousand dollar a month allowance, and my children educated in Europe. He gave each one of them five hundred dollars a month for four years to study, in addition to their air fare back and forth to the United States. I saw George once a week on Thursdays when the Bohemian Club had its weekly meetings. His wife wanted him to stay in town because she knew he would have too many drinks to drive safely, so we spent the night at the Fairmont. I went on trips with him to New York, Mexico and Phoenix. I got the trips his wife did not want. He did not take me for cruises on the QE II because, of course, that was what she wanted. And he sent me to Europe.

Now why in the world would a man as attractive and charming as he, with a very attractive wife, need a mistress? Why had he been going to the apartment of a madam in San Francisco for fifteen years? Every Monday he showed up with champagne for lunch and for the girl of the week — until he met me at the madam's apartment when I went there with a friend, a student in graduate school in anthropology at UC Berkeley, who worked for her. She went to return a book George had loaned her. We all had lunch together, and George asked me out to dinner. He never went back to the madam's. I am sure she never forgave me.

Well, the answer was really very simple. He and his wife put on the facade of the very happy couple, but they had not slept together for years. George was impotent. He simply could not get it up. And that meant oral sex. His wife would never do it. In fact, she was such a lady he would never dream of asking her. She was an alchoholic who went on serious binges, and then had to go to the hospital to get cleaned up. George loved oral sex and had a very educated tongue, and this was his his secret.

He took me on hunting trips with his Bohemian buddies and they all got the impression that he was a hell of a stud who couldn't live without it. That was his posture. The first summer after I met him, he rented a cottage at the Hexagon house while the Bohemian Grove was in session at Monte Rio. He also invited a prostitute from Los Angeles, whom he had seen every summer for twenty years, to share the cabin with me. He wanted me to see how things were done during the Grove Encampment. Frenchy would take me to the bar and introduce me to the Bo's and then we would entertain all of his friends, me in one bedroom, she in the one adjoining. He bought us cases of booze, and we bartended for the "boys" and then took them one by one into our respective bedrooms. Everybody was loaded and having a very good time. They had tossed aside Dull Care in the opening ceremony, and for the next two weeks, and particularly for the three weekends, the atmosphere was carnival. Frenchy knew not only all che "boys," but the girls as well. They came up every summer to make a lot of money. By the time the next summer rolled around, George's and my relationship had changed. He wanted me all to himself. I had a cabin alone at the Hexagon House and entertained nobody but him. He had his moment of playing at pimping and pandering the summer before. After each encounter, he would say, "Did he pay you? How much?" It was part of his kicks. It might have occurred to him that what he had done was a felony and worth several years in a state prison. But he would have brushed the thought aside. He knew that with his money, prestige, social position and connections it could never be a problem. For George there were no problems... he had enough money to take care of everything.

The Continuing Saga of Scarlot Harlot IV

Carol Leigh

Everyone wonders about the mysterious prostitutes who entertain the Bohemians who "travel across the river." Well, I am one of those prostitutes. I call myself Big Red, like the logo on the Wrigley's gum wrapper, which I paste on card stock and use for business cards. I try to amuse myself. "I'm Big Red! See, here's my card. Only there is no gum. You'll have to come back to my room if you wanna chew. . ."

We enter the bar at eight or nine at night. The festivities at The Grove are over at nine-thirty or ten, but if we're lucky, we can catch an early bird. Plus, we're bored. There's nothing else to do. We enter the bar, fresh from about an hour in front of the mirror. We look our best. We sit with our girlfriends who immediately begin raving about our appearances. We discuss each woman's good qualities and assure her that she will make a lot of money that night. To be sure, we are very beautiful, though ridiculously out-of-place at the informal golf club bar. We know it and flaunt it, yet we are disturbed that there are so many townies at the bar. They stare at us and snicker; when the town boys get drunk they insult us. We look around and wonder, who are the cops and who are the reporters? We discuss it...

We recall the old days at Hex, a casually elegant hotel bar. During the period of the "encampment," we had the bar to ourselves. The gay clientele went elsewhere and the call girls and Bohemians could proposition each other with delightful abandon. I had a reputation for being particularly "sex positive." I used any excuse to show the prospective clients a split-wet picture of my cunt. Another woman came dressed like a bird in a bikini top made of feathers...

Wealthy men pay only a little more than middle class men. We make less up here per hour than we might make at a massage parlor.

Sometimes we feel cheated. We say they're cheap. Bohemians tell me that a man is less of a man if he pays more than his friends for a whore. For some of them, swindling us is a sport. Others are gentle and kind. They leave the bar with us as soon as we ask, or they ask us — they ask how much we charge and pay what we want — in bed they are gentle and fast. They flatter us. Many promise to return to us and don't. Others come back and give us more money than we expected...

I moaned, "I haven't been out once tonight. I'm getting depressed." During a good evening a woman might see three or four men.

"Oh, don't worry about it, Red. No one's caught tonight. The guys are all window shopping." Jamie's always supportive. She's also very beautiful. If she didn't catch, no one did. "Keep your spirits up, sweetheart," she says with a sympathetic pout.

"Oh, I'm never gonna make any money!" I like to complain.

"You think you got problems?" Martha's a mountain woman and very colorful, but she's new in the business so she doesn't make very much money. "Last jerk I did only paid me half a' what he said."

"You gotta get the money up front, darling," Jamie reminded her. "You can't trust anyone 'cause there are some creeps around here who'll want to rip you off. I hate men," Jamie giggles.

"What about more money? I wanna get more money from these guys. I mean, somebody should pay for all the time we've been sitting here. How do you do it, Jamie?" I'm always asking.

"Just tell 'em you're worth it, Red," Martha offered, proud to be of help.

"Tell them that your specialty is oral sex and that you're the best," Jamie confided. "That's what I always say."

"Great idea, Jamie. But if you're supposed to be the best, I'll hafta be the second best. I'll tell 'em I try harder. . ." I grinned, trying to amuse myself.

"Peg, what do you do to get more?"

"I ask for it. If that doesn't work, I beg." Sweet, shy Peg is an accountant and an embezzler as well as a part-time prostitute. Later that evening, I tell a man that I give the second best head. I introduce him to Jamie and tell him she's the best. He sees me that night and sees Jamie the next. We try to help each other out . . .

One year we organized a union. We had one meeting in which we heatedly discussed whether or not we should make a pact to turn anything under two hundred down. We talked about "appropriate" versus "slut" behavior at the bar. Some of the women claimed to be embarassed by the behavior of others. We talked about approaching men only when they were unaccompanied by a woman. We didn't agree on anything. I was proud that we met like that . . .

One of us is a lawyer, one is an administrative assistant, many of us are mothers. I am an actress/writer/producer, one of us was an elementary school teacher (now a full-time pro), one of us has a daughter who is deaf and may be going blind, one of us was a Sunday school teacher who had herself hypnotized to believe she was beautiful and horny so she could have the confidence and inspiration she needed. She wanted to break down her inhibitions, but her plan backfired. At the end, she wound up giving it away. We laughed and teased her the next day . . .

When there's not much money around, we feel tense. Some girls fight, and some of us cry. One cries because her boyfriend stole money from her again! And after he promised to stop. One cries because she hasn't made any money all night, and the last trick she brought to her room told her he doesn't pay for it. One woman cries because a trick she likes favors another woman. I cry because I wound up doing too much for not enough cash, because I'm just not assertive enough and I don't know how to bargain and those two guys I did together were so demanding. When we are making enough money we feel elated and no one cries . . .

At the end of the evening we have parties "women only" in the larger rooms. We usually are giddy, some of us drunk, most of us anxious to tell our stories. We hug and tease and flatter each other. At one party we hugged and kissed in twos and threes on the beds. Last year only a few of us did coke; most of us smoke pot and drink. I perform at these parties, with my tape recorder and telephone, and my poetry. I try to amuse myself . . .

Interview with Debra

Carole

Debra worked in prostitution for nine years. She is thirty-two years old and is presently working as a paralegal.

Carole: Where did you grow up?
Debra: My mother had me in Louisiana. I never met my father. I have no desire to. He just wanted some pussy and my mother happened to be there. From what I understand he was a jackass. He was already married. My mother had me, didn't tell her parents and then gave me up for adoption. I was gone from my mother for nine months. But when she was getting the final papers for the adoption, she said, "No." Meanwhile she'd gotten pregnant again. She told me the reason she'd gotten pregnant a second time was that she'd gone through this birth, mine, and felt empty. Then she decided that she was going to have me, too. She went to court and to this day she cries when she talks about it. It was awful! They called her names in court.

My mother moved to Wisconsin. I lived with my grandmother, who is wonderful. I love my grandmother! But she was a product of her times and she lived in a very tight-knit German-Polish community in Milwaukee. She wanted to tell the neighbors that I was a foster child. My mother told her, "She's my daughter and I will never renounce her again." And she didn't. I've always loved my mother for that. Except when I was doing the prostitution. She had quite a problem with it. She tends to get religious. I'm not religious. I believe that a lot of religious beliefs are man-made myths to keep people down. I believe in some superior being, but not some blonde man who walked the earth.

My mother married when she had two children — my sister and me. As far as I'm concerned, he's my real father. I mean it's not hard to take a dick and put it in a pussy. It doesn't mean anything. What motherhood and fatherhood mean to me is the actual bringing up of the children and the love you give them.

We moved to Madison, where we lived until I was in the sixth grade. My mother always said that she'd have twelve children — six boys and six girls — by the time she turned forty. And she had her twelfth child five days before turning forty. She loves children.

I had a lot of responsibilities when I was a child, I think, almost *too* much. I remember making my first turkey dinner when I was in sixth grade. I did the babysitting for all the kids. I was a real responsible child mostly because I didn't have a choice. It wasn't, "Could you," it was, "Do this." Then we moved further out. Really in the boonies. We bought an old farmhouse with one acre. It didn't have any heat upstairs so we had to sleep downstairs — ten of us in the same bed.

My father was an alcoholic until I was about seventeen or eighteen. A really severe alcoholic. It was real hard for him to show affection. I always thought he hated me. Then he quit drinking with AA, his whole person changed. He became a more gentle, caring and thinking man. I couldn't believe it. I used to waitress in a bar where he used to drink. It was one of the hardest things I remember doing — serving him liquor when I knew he had a problem with it. He was spending money and we were broke. I remember being a kid and being hungry. I mean, I remember cutting up onions so that my stomach wouldn't hurt. But my parents did the best they could. We always had some place to stay and shoes and we never starved. I think it taught me a lot.

I've been working outside the home since I was thirteen. I've done a lot of jobs. My first farm work, I picked cucumbers for eight hours a day. It's back-breaking labor. And you didn't get paid shit for it. We worked for Del Monte, the pickle people. The older I got, after I left home, I realized that other kids didn't have to do so much. It kind of freaked me out. It made me realize how much I did do.

Carole: How did you get involved in prostitution?

Debra: Well, I turned my first trick a long time before I actually turned out as a prostitute. I had been in college for a while and I was working as a cocktail waitress because my parents couldn't afford to give me any money. And there was this assemblyman. Assemblymen really made me see what politicians were about — I'm telling you! — these men were disgusting. They were gross. But they run our state. The people in Washington are probably worse, and they're running the country! This one man, one night, seduced me. He was older, probably in his fifties, and I was eighteen. He knew that he shouldn't have been doing that. He was married. Anyway, he gave me crabs and I never saw him again except where I worked. He had had his conquest, so that was that. But then I decided that I wanted to be an assembly page. To do that I had to be sponsored by an assemblyman. That's when I first turned a trick. I went up to him and I said, "I want you to sponsor me." He looked in my face and he knew better than to deny me. He was a politician and he didn't want it to get out. I was using sex as a tool, although not consciously. I was sexually harassed as a page and left. But that's another story.

Later I went to art school. And graduated. I had a 3.6 average. I worked house painting. I've had a lot of different jobs. I've worked in canning factories, which is horrendous work. That's why prostitution was so nice for me. Because you got a lot of money. You didn't take harassment. You didn't allow it. You were in control of the situation. You know? If someone patted my bottom, I got money for it. They didn't expect it to be part of the job. Which is very basically what I was going through with a lot of the other jobs. Being told that I should be thankful for the job. Please kiss my ass and thank me for giving you this shit job. You know? And I was getting totally fed up with it. So I started prostitution and took to it immediately.

Carole: Where did you start working?

Debra: Here in California, in the Bay Area. I moved out here in 1976. I met some people who were into prostitution and I turned out in February 1977. I liked being an artist and I was a good commercial artist. But I walked downtown San Francisco for months and nobody would give me a job. Not only would they not give me a job, they wouldn't look at my portfolio. Because I didn't have the work experience they wanted me to have, they wouldn't give me a How-do-you-do. People are fairly rude in a large city.

I worked with a group of women and one man. Right away. Thank God! I learned how to protect myself and my body. Another woman stood behind me as I worked. I got tutored in how to be a prostitute. That's the only way. I turned out on University Avenue in Berkeley.

The man never came out. A black man and a white woman on a stroll just ain't cool. The police would have a heyday. He'd go to jail and I wouldn't. It's ludicrous the racism in this country. I learned about racism in the seventh grade because the kids at school thought I was Mexican — but I didn't really learn about it until I turned out. It's sick. I've just been reading some books and I realize that a lot of times in the course of history common people, decent people, have allowed fanatics to control the way the world is run, mainly because they didn't step in and stop it. Because they're not fanatics. You know what

I mean? I think racism is becoming more definite in this country because people who think like I do, or think like you do, aren't saying, "Hey, wait a minute, I'm not going for it."

Carole: Debra, what kind of violent incidents took place in your work?

Debra: Well, first of all, when I turned a trick, I did it the way I wanted to. I was in control. I was the boss. I didn't allow tricks to touch my genitals and I fucked them in my hand. I had a certain way that I tricked and if they didn't want to trick that way they could leave.

The only two times somebody did something to me personally were right after I turned out. It happened two weeks in a row. The first month I turned out, I had my women friends with me but I was young and naive. When you ride with a trick you're in their territory. You have to take special precautions even if it's three minutes or three blocks away. You have your own specific route that you take. When you get in the car, you search it — you look in the glovebox. You keep your hand on the door handle at all times. You make sure that the door opens and closes before you get in. You watch every move the trick makes. He keeps both of his hands on the steering wheel. If you tell him to take a right, and he doesn't you're out of the car.

The first time, I took this trick to the trick pad. It was evening time, probably 10:00 or 11:00. He was a young guy. It was really busy at the trick pad. He didn't want to wait. I didn't know you don't ride back with a trick who hasn't dated. So, I'm driving back and I'm looking out the window and the guy put a knife to my throat. He took me off for three, four hours in the hills of Albany. I tried every move I knew. I mean I cried, I pretended I liked it. I finally talked him into getting a room so that we'd spend the night together. Finally! So, we rode back to Berkeley and I jumped out of the car and I told him that he better get the fuck out of there and he drove away with his door flapping. He'd raped me numerous times.

Carole: Wasn't it hard to get into a car again after that?

Debra: No, I knew that I'd done it wrong. It's a dangerous business and you have to protect yourself. You know, the thing that saves a ho is her sixth sense. Her sense of people. You have to make up your mind about people within minutes. You get to be really good at that. Our rule is if someone looks at you the wrong way, and says hello how you don't like it, no matter how much money he's offering you, leave it alone. Follow your first mind. You can look in someone's eyes and see compassion or humaneness or you can see meanness or violence. And it works.

It happened to me another time, though, shortly after. This guy had apparently been doing it to other women in San Francisco, but I was in the Berkeley stroll, so we hadn't gotten the word yet. 'Cause normally if one ho knows, she'll let the other hos know. 'Cause you protect each other. This white, middle-aged, respectable looking man took me off and we were driving to the same trick pad. He pulled out a gun and said, "Bitch, you make a move and I'll blow your head off." I broke his windshield and I broke his glasses. But he kept driving and I was raped. That was the last time, though. And I was a ho for nine years.

Carole: Did you ever report these incidents to the police?

Debra: I can't tell you the countless times I've heard police say that a prostitute can't be raped. It really upsets me. I think a lot of men believe that. It's totally ridiculous. I've had friends who've gotten hurt. After a while you stop telling the police. Their attitude is, "Hey, that's part of your job." Probably a lot of women believe that, too. Though I've had less of that attitude from women than men — the attitude that a prostitute is putting herself out there and that she deserves what she gets, whether it's rape or getting beaten up.

Carole: Did you make a lot of money?

Debra: Yes! We made *beaucoup* money! My attitude was that I was going to get what I wanted. For so many years I'd been abused, mainly by men. Face it, the people who ran the factories and the jobs were mostly men. I got sick of men doing that to me. I made between three and five hundred dollars a night and sometimes more. I lived better than I did in my life. It was a going joke — "Feed Debbie." I was really little then. There had been so many times that I hadn't eaten before so I ate like a horse. And I had furs, leathers, silks. We rented yachts for New Year's Eve. It was great! But it was fast money and fast money goes fast. We didn't just blow it, though, we invested it in real estate. Then the Feds took everything. But that's a whole other story.

Leaving the Streets

Gloria Lockett

In 1978, I was working on the street in San Jose, California. The police kept on telling me and the other women I worked with how intelligent we were, and how we should not be working the street. They told us we should open a massage parlor, or run ads, or something, but that we were just too bright to work on the street.

So I got together with a few women I knew and trusted, and we decided to get an apartment together and run ads in an adult magazine. The telephone rang constantly. We had an idea that the San Jose vice were among our callers, but what we did not know was that from the first week we were under constant surveillance.

The apartment lasted three months. One day everything changed, and my life hasn't been the same since. The vice called, pretending to be a customer. He came to the apartment with a transmitter in his belt buckle, and solicited one of the women who worked there. They arrested her, me, and four other women. There were four men in the apartment, having paid money to engage in sex with us. None of them were arrested. They only had to promise to be witnesses against us.

We were charged with four misdemeanors: 647(a), soliciting or engaging in a lewd act in a public place; 647(b), soliciting or engaging in an act of prostitution; 315, keeping a house of ill fame (i.e., a house of prostitution); and 318, prevailing upon someone to visit a place for the purpose of prostitution. We were also charged with two felonies: living off the earnings of a prostitute (i.e., pimping); and conspiracy.

I was charged with pimping because one of the women had given me money to put away for her, which is a very common practice among women who work together. She asked for it back, because it was money the vice officer had given her, and it was to be used in evidence. The police immediately told me I was under arrest for pimping. I was not at the time, nor have I ever been, a pimp.

The case stayed in court for two years, at a cost to the taxpayers of approximately one million dollars — the estimate of the prosecutor and the police officer in charge.

We were willing to plead guilty to being in a house of prostitution, but the prosecutor would not allow that. He wanted a felony conviction. Finally, we were found guilty only of being in a house of prostitution. We were put on probation, and charged a fine, but we were not sentenced to do time in jail. Needless to say, the police were very upset. They vowed to get us.

In 1983, my lover of nineteen years, a very good friend of mine, and I — the only Blacks in our group — were arrested on twenty-four counts of violating federal laws, including three counts of tax evasion, nine counts of violating the interstate travel act, ten counts of mail fraud, one count of a known felon having possession of a weapon, two counts of harboring witnesses, and two counts of racketeering. All the white people in our group were granted immunity in an effort to make them testify against us. My lover was found guilty of twelve of those counts, and is now doing twenty years in a federal prison in New York State. My friend pled guilty and got three years in a federal prison in California, and five years probation. I was fortunate enough to be acquitted.

When my lover and I got together, my children were two and three. This wonderful man is the only father my children have ever known, and now he is in prison thirty-five hundred miles from them.

The Continuing Saga
of Scarlot Harlot V

Carol Leigh

Hank just stopped by. I've seen him for several years and he's one of my favorites. We've never actually had a conversation, but I think he has a sense of humor because he smiles when I make jokes. Today I greeted him in my apron (saves time dressing) and I told him that I was just cleaning the house and forgot to put on my clothes. He seemed amused. We embraced at the door. I turned around and said, "Look, no panties. And I've been exercising."

We discussed my muscles and flab as he fell to his knees and kissed me all over.

"Take off your clothes," I said, and hopped like a bunny into bed.

He stroked and kissed and massaged me everywhere. I said it was good, and it was, because Hank has a warm, loving touch and no ejaculatory control. Within minutes he was up, dressed and darting out my front door. Easy come, easy go, as we used to say in the Tenderloin.

"See you soon, darling," I called after him. I do have a fondness for this man. But he makes me a little nervous. I mean, who is he?

Silence Again

Judy Helfand

I have worked with Women Against Rape for nine years now and in all that time I have talked with only three women about my experiences as a nude model and topless dancer. I was never ashamed of myself while working — I felt proud, cocky and powerful. But today I feel ashamed and afraid to bring it up. We're not a bunch of social service minded liberals, either, but a group of women out to change the world. We talk about rape, racism, incest, classism, homophobia, pornography, fat oppression, wife beating, lesbian battery and, of course, sexism. We do not talk about our experience of prostitution — selling our sexual selves or bodies to make it in the world.

In reading *off our backs* I came across the following: "Cleis Press is now accepting contributions to an anthology by women who have worked or are working in the sex industry." My stomach jumped. A book from a feminist press by women who may have shared my feelings and experiences. I could read their writings. I could submit an article, too! Finally, a release from that sense of isolation. Cleis Press has recognized this as an important area for feminist discourse.

Then I read on: "massage parlors, encounter studios, escort services, pornography, street prostitution, as well as other areas of sex work." Another clench of the stomach as I saw that topless dancing wasn't in there. Neither was nude modeling. Maybe my experiences weren't really "sex industry." I couldn't waste people's time with my writing because what I had done was too "tame" to be legitimate. And anyway, my experience didn't really count because I was a college student; I wasn't tied to it; I was really above it all, not part of it.

Then I affirmed, yes, I had been part of the sex industry. My denial was part of what needed to be examined. I needed to share my experiences if for no other reason than to find other women who felt the same. In our own experience we hold the keys to deeper understanding of the oppression of women in the world. Silence. Guilt. Isolation. I needed to participate in breaking through these three barriers.

The summer I was to be twenty-one, my boyfriend and I got an apartment together, a daring counter-culture move for me in 1966. In the back of our duplex lived a woman who worked as a nude model and topless dancer. To me she was exotic, exciting, extremely independent and powerful. I wanted the same assurance she expressed about the sexual attractiveness of her body, her allure to men. By the end of the summer, I was working as a topless dancer on Broadway in San Francisco, and as a nude model for an art professor/photographer. The money was lots better than I'd been making as a bookkeeper's assistant and countergirl.

Working in the sex industry, I experienced many different, often contradictory feelings, some of which I've never fully acknowledged before. My expressed feelings at the time were total ease and a kind of sarcastic humor about how ridiculous men were if I would make twenty-five dollars a night for showing my tits for thirty minutes max. At the topless club, I spent my time off stage studying, or sitting at the bar feeling superior to the poor jerks who patronized the place. Occasionally, I visited the snake dancer and her snakes upstairs.

Tasha, the snake dancer, was small breasted, athletic and trim. She was my idol. At the time I looked down on women who injected silicon to increase their breast size. I never considered dieting to maintain my five foot seven frame at one hundred and ten pounds. I was proud of my athletic, small breasted body in such a sea of breast-mania. Somehow it tied in with my independence, my stubborn refusal to see myself as an exploited woman, a down-and-outer like the other "topless co-eds." Having a more masculine figure was the final hold out against victim status. What I never did see was that my body type was in vogue at that time, emphasizing my look of youth and innocence which was a real turn-on to men. They were probably not seeing the independent, powerful, sexy butch I wanted myself to be.

The independence was definitely tied to money. I felt I'd solved the dilemma of how to go to school and earn a living, too. Twenty-five dollars a night as a topless dancer. Ten dollars an hour as a model. I took one job for moving rather than still pictures but it was too sleazy for me. The guy was really creepy. He did all my make-up and then had me dress in black lace underwear. He filmed fifteen minutes of me taking off stockings. The pay was fantastic but I couldn't maintain my illusion of the proud, independent woman in such circumstances. I stuck with "art" photography.

The issue of power interests me a lot. Having a presence and physical body which men found sexually attractive was important to my self-esteem. Having men pay to get turned on by me was an affirmation of my sexual power. At times I would dance for a certain man, trying to make him uncomfortable by flaunting my body at him. I really liked to win the amateur contests. Men could want and need me. I wouldn't fall into the traditional female role of pining after men, trying to ensnare them with various schemes. I'd just be so sexy I could have any man I wanted. Although, of course, I didn't want any of them. What I never saw was that in basing my self worth on men's desire I was far from developing a true sense of worth based on self love.

I see this false sense of power as one way internalized oppression keeps us down. For years I isolated myself from other women and put my considerable energies into men. I wanted to feel on a par with the most important, powerful people. Being sexually desired was the fix I needed to feel in control, to feel powerful. Now I see how this worked against the recognition of my own real oppression as a woman. I see that wanting men to want you sexually is what men want.

There has been so much silence surrounding this issue. As feminists we have learned to talk about how sex is taken from us by force, manipulation, coercion, and whatever else conveys "taking." We do not discuss how we find giving it away necessary to our self-esteem. Shame seems to be a factor. Although I thought I wasn't ashamed of my sex industry jobs I never told my mother. I told her I smoked dope and took drugs, that I had sex with my boy friends, but I didn't want to upset her needlessly by telling her I showed my bare body to men for money.

Somehow we need to find a way to talk about what we do of our own volition. Possibly we can come to see our participation not as collaboration but as — what? Self-illusion? Making it in the system? Finding a way to feel good about being a woman given the few options offered? I want to understand the process whereby I refused to buy into the lies of wifehood, self-sacrifice and living for a man, but never saw that the mirror-image lies in buying into the patriarchal version of independence — power and not needing a man.

It makes me angry when feminists lump all sex industry workers into a pile of poor, exploited, brainwashed victims without minds of their own. I was a young woman who needed to earn a living and chose to pursue the highest paying, least demanding jobs I knew of. I was successful. I felt good about myself. Today I have different values and a clearer understanding of my position as a woman in the world, but this doesn't invalidate my past experience. What I can do today is examine those unexpressed, unacknowledged feelings from the past, the feelings which co-existed with my previously discussed feelings of power, independence, sexiness and ease. This is the hardest part, the home of those barriers of silence, guilt and isolation.

I never felt a part of my work world. I had no friends, talked with few of my co-workers, and never interacted with any of them outside work. To some degree I felt superior: I was a college student doing this temporarily. But in truth, I didn't know how to relate to people other than sexually or intellectually. To have sexual passion enter my workplace would have been too scary. It would have threatened my "tough-girl-don't-touch" stance. I also played on my "sweet-young-thing" looks, another image which would have been hard to to maintain in a sexual relationship. I did find a couple of men to discuss "intellectual" issues with, existentialism or the Free Speech Movement, but the North Beach sex industry was quite different from the university. I know now that to maintain my positive outlook and self-esteem in that environment I had to remove myself from my deeper feelings and essentially wall myself off.

Guilt and shame were certainly among those walled off feelings. I worked in sleazy places with people I had no respect for. Of course, I didn't really know the people, but because of their work I saw them as failures, as society's dregs. With few exceptions I felt superior to all around me. This was how I protected myself from the shame and guilt of offering myself visually to men, doing what I had been raised to think was socially degenerate. Somehow, it seems to me that being a sex worker was a way of denying the feelings which were tied to sex at an unconscious level. This is still an open question for me. Topless dancing, nude modeling were never neutral experiences. Despite my avowed ease there was always a certain stridency, a feeling of daring which must have been the cover for fear and vulnerability. I was a lost young girl co-existing with a powerful, independent woman.

Guilt and isolation contributed to the silence. My isolation kept me from talking with the other workers, learning how they felt, exploring our roles as sex workers. And although I didn't keep my work a secret I didn't talk about it a lot. I was really terrified my parents would find out and I simply didn't know how I would handle that. Embarrassment was the closest I got to naming that confusing well of emotions which rose up at the thought of my parents judgment. Embarrassment is what rises up today in trying to talk openly about my sex worker experiences. I feel like a naughty little girl, half confessing to, half bragging about, some misdeed. What is the well-spring of this embarrassment? Another very open question for me.

People have always been shocked to learn that a nice girl like me could have been a sex industry worker. "I never would have thought. . ." For years I found a kind of defiant pleasure in their astonishment. Now I want to shout "Why not? What are your stupid stereotypes that deny my experience?" But I realize that I shared in the denial, felt as if my work was not the true me but a part I was playing. Now I know it was truly a part of me. I'm learning to know that part concurrent with becoming aware of other aspects of my inner self. In time I may be able to integrate all my parts, to understand how I got here. This article is only the beginning, raising far more questions than it answers. But in overcoming the silence and isolation it's a very important first step.

Coming Out of Denial

Sharon Kaiser

Fourteen or fifteen years ago, for about three years, I worked as a porno actress and did a little prostitution. I rarely told anyone, and when I did, I played it down or lied about it. Then a few years ago, one of the few friends who knew introduced me to Margo St. James, who in turn introduced me to COYOTE.

I came out of the closet, and began to reclaim a part of me I denied and saw as bad. For the first time I had support for that part of my life, that part of me.

I got into pornography as a fluke. I had been a struggling actress for years, and had decided to get on the other side of the camera, into film production. I got an opportunity to learn some of the craft by filming hard core pornos. I did learn behind-the-camera craft, and it did lead to more straight film jobs, but in the meantime, one thing led to another and I did a lot of work in front of the camera as well. I called it experimenting; it was the late sixties, early seventies, and experimenting was "in."

I'm not going to say it was great . . . it wasn't; it wasn't bad either. I was dealing with a stigma, something that had been pounded into my head as bad and dirty. So no matter what I called it, no matter how I did it, or what I did (behind or in front of the camera), I was bad. I don't know how to explain it. It's not the act that makes it bad; the people were clean and respectful, but the stigma made it bad.

I dealt with it by denial. Later I would deal with prostitution the same way.

It's funny, I've been a lesbian all my life, and the stigma surrounding homosexuality in the middle sixties when I came out was never even half as bad as it was around being a prostitute or doing pornography. I dated women who did prostitution in corporations, and the denial was so great that we never told each other what we were doing. We lied. . . mostly to ourselves.

I never called myself a prostitute; I never called myself a porno actress either. I was a filmmaker. I didn't work the streets, I didn't work every day, my customers were repeats, referrals. I called them my friends. . . it was an easy lie. They didn't pay me, I would tell myself; they helped me out with my rent and bills, and they would land me film jobs. And I liked them; you're never a prostitute when you like them. Besides, I was a lesbian, and I was experimenting, and it was safe. . . I could get out or stop anytime I wanted. . . I was on top.

In those days I wore make-up and sexy dresses or shorts with slits going up my hips. I loved dressing, and in those days I loved performing. When I stopped I went just the opposite. I began wearing jeans and plaid shirts with t-shirts, and quit wearing make-up. And this was my costume until three years ago.

The women in COYOTE reminded me of how much I enjoyed dressing up and how much I enjoyed wearing make-up. . . how much I enjoyed looking and being sexy. They reminded me of this whole part of me I had denied and had hoped was dead.

Oppression does funny things. The people to whom I most feared revealing my history were lesbians. They don't necessarily see prostitution and pornography as immoral. . . but they are revolted. And I think this is because of the way we've been oppressed as homosexuals; we've been conditioned to view sex acts between members of the same sex as revolting and immoral. Because we've been hurt in that way, we in turn hurt in the same way.

So I had nowhere to go. I'd heard of COYOTE, but because I'd done so much denial for all these years I didn't see myself as an ex-prostitute, or even as an ex-porno actress.

When I finally went to this group, for the first time I met women who proudly called themselves prostitutes. I met women who supported each other and supported me. I had known only one woman when I was working who called herself a prostitute, and I couldn't even come out to her then.

My whole life has changed as a result of meeting these women and working with them. If I had had that support then, so many things would have been different. I wouldn't have had to think I was bad. I would have loved myself a little more.

The Continuing Saga
of Scarlot Harlot VI

Carol Leigh

Brrrring...Brrrring...

Wow! Maybe it's an activist prostitute, calling to help me plan the revolution.

"Hi, honey. What ya up to?"

Oh, shit. It's Frank. Should I or shouldn't I? I am so immersed. I don't feel like working. I just get in this really sensitive space. I'm an artist! I shouldn't have to. And he's really an effort. But I need the money.

"Oh, I'm great darling. I was just hanging around. Why don't you come over. I'd love it."

"Be right there." He's happy.

"Just give me a half hour to get dressed and clean my apartment."

"Don't bother for me."

"No, I have to. See ya."

I straighten up my desk, make my bed, shower and set my hair with electric rollers. Whore Magic. That would be a great brand name, I think as I smear my lips and cheeks with Wild Cherry.

I should start a business and sell cosmetics, oils and sex toys by Whore Magic. I'd make a fortune. I lament as I choose matching bra and garters and a lowcut dress — sadly, because I know that tail is more profitable than retail. I choose music and light and incense. The doorbell rings. Frank appears in tennis drag (the alibi to his wife) but this is not a matter of love.

We kiss and hug. I drag him into the bath and wash him with ritualistic tenderness, sponging and sucking and cooing. I drag him back to bed and proceed with the oral sex. Maybe he'll just come like this and leave real fast so I can get back to my art and politics. But I tease to extend his pleasure so that he'll come back again. Hurry up, hurry up, I think as my mouth and fingers linger.

"What about sixty-nine?" he asks, as if I might refuse him.

"Mmmmm. Oh yes, yes," I whisper. Shit. I don't want to get all involved. I don't feel like getting off. I never feel like it, but I'd rather come than fake it and the clients in my call girl network expect us to act like we like it. I wish I worked turnover like in a brothel or massage parlor. Regulars are so much pressure, but I work this way to avoid police.

"It's great you love to fuck and suck so much. You really like it, don't you!" he moans to my crotch.

"Oh, yeah, I do etcetera . . ."

"Do you like my cock?"

"Oh, yeah, I do etcetera . . ." Oh, c'mon, I think. Now, if sex workers had status as actresses, I wouldn't suffer from the tension of these lies. "I like it. Please fuck me."

"I can tell you really do. I think the women should enjoy it. I know you really do. That's what turns me on."

"Oh, yeah. I love it. I love it." I say. What I hate the most is that these guys think we're sex-crazed. They think we're aching for a hot time in the sack. I don't know why he keeps asking. I certainly respond passionately enough. Frank comes. He rolls off and hugs me.

"How many times did you come?" he asks.

"Oh, yeah, I don't know. I lost count."

Frank's a nice guy and a good lover, but my mind is somewhere else. My call girl friends agree: sex work is a lot easier when you see a lot of men. When one sees three or four men a day for several days, one enters a sexually-open state. But I don't have time for that, so I find the work irritating.

I know! I should write a book for tricks about how we really feel about these encounters. I could interview all my friends. Ah, when whores start telling the truth and lifting the burden of these lies we will become so powerful and the future of prostitution will be so rosy. . .

Dream Turned Nightmare

Cecelia Wardlaw

I was born forty-eight years ago to a Roman Catholic and alcoholic family. I am a recovering addict, and I recently learned that I was an incest victim.

As I was growing up, I remember pouring over any books which offered me information about sex. My mother hid the medical books I was reading, so I retreated to dictionaries and encyclopedias which I found at the library. As a young teenager in the 1950's, I tried unsuccessfully to seduce the neighborhood boys. They, too, were Roman Catholics, and Roman Catholics in the era of "Father Knows Best" saved themselves for marriage. In 1960, I was a virgin bride and hot as hell. My husband could not match my sexual appetite, and I thought the problem was due to some fault of mine. I began reading again. I found sex manuals, which were relatively new then, but my husband said they gave me "too many ideas." When articles about massage parlors first appeared in magazines, I was fascinated. I fantasized about what it would be like to be a prostitute, but thought my chances of ever becoming one were slim. Little did I know.

As my children grew older, I became more involved in their lives and my own expanded. I began doing volunteer work in the community and found people who thought the way I did. I found support for my ideas. I also discovered I loved women. My life was full and content. Even sex was not as frustrating.

Then we were transferred to the south.

I remember kneeling in front of the Blessed Mother's statue that first evening in our new city, and sobbing. A few weeks later, on our twelfth anniversary, my husband and I went out to dinner. I remember sitting across the table from him, thinking, "I have nothing in common with you."

It took me a year to work up the courage to leave.

When I eventually left, I discovered that I had not the faintest idea about living alone and taking care of myself. Alcohol and pills entered my life. It took at least one joint to work up the courage I needed to go into a bar. The men I met just wanted sex. Free sex. I went along with that, but not for long. In the meantime, a woman I had grown to love while I was still married came to visit me. Our first night together, we got high, laughed and talked about old times. The second night, we made love. Then she left. I didn't know what to do. I was far too timid to go to a gay bar, even high.

I was a registered nurse and worked in a methadone maintenance center as a nurse/therapist. Just as the magazine articles about prostitution had fascinated me, tales of the streets and street life now caught my attention. In my vulnerable state, it did not take me very long to become romantically involved with one of my male patients. I began stealing drugs for him. My man ended up in the penitentiary, and I was once again on my own.

I found my way back to the north, and ended up back in the bars. I began turning tricks, not so much to make money, but to avoid giving away sex. I met a woman who was street wise, beautiful, shot drugs, and wanted to be with me. I was in love. She introduced me to heroin, and, for the first time, I developed a physical dependency.

Linda and I lived together in a house I had bought just to get her under my roof. Once I became addicted to heroin, there were two habits to support and we needed more money. My criminal activity increased and, in time, I was arrested. After I was released from jail, we needed fast money, badly. I was no longer employable as a registered nurse, and besides, the money was too slow in coming. We sat down one day with the phone book, looking for massage parlors, and found several. Linda's cousin and I went out the next day to check them out.

The parlors weren't located in the best section of town. At the first one, we climbed a dark, dismal stairway to the second floor where we found a hulk of a man sitting at a desk. He glared as we approached him. There were five or six scantily clad women lounging in a variety of poses on couches and chairs. They all smiled as we entered. The man instructed us to fill out an index card with our names, addresses, and phone numbers, and said that he would call us.

The next parlor was further uptown, on a street laden with bars. Again, we climbed to the second floor of a seedy looking building. This time we were told to return that night at 11:00 to see the manager.

We went back to the street and entered a pick-up place. I perched on a bar stool, and soon, a man began playing with my leg. A voice said, "Watch it." I turned to the door and saw a monster-sized cop. I slid off the bar stool, and told Linda's cousin I was heading home. She decided to stay and try her luck at another joint. She called us later that night from jail. She had been arrested.

I returned to the parlor at 11:00. I was told to go down a hallway — even darker and more dismal than the stairway — and into a back room to take off my clothes. In the room I found a bed made up with a single sheet and a towel. The walls were covered with mirrors. What little plaster was exposed was painted black and red. I stripped down to my panty hose and blouse. The manager knocked on the door, told me to remove the rest of my clothes, and left. When he returned, he laid down, after removing his clothing, and told me to sit down, indicating the edge of the bed. He told me to do anything I liked. I remember looking at him questioningly, but got no further instruction from him. I shrugged my shoulders and began handling his genitals. I gave him head. He tapped me on the shoulder and told me that I had done fine, and that I should report for work in the morning. I was so relieved. Since my release from jail, Linda and I had no source of income except welfare checks and the few tricks I was able to turn. I did not want Linda to whore. My skin crawled at the thought of her being touched by a man.

I turned up late on my first day in the parlor. As soon as I got home the night before, Linda and I got high, and we continued until morning when we ran out of drugs. I had to wait for her to get more so that I could make it through the day. I guess that by the time I arrived at work, the women really weren't expecting me. They looked surprised when I came into the room.

I was sent to a dressing room, with a dresser, a bald light bulb hanging overhead, and hooks on the wall for street clothes. As many as six women at a time used this room — which measured only about eight by ten feet — to change clothes. Next door was a laundry room with washers and dryers that ran continuously. The parlor never closed, and we were frequently on the floor for sixteen hours without a break.

Apparently I was taking too long in the dressing room, because a beautiful black woman was sent after me. They thought I was shy, or afraid. In fact, I was so high I couldn't move very fast and I was unnecessarily repeating a lot of motions.

I made it to the front sitting room and took the last seat on the couch. The women engaged in small talk until Daisy, who worked

110

the desk, observed a john through a strategically placed mirror outside the steel, electronic door. When Daisy called, "Customer," a flurry of activity ensued. Women sat up straight, applied lipstick, pulled up or pulled down clothing, smiled on command, and struck seductive poses — all in a matter of seconds.

Customers came and went all day, and I remained unchosen. When a man was buzzed in, he approached the desk, exchanged a few words with Daisy, and pulled out some money. Then he turned to us, and we smiled and struck poses. I learned all of this by observation. No one gave me any verbal instructions, although I was sent in on a few sessions that first day to watch. The john would select a woman, who would lead him to a large, gaudily decorated room. Large mirrors were standard, walls were painted in dark reds, blues, greens and black, and there was plenty of gilded trim on walls, mirrors, and bathroom fixtures. Most rooms included a large, raised bathtub, used for the most expensive sessions, which lasted an hour. Standard sessions began at fifteen minutes for a hand job at twenty-five dollars, or half-and-half (a fuck-and-suck session) at forty dollars. Prices and times varied according to the desires of the customers. The longest session available was one hour, included the use of the tub and a half-and-half, at one hundred dollars. English sessions (s/m) were strictly tailored both in cost and content by the desires and pocketbooks of the customers. Only certain women did s/m sessions, and I was told early on that I would be good at it. I think it was because I looked so angry.

I remained unchosen well into that first evening, until a very high young man was buzzed in. All of the other women were busy with customers. He sat, or rather, fell to the couch beside me, and I began talking to him. Before I knew it, I had him talked into a hundred dollar session. I became the favorite of the "drunk crowd" after that. I wasn't afraid of them and found I could talk them into just about anything.

Several months after I began working, very early one morning, an extremely intoxicated man was buzzed into the room. He ended up spending the rest of the night with me and subsequently became a regular customer. I had several regulars by this time and even was occasionally the "top booker." My trips to the street were far less frequent, but life at home was getting worse and worse.

Linda said that her lack of interest in sex was due to her increasing dependence on heroin. I suspected it was due to my sexual involvement with men. When I would try to quit my work, she would pick a fight, and I would end up getting beaten.

Money was a constant problem. There was just never enough. If I made two hundred or two thousand a week — and it varied that much — the money disappeared. That's how we arrived at Christmas of that year with no money. Our Christmas dinner consisted of a half pound of ham and three scrambled eggs. We were both sick — dope sick. Linda said that if we weren't together, we'd each be having a merry Christmas. She always said that it was our racial difference that caused us problems. I knew that it was drugs. I was in such denial that I remember wishing for Santa Claus to magically appear before morning with a tree and train. He didn't, of course, and I never felt so stuck in my life.

The months lumbered on. I lost my house because no mortgage payments had been made for over fourteen months. We moved to an apartment and I began seeing my early morning visitor on my own time. I lived with constant paranoia. Eventually I was fired from the parlor. I was taking too much time off work and coming in beaten. This is a very difficult period for me to put on paper, although I talk about it a lot. Losing my house was deadening. When I bought my house — during a period of sobriety in 1980 — I was the proudest woman around. I had so many hopes for Linda and me. Losing my house meant losing all hope that she and I would work out our life together.

After I was fired, I managed to land a nursing position with a temporary agency. I was also seeing my john three or four times a week. Money was better than ever, but life was hell. My john was paying the rent, buying the groceries and giving me two hundred dollars each time I saw him. I was on methadone, which meant that my physical need for heroin was no longer a factor. Linda and I fought constantly about that fact. I was being beaten regularly and made several feeble attempts at suicide.

There was one counselor at the meth clinic whom I would call whenever I had been brutally beaten. She said, "When you've had enough, you'll do something about it." And I did. It took months, but I did leave.

Prostitution

Rosie Summers

Today I watched a black bird come down to the broken tree in front of me and stare at me for more than five minutes while I tried to begin this article. She stood so close, and cawed for so long, I believed she wanted to tell me something.

When she left, my eyes stayed on the tree trunk, and its ridges and brown wrinkles looked so much like a woman's labia. There was even a long, oblong hole in it, with the sky and the clouds showing through.

Almost everything in nature — the tiny, prickly hairs on plants; soft, huge mountains in the distance; and the way that plants can respond by moving if you stare at them long enough, reminds me of women's bodies. Is there something important about women, who carry life in their bodies and who are so much more orgasmic than men, that our society has almost been able to hide?

I remember being a New York City prostitute, and coming home every evening to my East Village apartment to chain smoke cigarettes and sing the aching, lonely kind of pain songs that rock and roll radio stations still play. These are songs that're sung by male voices — not women's songs about being broken hearted and dumped — but aching, searching kinds of songs about being alone in the city or alone on the road.

The neighbors recognized me as a woman who was probably crazy and also probably a whore, and they'd pass me on the narrow staircases without greeting me. Several times, though, I thought I heard people talking about me when I passed the other apartment doors.

Every morning I'd get dressed in my Chanel No. 5, heels, and short dresses. My expensive shoes would be so high and so difficult to walk in that after hobbling down the stairs, I'd flag down a taxi to go to work.

Although I worked in a massage parlor with other hookers, I experienced as much hatred there as I did in the outside world. Whenever I heard the phrase motherfucker, I listened real hard, because I came to think of that as my nickname.

The large, black madam, who wore a nurse's uniform and white shoes, would lean back against the icy blue walls and direct the conversation.

"That motherfucker thinks she some kinda good whore, but I saw her lick that old man's dick for five dollars. She ain't no big money."

"Shit. Barbie? She ain't no money."

"Shit. If I was a man, I wouldn't spend no more than five dollars on that whore's pussy, neither."

Nobody who isn't locked up puts up with constant oppression, and the clever madam balanced her insults with kindness. Sometimes when I'd be walking back to the massage room, intent on giving some man pleasure (and intent on it, I believe, because I wanted to be loved) I'd hear other conversations.

Madam: "That poor Barbie. I feel sorry for her. She's adopted, you know."

C, my only enemy, who would be talking in a husky voice and making poor-baby eyes at me: "You're just kind of an orphan, ain't you baby?"

Madam: "Shoot. If I was her mama, I wouldn't give her up for nothing."

C: "Must've been a pretty little baby."

I'd skip off to the massage room, feeling loved for that entire trick, but then sometimes I'd come back to the other side of mind-bending, the cruel side.

Me: "Somebody's been calling me up all night, and scaring me by threatening me!"

Madam: (Aside) "And that's the only call that motherfucker ever gonna get, too."

I felt cut off from people, although I had sex with five or more men every day. At night, instead of counting sheep, I put myself to sleep with fantasy machine gun dreams. I'd shoot first the madam, and then all the tricks I could remember, until I fell asleep.

"Was she any good? You don't like that girl, do you, Mister Jones?" It was painful to have my insides used by someone and then a few minutes later to hear another prostitute loudly talking him into disliking me, so he'd like her better.

"That whore ain't givin' out no good pussy. Mister Jones complained," the madam'd sometimes say. The trick was always mister, but we were always either that whore, that bitch, or else baby or honey.

After having had so many men inside me, poking in me without liking me, I began to get nervous and to do odd things. Several times I drove to visit a trick who paid me only twenty dollars and who lived seventy miles away from where I was, by then, walking the streets. Every time he laughed at me, enjoying himself for having made me come so far.

Before I went to see him, I stopped in a diner, and in that small town, my walk, my short dress, my nervousness, and my being out of doors so long after dark, marked me as a hooker. I set off a sort of giggling hysteria in a group of men, who started excitedly talking about me and making jokes. "I wouldn't touch her with a ten foot pole!" one of them said. And then, unless my pain has distorted my memory, he took a long mop pole and came up closer and waved the pole around at me, a woman who had been used to the point where she wasn't "pretty" any more.

He knew that any one of them could have slept with me that night, and that's what made me something to hate. When I was on the street, I sometimes was subjected to men amusing themselves by honking for me, and then screaming or making ugly faces when I came close to the car, then racing off. Maybe it was because I looked men in their faces, which is something non-prostitute women train themselves not to do, and which I don't do now, but I remember men on the street insulting me. I remember the New York City gay man staring at me a long time, and then loudly telling his friends, "Honestly, the things some men will buy!" And, as I write this, I suddenly remember a man in San Francisco who spat at me.

***

In the desert of New Mexico, there's a women's commune where the women dress mostly in glass Indian beads and turquoise, and live in teepees. When they have gatherings, women slowly climb up the cliffy, sky-surrounded mountains to chant and to sing to Mother Nature. They travel in beat up old pick-up trucks that have crystals and charms dangling from their rearview mirrors, and they come from adobe towns with Indian and Mexican names, towns that are famous for mystical visions.

In the summer women sit naked in peyote circles, and each woman sings out her life, even if it takes her hours.

115

My name is Rosie, And I know every man. I know their bodies, and they say they know mine. But I'm like the wind on a hard, stormy night. I'm like the sun and the skies. I'm someone whom men will never know, I'm someone who's pulsing with life I'm someone who's filled with joy.

***

Picturing it, I see him lying on the massage table, and reaching out to touch my breasts. First I see the textured, green body suit, protecting my body like my body protects a sigh, which it does not express. He pulls at the body suit, and gets it to hang down from my waist. Then he reaches out, and begins to squeeze my breasts.

Where do I go, then? Do I go into my fantasy — he is a woman with a dildo, who's going to be fucking me — or do I actually travel here, somehow, into my future, to give myself strength?

The man pulls my body suit down farther while he's still sucking on my breasts. His hands are white against the green suit, and they squeeze themselves under the stocking, and finally under my underpants, into my vagina.

He follows the ritual until he climaxes. "You were very good, Barbie," he says, and he reaches out to touch my vagina, and give it an extra, free squeeze. "That's a good little thing you've got there," he says. "You try and keep it clean."

***

I belong to a women's theater group, and for several weeks in a row, I arrived with a new five minute play about prostitution.

I wrote about two cops illegally trying to set me up for a felony by showing me a wallet full of hundreds and then leaving me alone in a room with it. I wrote about the same cops trying to recruit me for a brothel where they would get a commission, and also about their bragging to me about other hookers they had beaten up. I wrote about tricks trying to kill me and pimps trying to sweet talk me and threaten me. I wrote that when judges and cops deal with hookers, they drop the chivalry and the phony, overdone sexuality men pretend to, and instead make loud jokes about the women to punish them for having had so much sex.

When I finished reading these pieces, the women either changed the subject, were completely silent or laughed. Although they showed no sympathy when I talked about men trying to kill me, they became very sympathetic when other women talked about car repair bills, or broken xerox machines at work.

116

When I was in a crummy New York hotel, I remember overhearing the police discussing the death of a hooker with the hotel manager. All three men were laughing, and making jokes about the parts of her body that had been found in garbage cans. I also remember the first week I got to California, and reading a front page news story about a blonde Berkeley co-ed who was killed. She was in the news for nearly a week, although the hooker's death, of course, got no news coverage at all.

I can't help but feel that when feminists laugh or change the subject when I talk about experiences that nearly killed me, they are reflecting society's feelings that hookers' deaths — and lives — are unimportant.

There were eighty-one hookers and possible hookers murdered in the Seattle area between 1983 and 1986, and I think the chances are good you've never read about it in the newspaper. Right now, as you're reading this, some runaway may be standing in a bus depot, being recruited by a pimp. Runaways who end up as street walkers are not expected to live more than three years, according to Trudee Able-Peterson, author of *Children of the Evening*.

When I tell other women these stories, they usually respond with silence, and when I try to talk to men, it can be even worse. I once had a boyfriend who felt his penis was too small, and he was upset and jealous when I told him a man with an elephant penis told me he had killed women with it and he wanted to kill me with it, too. "Gee," he whined, in his envious little boy's voice, "If you met a guy with a dick that big, what chance do I have of impressing you?" It didn't, of course, ever occur to him to sympathize with me or to comfort me because I had once been someone whose life was considered so worthless that men often tried to kill me.

***

Some people believe that at one time women's bodies were considered sacred, because they are the origin of human life. I believe that if we women didn't repress our psychic and sexual energies — so much stronger than men's — we might live in such a different world it'd be hard for us to recognize.

We live in a culture that worships death through war, through an economic system that keeps most people starving while a small percentage of people focus on expensive drugs like cocaine and on sex with strangers. We live in a culture that encourages people to be shallow and soulless, or to focus on possessions and repressing others and themselves. Sex in this culture often takes the form of prostitution — on a person turning off her emotions, being psychically someplace else while someone who despises her is making love to her.

Maybe someday we'll live in a world that doesn't require prostitution. Maybe the rushes of orgasms some female dowsers feel while getting into trance states won't be considered abnormal, even though only women can do it. Maybe someday women won't become housewives, and sit in square houses on square blocks, watching square boxes with pictures of men killing each other. Maybe instead, seeing auras will be common, and talking to plants and animals will be easy. Maybe someday heterosexual sex won't be considered something that a woman does for a man in exchange for money, dinner and wine, or a lifetime job as a housewife. Maybe someday we'll all treat each other with respect and dignity.

One for Ripley's

Phyllis Luman Metal

*Well, my dear, I must admit your story seems somewhat unusual
. . . quite unusual as a matter of fact. I would never imagine a woman
would begin being a prostitute at the age of fifty-five. I think that's
one for Ripley's, if you don't mind my saying so. I guess I thought of
prostitution as something unfortunate young girls got talked into by
unscrupulous men. That was my impression. But to get into it at that
age and of your own free will, although it does seem there was some
financial pressure. . . Still, there must have been something else you
could have done. Tell me, what did you feel about it? Were you
overwhelmed by guilt?*

No, I was not. It was a hell of a lot better than marriage. And I tried
that five times.

*Well, I just don't understand. You seem quite normal. You are an
attractive woman, of good family, well brought up. The men you
married must have been monsters. But five of them? Something just
does not fit.*

Well. . . I found it very liberating to be a prostitute, and the men
must have found it liberating too, for they were much better lovers
than my husbands. They seemed to feel free with me and I with them.
Why are you so upset? You don't think sex is wrong do you?

Well, no, I don't think sex is wrong between two consenting adults.

You don't think it's wrong to earn a living, for a woman to earn a
living that is?

*Why no my dear, of course not. Women have jobs now, all sorts of
jobs, married or unmarried.*

Well then, why is it wrong to get paid for sex? You must be getting
upset about putting the two together.

It would be like selling your organs. Some part of your body.
Well, what about selling blood? That doesn't seem to bother you.
Well, that is to save lives.

True, but you would be amazed at how desperate some of the men are to have sex in the way they need to have sex, and how uptight they are about telling their wives what they need. And then there are always the guys who are between relationships, or can't seem to get anything going.

Well, my dear, the whole subject is quite confusing. Why don't we just go to a hotel and have some relaxation.

Are you willing to pay me?

Well now, we are good friends. You wouldn't charge me would you?

Do you treat your patients who are your friends for nothing? My body is my source of livelihood. I have upkeep to be available and appealing.

I just wouldn't feel right about paying you. It would spoil it for me. I think you should give it to me.

Sorry. We can be good friends but forget the sex then. When I first charged for it, I had much more self respect and self worth than I ever had before. I felt appreciated. When I was a wife I was expected to do a lot of shit work and service my husbands and their desire, not mine. I felt used and abused. No trick ever broke my ribs like my husband did. No trick ever took all my money and left me when it was all gone — another husband did that. No trick ever urged me to neglect my children to accommodate him. No trick ever threw a bunch of in-laws who made my life miserable at me. No trick ever came home drunk every night like one of my husbands did. And I always had money, which I did not when I was married. And I never got a venereal disease. And something else. I got to know people of all nationalities in a way I never could have otherwise. My customers in Paris were from all nations. They were Swiss, British, German, Norwegian, Italian, Spanish, French, Syrian, Berber, Algerian, Sengalese, Saudi, Iranian, Japanese. I felt like a citizen of the world. Prostitution made me feel that all of us on the planet were one family.

Well, my dear, it is all very interesting. But I am sure you are an anomaly. I can't believe this is how it usually goes. There is something wrong about it. What would happen to the family if it were legal?

I think it is much more prevalent and accepted in Catholic countries where the family is much stronger than here.

Well, my dear, let's have a drink and talk about something else. There are so many other aspects to you. You have such a varied life.

This surely isn't that important to you. Why don't you just forget about it. Why make an issue of it? I think you just like to take up controversial issues for causes. You just like the role of being a social reformer. What in the world do you have in common with all those girls who stand on corners? They can't do anything else. Don't tell me you are a feminist.

Attitudes

Sharon Kaiser

I was watching a talk show a few weeks ago, and they had a panel of four they were interviewing, and one of the women on the panel was a prostitute. The show's host was soliciting questions from the audience.

The audience questions centered around *why* this woman was a prostitute. Her response was that she liked it, that she saw it as therapeutic, and of value in this society.

During this question and answer sequence the camera cut back and forth from the prostitute to the audience. Every time it cut to the audience, it focused in on one woman sitting in the aisle. I remember thinking that she was very beautiful, and well-dressed, like she had money. She looked educated, and as though she had come from a good, loving home. That sort of all-American sparkle look.

At one point she made a comment under her breath, and the show's host picked it up and asked her to repeat it over the mike. I don't remember what she said, but she began this hostile attack on the prostitute. Soon, others began attacking the prostitute too. The first woman came up to the mike and said something about a whore only being able to think between her legs.

I remember feeling this helpless, surging rage. I wanted to cry. It never seems to matter how long I've lived with the stigma of being a prostitute or being a lesbian, or being something someone didn't think I should be. I can't seem to get used to being treated as though I am less than human. I don't think I ever will. It's always a shock to me.

The Continuing Saga of Scarlot Harlot VII

Carol Leigh

Well, here I am again. The Whore. I admit it.

Oh, no. This can't be, you think. Not an actual, real-live prostitute spilling the beans? Isn't that dangerous? Won't she be arrested? What if her mother finds out?

And dangerous it is. Yet I forsake my well-being in an effort to satisfy your overwhelming curiosity about what prostitution looks like from the inside out.

Besides, I'm proud. Sex work is nurturing, healing work. It could be considered a high calling. Prostitutes are great women, veritable priestesses. Maybe that's an exaggeration.

"Prostitutes always glorify their work," says X. "They have to glorify it or they couldn't stand to do it."

X is an ex-prostitute. Ex-prostitutes are out of touch with the true glories of the trade. Plus, they were never very good at it. That's why they're ex-prostitutes. But I suppose everyone has their prejudices.

And so I strive to sift these complexities, to seek and present The Truth. Naturally, I've been barraged with letters from the curious masses. I've edited their substance to the quintessential. For instance:

Dear Scarlot:

Is it true that women made prostitution illegal? You said so once.
— *Doubtful*

Dear Doubtful,

No. I was over-reacting. I exaggerated. I guess I'm just angry at everyone. But some women helped.

Dear Harlot,

Is anything you say true?
— *Just Wondering*

Dear Wondering,
Yes.

Dear Whore,
Me and my friends never even think about prostitution. You shouldn't assume everyone is curious. By the way, what is truth?
— Socrates

New York City Tonight

Sapphire

1.

I'm talkin' about
  a sickness
        inside
A feelin' I can
no longer
     hide
I've gone the
   way of
      serpents
an' can no
   longer find
         my way home
2.
I need the
wisdom of the
      ancients
The sight of
the soothsayers
The salve of
   blues
A spiritual cathartic
   or
I will strangle
in my own
           filth
I will be but

a parody
    of a woman
livin' a death
    and life
        that ends
            with me,
with an aversion
    to pain
        that only allows for
a shallow
    mediocrity; not
        havin' the courage
        to move past
            old hurts I
remain bound in a
    Peter Pan pubescence
And I am at once lost
and found unsure
    of what is mine,
what is creation or
    imitation, forward or
    backward
        I have lost sight
            of the Blk. Will
                the seventies be
                the times of
                    the Blind
Groping lost where is the vision?
    All I see is the
        cracker's wasteland
        a toilet left
        unflushed
Malcolm! And I'm a thousand years
    behind the times
Nothin' has changed
    ten years ago today I was
        trickin' in L.A. now
            I'm in New York and
            I repeat nothin'
                has changed!
I can't find my dreams
    I don't know what
        nothin' means.

I am alone. So ashamed
I keep goin' but
want to come
home.
3.
Across the aisle from
me on the subway
a nigger in pink
jeans reads Ebony
magazine his
hair pressed and
curled
Elijah why did you leave us
All I think of is gigs
costumes, gettin' slim, tryin' to MAKE
IT actin', dancin', maybe a play
on Broadway like Zaki
All the while the race
among the races is
at a crucial point
the survival of my people
is at stake
and I have elected
to spend my days
in petty pursuit
of pieces of the
pie. The shit
pie. I
am sick. I don't know
what it will take
to get me
well. Malcolm is not goin' to rise
again. Panthers played out. Elijah is dead.
Processes is back. I can't talk about nobodi cause
I wear wigs. I can't write warrior poems talkin'
bout clean up the community cause I would
have to wash myself away. I am
part of the perversion that
permeates our
existence
Blk children can
pass by taverns

and see me
   on a platform
      g-stringed and gyratin', hear me
         cursin' on subways
            and street corners
               see me wid wite boys
                  and women.
I repeat
               I am sick
and do not know
   what to do about
      it. I have
come from the sixties to the
   seventies. From being
      the solution to
         being the
            problem.
   They should stone me/US
   I did not get this way ALONE.
   I am a product of
      humiliations, drowned dreams
         and betrayals. It is
            not all the time what
               it seems. I tried/
                  tryin' and am still
                     gettin' up
I know in the end it will be better
   than it was an' I
      cannot berate myself
         cause of limited
            survival mechanisms
I am gettin' up
   and gettin' on
Comin' home!
      and don't
         want no static
            bout where
               I been. I'm
comin' HOME an'
like the bible say
      'let he who is
         without sin

cast the first
stone'
I got to move past old ways
sometimes I jus' don't know how —
I could be doin' better
but I could be doin'
worse
I have heard of those
who walk the way
of the new world. I don't
know how I came to always
be on the outside
lookin' in. Enlightened ones
do not leave us. Oh robe
wearin'/Blk talkin'/knowledgeable
ones love us be
like my grandmother
whose prayers have
endured past all things
when the dancers stopped dancin'
poets stopped poetin'
men stopped lovin'
her prayers endured
I remember her when
ideologies, Kings and
other things had let
me down and if you
can be like she
and never turn
your back on
your children
She said, 'go grow but don't
forget you can/must always
come home.'

4.
I have much
good to give
But don't feel
I have long
to live

5.
changes pain

6.
On the subway
   home
people look at u
   like u crazy
Black mutherfuckers!
I was with a trick
   last night
Oh god! ain't no use
   me even talkin' about it
   cause u can't know 'less u
      been there.
This nauseating monkey/factory hands/half his fingers missin'/
cadillac/whiskey drinkin'/talkin' bout is it good?/
u got some good pussy girl/tight stuff/lemme rub it/
lemme suck it good
for you baby/lemme grab some of that tittie/lemme rub — I'm not
gonna put it back in — come on now I'm gonna give you two twenty
dollar bills/
do you suck?/Aw honey u sumptin' else/I sho likes u/yo skin
smooth as butter/come to daddy lemme suck some of dat tittie
It was makin' me wanna die vomit but the rent/tokens/dance
classes/food/
taxis/clothes/telephone/gas/lites/books/food/rent/
entertainment made me bite my lip an' say Oh baby/it feels so good/
   Ahhh/oh yeah honey/do it daddy
7.
I feel empty
   unfinished like
      this poem
         which has
            no appropriate
            end.

Good Girls Go to Heaven, Bad Girls Go Everywhere

Aline

I'm an American who was bred and raised in Colorado. I'm of English, Welsh, Scot and Massachusetts Indian ancestry. I'm a woman who chose not to have children in this lifetime.

I'm a direct descendant of one of the women who lived in early white-America and was burned at the stake in Salem, Massachusetts, after being persecuted and accused of being a "witch," along with numerous other women and men who were murdered in the name of God.

No doubt I'd be labeled a witch if I lived during that weird, proudless time in history. Why? I've rejected motherhood, though I continue to nurture and "mother" other human beings, and look forward to doing so throughout my life. I've enjoyed a career for over a decade nurturing and entertaining adult males.

No, I hardly fit the stereotypical image of a lady of the night. I've never "prowled," and over half my "business" has been conducted in glorious sunlight. I contemptuously reject marriage, which is all too often a form of unpaid, or indirectly paid, licensed, sanctioned, prostitution. Am I bound to become some kind of quasi-quaint old maid? Hardly. I'd rather suck cock than kiss ass!

I am the eldest of four children and helped look after the youngest two, a girl and a boy. I was what is described in psycho babble as a deputy mother within a dysfunctional family. My parents would have been better off without kids.

In 1970, I happily experienced being paid for performing a form of legal prostitution — the ageless sex work known as strip tease, or erotic dancing. To be more precise, I worked as a topless dancer.

It was fun at the time and the wage and tips were good. I much preferred exhibiting myself, flirting, showing off my body than

131

working at some shit-job cleaning somebody else's toilet for a poverty level income.

The tips often totaled more than the fixed three dollars and fifty cents an hour payment, which back then was good pay. The money flowed freely from the mostly-married, bored, horny, over-worked, middle aged, male executives and their male flunkies. There were always a few Air Force men frequenting the tacky, nightclub-bar-restaurant.

I didn't much relate to the other "girls." They were a bit older, and they reminded me of the hoody-looking, so-called low class girls in my high school. You know, the stereotype that existed in most all high schools in the sixties. Now they're "punks" and they're from all levels of social classes. They'd hang out in the bathroom constantly, through breaks between classes, and throughout lunch period. They didn't eat anything. They just smoked. And smoked. I remember them laughing at me because I didn't know how to inhale. I remember their gobs of make-up and black mascara, and the ugly, ratted hair all piled up on their heads, making them appear five inches taller than they were. They looked — well, evil. They looked threatening. They *were* threatening. Of course they learned their hostile attitude from their idiot parents who had brutal, idiot parents, who had — and so on. To society at large, they looked like "whores," right?

In fact, they ended up becoming very conforming women who got married, believed in "God," went to church, had virginal or near-virginal weddings, and most likely became over-breeders. Some are still married to the same guys. Others had violent divorces and re-married a second or third time. When I went to my high school fifteenth year reunion, the "whore-y" women had turned out no different as adults than most of the Suzy-co-ed-white-middle-class women who had not dropped out or gotten pregnant before gradua-tion. They all had followed the yellow brick road to find a prince charming, get stud-service, make babies, play house, and hopefully live happily ever after. I was the only one, in my autobiographical note, to mention that I was a prostitute. Out of my fifty or sixty graduating classmates, I was, by far, the most "deviant" of all.

Back at the club — we were all sex workers, exhibiting our nearly nude bodies, erotically moving our torsos, hips, pelvises. From the stage, we literally looked down upon the men, with their beaming, grinning faces. Their howls, horny male barks, whistles and cat calls made them look like a pack of dogs or wolves, all waiting to get at some fresh meat or to get it on with a "bitch in heat." We felt as if we were above it all, because we were sexy, desirable, young, gorgeous, confident, and proud to be female. Knowing their eyes were all on me, I was empowered, in control. I soon realized that they were playing a social game, pretending to be ready to mount any of us if we had asked them to do so. It was part of the ritual. In the nightclub and at "stag parties," booze, grass or whatever it took to shut off the real world was always available. I was another diversion, an erotic intoxicant that pulled them from reality for awhile.

A few times, in the course of a one-to-one private session, I was paid for masturbating in the privacy of my own home, on my own bed, with a man happily and quietly watching while I brought myself to orgasm. No, I never faked it, but I was somewhat quiet about it and always worried about what the neighbors might think. You see, of course, that was illegal, a social no-no! I could be a "nasty" girl in a "nasty" nightclub run by "nasty" men. But I couldn't be a "nasty" or "bad" girl having fun with herself with a gentleman willing to give me money directly, as opposed to indirectly, through a cover charge, drinks, in a male-owned enterprise.

I did not stay at the nightclub long. I was ready for new adventures and couldn't see myself forever undulating in front of a pack of wolves. I couldn't happily endure the mind-games, greed, drunkenness, loaded words. It was draining me of my own energy and creativity. It was time to clean toilets for a while. I now do occasional massages for seniors of both sexes, and once in a while genital-gratification work on men of various ages. I also do chore-work and odd jobs for old folks, very often women, sometimes men. I love them all. I have been politically and socially active around various issues, including prostitution, for over a decade. The most meaningful work I have done has been, with few exceptions, all volunteer, unfortunately. Not so ironically, considering our culture, the best money I've earned has been through sexual services.

When I think back on my work at the topless club, I realize that I was probably hired because of my youth and my small bosoms. I was only twenty-one, younger than the other dancers. I could have looked even younger — eighteen, sixteen or even fourteen to some of the customers, according to their fantasies. I may have been masturbation material for some men lusting after teenaged women and girls. I regret this possibility. As a woman now in my thirties, I realize I may have projected or unknowingly portrayed an image which reflects a sick societal fact. Although I did not experience incest in my family, I know that it has been and still is a traumatic reality for a great number of women. Some became sex workers and some did not. However, it is absurd to generalize, as has been done in fiction, television and movies, that all, or nearly all sex workers are victims of incest or have been sexually molested as children.

133

There is a belief that sex workers spread sexually transmitted diseases, AIDS, herpes and crabs. I, for one, never contracted a bug from a customer, nor did I ever pass one to a customer.

There is a belief that most "whores" are addicted to drugs, dope and booze. I don't do any narcotics. I'm not even addicted to coffee. That shit causes heart attacks and strokes, but it's oh-so-legal. I quit smoking cigarettes. Once in a while, I'll lust over chocolate and French pastries. I drink beer and wine socially and infrequently. I'm dead set against cocaine use and abuse. In my twenties, I experimented with LSD and mescaline. Now I'm a member of Smokers Anonymous. No kidding.

There is a belief that sex workers hate all men. I don't hate men, not even Prez Reagan. I can feel disgust, repulsion, impatience, alarm, dismay, pity, horror, disapproval or frustration toward other human beings, but I don't feel hatred. I am not hostile by nature. Honesty, openness, sensitivity, are qualities I seek in others. They are qualities much needed in the work/employment known as prostitution, which is not unlike being a counselor, a pyschologist, a good listener. Like doctors or nurses, we try to be sensitive to the men who come to us, and also remain emotionally detached.

To think of us as thriving on lust is another myth created by men and perpetuated by horny priests, ministers, two-faced religious enthusiasts and Bible-beaters. By the way, there is plenty of sex and violence in the Bible, may I remind you.

I firmly believe that all human beings are primarily bisexual. We are all sexual creatures, period. This damn country is touch deprived. Unfortunately, our sexual behaviors and beliefs are being dictated by peer pressure, media and religion. The word "whore" expressed as an insult, a put down, a cut, is a broad floating term used to perpetuate social myths and hatred and fear of women.

I don't like labels, really. I'm getting tired of tags, categories, slots. I have always been curious and willing to share sexual intimacy for fun and socializing with people of different races and classes. Does this mean my life is a parade of sexual encounters with no meaningful relationships? Not at all.

I will continue to be fascinated by the opposite sex as much as I am by my own. I will probably never marry, and I made sure I would not reproduce by getting a tubal ligation a few years back. I will continue to love and be loved as much as I am able, and with whom I choose. I'm talking about love, not sex. I am a woman who knows the difference between the sweet, heavenly passion shared with another person, and the simple, uncomplicated get-laid genital exchange.

Making Movies

Jane Smith

When I saw the call for writing by women who have worked in the sex industry, I thought, "Great!" Here was the spur I needed to write about my movie experience. Then I started wondering. Would it be fair? With my education and upper middle class Jewish background, I couldn't possibly be typical of women in the sex industry.

I argued it out with myself. No one's typical, I thought. Women come to the sex business from all kinds of backgrounds, and for all kinds of reasons. I bet we're as diverse as women in society at large.

I wrote a first draft and showed it to some writer friends. They liked it, but advised me to cut out the parts where I tried to excuse myself, to justify. "Just tell your story as honestly as you can," they said. "You don't have to keep insisting that pornography is evil. Who you are will come through. Trust yourself." Truth is made of many voices, they said, and my voice is as valid as anyone else's.

So I feel free to say that although pimps, kidnapings, and beatings may be part of other women's stories, no one forced, tricked, or addicted me into the business. No one owned me, took my profits, or beat me when I tried to leave. I was not hurt or raped by the film-makers. I got into the business as a sort of lark, to try something different and make some quick, easy money. And I was lucky. I got out.

It was 1967. I was a hippie, an on-and-off drug user, a nineteen-year-old college dropout from New York. Having read the Beat writers in high school, I was drawn to San Francisco, so when I left college, that's where I headed.

I found what I was looking for. People smoking pot, taking psychedelics, and spreading the word that careers, jobs and the rat race were irrelevant and poisonous; that love for people and respect for the natural world were basic; that straight people should be turned on so *they'd* understand too. Today I realize that the vision I thought one hundred thousand people shared was different for each one. I see the white, North American, middle class arrogance of those days. I also realize that in Haight-Ashbury, as in suburbia, the women did the cooking, laundry, and typing — and also often earned the money so men could live a free life. But that's another story.

My friends and I agreed that regular jobs were stultifying and, in most cases, helped the enemy. Besides, what would we do with all that money? We lived communally. Our food came from the dented-can store, and our clothes from Goodwill. San Francisco General provided free medical care. Our cars needed little maintenance. I remember one baby blue 1954 Chevy, a communal car, unregistered, uninsured. It had no key. You started it by inserting a spoon in the ignition and twisting a certain way. The spoon was kept on the dashboard; we figured no car thief would be oddball enough to figure out what it was for.

I got money by stringing beads and selling them at hippie shops, and sometimes by working as a temporary secretary. For three months, I earned two dollars and eighty cents an hour working at the post office during the Christmas rush, which made me a plutocrat in hippie circles.

My friend Ruby told me about the movies. "They're always looking for new chicks," she said. "You get twenty-five dollars, and they pay you right on the spot." Twenty-five dollars was a lot of money in 1967. Hamburger was three pounds for a dollar; a loaf of bread was a quarter. Minimum wage was a dollar and forty cents an hour.

"I'm not pretty enough," I told blonde, blue-eyed Ruby.

"Nah, you're fine." She appraised me. "Your tits are bigger than mine — Joe likes that."

"Do they take out social security and everything?" I asked.

"No, it's cash — under the table."

"You don't have to fuck anyone?"

She laughed. "For that, you get a lot more money. These are just girlie shows."

Did it bother me that strangers, men I wouldn't like or respect if I knew them, were going to ogle my naked body? As far as I can remember, it didn't, but even if I had felt squeamish, I wouldn't have let on. No hippie chick wanted to be thought of as hung up. No hippie chick wanted to *be* hung up. I figured that sex with strangers, whether real or celluloid, couldn't hurt me, the real, essential, me, unless I let it.

Ruby and I rode the bus to the Tenderloin. I expected the theatre to be decorated with garish posters, but the facade was understated: a name, a ticket window, and a door. Ruby told the expressionless ticket taker that we were looking for Joe, and he gestured at the door. Inside, light streamed into the dark lobby from a side office. We waited outside the door; Joe was on the phone.

Are these details accurate? I don't know. I've tried to bring back the physical surroundings, but in those days, my focus was on the inner light, the Tao, or something like that. I thought I should be above the physical world. External things were just trappings. Anyway, Ruby handed me over to Joe and said she'd be back in an hour.

Joe was completely impersonal. I felt no fear or concern as I took off everything but my underpants. The movie was to represent what a man might see as he watched a girl get ready for bed, supposing she'd left the shade up and the light on in her apartment. So I walked around in bikini panties, bending over, stretching, reaching for things, turning, lying down on the couch in a splay of abandon, getting up again, bending over. . . all with the lights hot on my bare breasts, the camera running and Joe directing me.

"Okay, now stand up. . .You dropped something on the floor, bend down and get it. Reach up to your right for something on the shelf. Now take off your panties. . .slowly. Walk toward the camera, you're going to pull down the shade — no, you changed your mind. Go back to the couch. Kneel on the couch. . .spread your heels. Lie on your back. Dangle one leg over the side. Okay, now turn on your front. Look at the camera. Open you mouth. Lick your lips. On your side now, away from me. . .put your right knee up. That's it; show some crotch. Now move your butt from side to side, like that, that's good. . ."

After an hour, Joe said it was enough. He handed me twenty-five dollars, saying, "Tell your friends, and if you find anyone else, give me a call and you'll get five bucks." I hadn't known that.

When Ruby came, I didn't tell her I'd enjoyed the session. The proper attitude seemed to be, "Oh, it's awful, and you wouldn't want anyone in your home town to see you, but it's good money." I didn't think it was so awful. I thought it was rather fun. I had always believed I was ugly, and too fat, and it seemed wondrous that anyone would actually pay me money to look at my body. It gave me a new confidence. Also, this seamy movie world was one place where my big breasts were an asset.

I passed the word to Kate, a mother of three, whose artist husband was always unemployed. "I've heard about those movies," she said. "Do you think we could make one together?" I called Joe. He said to bring her down the next morning. Kate and I dressed in our matching velveteen minidresses — hers blue, mine red — and took the bus downtown in high spirits, pleased to be able to have an outing together, without her kids. Joe agreed to pay us fifty dollars for a double, and we took off our clothes.

While we waited for the camera, we agreed to try to make this movie a little special, a little artsy, with movements that were vaguely Indian, vaguely yogic, vaguely ballet-like. "Our bodies are beautiful," Kate said. "We shouldn't be ashamed of them." She said as much to Joe, who agreed, as long as we were undressed. Kate knelt and I danced before her; I sat cross-legged and she danced for me. Joe made an occasional suggestion. When we were done, Kate said, "Maybe we'll turn on some guys. Maybe they'll see the light." We always wondered what the finished show looked like, but we never returned to see it.

Joe said he couldn't use me again. But Ruby knew other movie makers. For my next film, a solo, I dressed carefully in a tangerine-colored sheath, which came to mid-thigh, and crotchless beige mesh pantyhose. I thought I might do a strip for the camera.

But Harry snorted. "A strip? What are you gonna take off? You hardly have anything on. I don't know what I'm gonna do with you. You're nothin' special to look at, and I've already done everything I can think of."

My face burned, but I showed him the crotchless stockings. "Can you do anything with these?"

"Hmm. Lemme see. Take off your dress." I did. "Now lie down here."

I lay on a pile of pillows, and he wheeled the camera over. "Okay, raise your left leg . . . slowly." The lights felt hot on my inner thighs. The camera zeroed in on my crotch, my genitals open to the lights, and involuntarily, I clenched my vagina. "Huh?" said Harry. "Do that again." I clenched it again; open, close, open, close. "How'd ya do that? I never saw anyone do that before," he said.

"I don't know — I've always done it."

"Hold on. This could be interesting." He brought the camera closer. "Okay, now, do it again. Slow." For the next quarter hour, I tightened and loosened, clenched and unclenched those muscles. I've always wondered what Harry did with the footage. Cut it in with standard peep show shots? Superimposed the giant vagina on other images? I don't know. The edges of the no-crotch mesh stockings must have made a provocative frame. "Okay, that's enough." I sat up and put on my dress, and he paid me.

My last two productions were imitation lesbian movies. The first, with Lee, the wife of a friend, was filmed in the living room of a Buena Vista mansion, on a leopard skin sofa and on maroon shag carpet four inches thick. Leaning against satin throw pillows, Lee and I, who disliked each other, stroked one another's arms, legs, and breasts. This kind of intimate touching would have been fine with Kate or even Ruby, but with Lee, it was unpleasant. She kept watching me with narrowed eyes. We each got forty dollars, however, so I told myself it was tolerable. Lesbian films paid more than the peep shows; maybe some women refused to make them.

The other was an ersatz lesbian fight film. The deal was arranged by Maureen, a writer and friend of a friend. "I'll meet you at Ken's," she said on the phone. "Take the bus — it's about forty miles up the coast."

"Are you taking the bus?" I asked, thinking maybe we could ride together.

"Nah — my old man's taking me. I'm allergic to the bus."

"But —" I stopped. She had hung up.

Like all the movie makers I dealt with, Ken was impersonal, professional, and indifferent to me as an individual. Maureen had worked with him before, so I felt left out. "I don't want anyone getting hurt," he told us as we stripped to underpants. "Pretend to scratch, bite, kick...but no real scratching. Sometimes chicks get carried away." He appraised us: Maureen, blonde and statuesque; me, short and dark and sturdy. "Careful," he told Maureen, "you're twice her size."

We stood around, smoking, saying little, as Ken got the equipment ready. Again the props included thick carpet, throw pillows, leopard skin. "All right, Maureen, grab her and throw her down — gently! Don't hurt her! Just make it look good. Jane, push her away." But he didn't have to tell me. At that first unfair attack, adrenalin poured through me. I easily broke her hold — easily because she wasn't really trying — and entered enthusiastically into my part.

She grabbed me; I kicked her away. "Okay, Maureen, pretend you're scratching her breasts. Good. Jane, you're gonna bite her knee. Fine. Now Maureen, get your legs around her — you want her in a scissor lock. Jane, push her legs away."

"Ow! Not so hard!" Maureen cried.

"Sorry." Panting, I lunged for her ample chest.

"Maureen, you're gonna pull her hair — not really! Jane, jerk your head away, bite her hand, they like a lotta biting. That's good. . .No! Don't hurt her!" I eased my hold. "Okay, scratch her back. Fine. Now wind your legs around her chest. . .that's good. . .Maureen, push her away. Run your hands up her legs. . .Good, good."

Finally, Ken said, "Enough!" and stopped the camera. Maureen stood up, dusting off her hands. "I don't know if I could beat her in a real fight," she told the cameraman. "She's a real tiger." I stood there smirking until Maureen went off to get dressed.

Ken paid us each fifty dollars and asked me if I'd like to do a real fuck movie. "I pay one hundred and fifty; seventy-five each for your and your partner."

"I don't know — do I get to bring my own guy?" He nodded. "I'll see," I said, intrigued by the money. That night, I asked a friend, not a lover, if he was interested.

"That's a lot of money, but I don't know if I could get it up for the camera," he said. I understood that this was a serious question. For a few weeks, whenever I saw him, one of us would mention the subject, usually when we needed money to get high. But talk was one thing. To say, "Okay, let's do it!" was somehow to cross a critical line. By then, anyway, I had a steady boyfriend who didn't like the idea of my making skin movies. So the fight with Maureen was my last appearance on film.

***

I'm not glad I contributed to the pornography industry, although I admit I'm proud that I once did something so inconsistent with my present respectable persona. I've read a lot of feminist theory, however, and I feel disloyal when I say that my movie experiences were not brutal and degrading. I can imagine the reaction of someone who works in the business for a living: "She doesn't know what she's talking about. She's living in a fool's world. She just dabbled in the business. She was lucky."

That's probably true. Also, I was armored by social class and education. I could type; I could express myself; I could write. In straight clothes, I could present the image of an educated girl from a middle class family. Without those "coulds" a woman is far more vulnerable.

Moreover, I managed to stay out of the hard core. Twenty years ago, hard core meant sexual intercourse. I understand that today, intercourse is soft core, and hard core pornography depicts beatings, bondage, mutilation, even murder.

The last thing I want is for some young woman to read my essay and say, "See? It's perfectly okay to be a porn model — it sounds like fun." But does that mean I should keep my story secret, or invent a brutality I didn't experience?

Even from my rather mild story, it's evident that men ran the business for men. Women were only the raw material. The filmmakers set the terms, ordered us around, and decreed what would sell. None of that surprised me. In my experience, men ran everything. I didn't mind being raw material, because I felt that my core was untouched. It certainly never occurred to me that women could make movies for women's pleasure.

I think the way I reacted to being raped, that same year, illuminates the way I felt about the movies. I was raped at three in the morning as I walked through a rough section of San Francisco — at knife point, on the ground in an alley. Afterwards the rapist said, "You just wanted some cock, like I wanted some pussy," and took off. I couldn't quite see it that way — I'll never forget the terror I felt as he followed me for a block and a half, an arm's length back — but all I did was dust off my miniskirt and go home to bed. I didn't tell my housemates until the next day.

They were horrified. Was I all right? Did I want to go to the police, a doctor, the free clinic? "I'm fine, it was nothing," I said, surprised and a bit indignant that they thought I wasn't tough enough to ignore a rape. I suppose I believed that taking a rape in stride proved I was hip. If I admitted I was shaken, if I allowed myself to be shaken, someone might suspect that I was hung up. For a woman, being hung up was the ultimate indictment.

It has taken me twenty years to acknowledge that being used as raw material, being raped, did affect me. In 1967, my hippie ideals told me the real, inner Jane was inviolate. Today, the grown up woman knows it was Jane that was manhandled, raped, used. That's a heavy knowledge. I'll be dealing with it the rest of my life.

Confessions of a Feminist Porno Star

Nina Hartley

"A feminist porno star?" Right, tell me another one, I can hear some feminists saying. I hear a chorus of disbelief, a lot like the two crows in the Disney movie "Dumbo" — "I thought I'd seen everything till I saw an elephant fly." On the surface, contradictions seem to abound. But one of the most basic tenents of feminism, a tenent with which I was inculcated by the age of ten, was the *right* to sexual free expression, without being told by society (or men) what was right, wrong, good, or bad. But why porno? Simple — I'm an exhibitionist with a cause: to make sexually graphic (hard core) erotica, and today's porno is the only game in town. But it's a game where there is a possibility of the players, over time, getting some of the rules changed.

As I examine my life, I uncover the myriad influences that led me to conclude that it was perfectly natural for me to choose a career in adult films. I find perfoming in sexually explicit material satisfying on a number of levels. First, it provides a physically and psychically safe environment for me to live out my exhibitionistic fantasies. Secondly, it provides a surprisingly flexible and supportive arena for me to grow in as a *performer*, both sexually and non-sexually. Thirdly, it provides me with erotic material that I like to watch for my own pleasure. Finally, the medium allows me to explore the theme of celebrating a positive female sexuality — a sexuality that has heretofore been denied us. In choosing my roles and characterizations carefully, I strive to show, always, women who thoroughly enjoy sex and are forceful, self-satisfying and guilt-free without also being neurotic, unhappy or somehow unfulfilled.

In order to understand why I can be so happily involved in a busi-

142

ness that is anathema to so many feminists today, it's important for me to explain the uniqueness of my early life experiences. My parents were ex-communists, having left the party in 1956, seven years before I was born. My father's subsequent blacklisting in 1957 cut short a promising career in radio. My mother put her double major in chemistry and statistics to work in a long career for the State Health Department. By the time I, the youngest of four, was in grade school, my father stayed home to write and my mother worked full time. I grew up assuming that I, too, could "have it all": education, career, mate and family.

My parents were very liberal and never censored my reading material. By the time I was twelve, I was checking out books on the subjects of puberty, pregnancy and sex. I was doubly lucky to live in Berkeley, California, during the sixties and seventies, as the librarians never tried to disocurage me from checking out "unsuitable" books. This access to factual, non-judgmental biological information is the basis now for my "surprising" lack of shame and guilt: since sex is so natural, and since I demystified sex early on, having sex on screen, if that's what I wanted to do, was not traumatic at all.

Once I passed puberty, two books in particular were very influential in the continuing development of my personal sexual philosophy: *Our Bodies, Ourselves*, and *The Happy Hooker*. The former taught me that women deserved to be happy sexually, that their bodies were wonderful and strong, and that all sexual fantasies were natural and okay as long as coercion was not involved. The latter book taught me that an intelligent, sexual woman could choose a job in the sex industry and not be a victim, but instead emerge even stronger and more self-confident, with a feeling, even, of self-actualization.

High school was uneventful — I became deeply involved in the excellent drama department at Berkeley High, exploring a long-standing interest in the theater arts. Contrary to a lot of adolescents' experiences with peer pressure in the realm of sex and drugs, I was lucky to have no pressure placed on me one way or another, because that was the norm in Berkeley in the seventies. Consequently, I had a more active fantasy life than sex life, and was very ripe when I lost my virginity at eighteen to a man with whom I had my first long term relationship. This, unfortunately, had more forgettable moments than memorable ones. The sex and intimacy were mediocre at best, and I realized that my libido was not to have a good future with this man. My present husband is just the opposite. He gave full support for my long-dormant lesbian side; for the past four years I have lived with him and his long term woman lover in a close-knit, loving, supportive and intellectually stimulating *menage-a-trois*.

I stripped once a week while getting my bachelor's degree in nursing, magna cum laude, enjoying it to the fullest and using the performance opportunity to develop the public side of my sexuality. I went into full time movie work immediately following graduation, having done a few movies while still in school.

I know there are people who wonder, "Is she naive or something? What kind of a cause is porno?" But let's face it, folks: while the sex drive may be innate, modes of sexual behavior are learned, and I don't see Nancy Reagan setting up any "Happy, Healthy, Sex Life" institutes in the near future. If the media can have an effect on people's behavior, and I believe it does, why is it assumed that sex movies must always reinforce the most negative imagery of women? That certainly isn't what I'm about. From my very first movie I have always refused to portray rape, coercion, pain-as-pleasure, woman-as-victim, domination, humiliation and other forms of non-consensual sex.

I can look back on all of my performances and see that I have not contributed to any negative images or depictions of women; and the feedback I get from men and women of all ages supports my contention. I get a lot of satisfaction from my job — for me it is a job of choice. As feminists, we must all fight to change our society so that women who don't want to do gender-stereotyped jobs can be free to work, support their families decently, and fulfill their potential in whatever job they choose. This includes not feeling compelled to do sex work because other well-paying options are severely limited.

Each of us has some idea or action that we hate but that is still protected by the First Amendment. I consider myself a reformer, and as a reformer I need a broad interpretation of the First Amendment to make my point. As a feminist I have principles that won't allow me to take license with that precious right to free speech. There have always been, and to some degree will always be, extremists who see the First Amendment as their license to do or say whatever, and not as a right which has implied responsibilities. Of course the sexual entertainment medium is no exception to this. I say censure them, but do not censor me.

The Right to Protection from Rape

Karen

Several years ago, I was working as a prostitute on the streets, in Fresno, California. I was walking to my hotel room with a birthday cake when I met a man who said he wanted to do business with me for fifty dollars. He proceeded to pull an ice pick out and rape me. He kept me about three hours, and then was walking me to a park, not far away, where he said he was going to kill me. Suddenly, my friend Alice spotted me. She jumped out of the car she was in, approached the man who had raped me, and pulled me away from him. We went back to the hotel room and were sitting on the bed. They were trying to calm me down, when suddenly I saw him walking down the driveway, again. I screamed and pointed to him and my friends took off after him. They cornered him and he pulled out his ice pick, again. Somebody got it away from him, and they held him there for the police. We went back to our room, where there was a loud banging on the door. Alice asked who it was.

It was the police. They said, "Open the goddamn door or we will break it down." Less than five seconds later, the door came crashing in, hitting Alice. They barged in, and four shotguns and two hand-guns were staring us in the face. They said we were under arrest for assault on the man who had just raped me repeatedly. Alice went outside with one of the officers and was explaining what had happened. He, in turn, told her it was impossible because I was a prostitute and could not be raped. He also said the man was too drunk to do anything. We told the officer where the ice pick was, and he tried to make one of us go on the roof to get it, because he did not believe there was an ice pick. When someone finally got it down, they grudgingly decided it had happened.

When I told them I wanted to press charges for rape, the officer would not take a police report. They just took him to jail for being drunk in public. After three hours he was released. I was very disappointed and outraged at the police for their callous and uncaring attitude. At the time I was only seventeen years old and still believed in our justice system. Even though I am a prostitute, I feel I should still be entitled to protection from the police.

The Continuing Saga of Scarlot Harlot VIII

Carol Leigh

I sit at my typewriter and try to figure out what I can do to make the world safe for prostitution. That doesn't sound so good. I know why. It's the word prostitution. I looked it up in the dictionary:

1. Trading sexual services for money or goods;
2. Selling one's talents for an unworthy cause.

That second definition tarnishes our reputation. There's plenty of causes less worthy than survival or feeding your family. What about Porsche-titution? That's selling one's talents for a Porsche.

Oh, how I love wallowing in these complications. But, seriously, there are women for whom providing sexual services is not synonymous with compromise. Some women seem to relish careers as sexual facilitators. They enjoy their work and make lots of money. I think they should be afforded the same status as doctors. And me? Well, I don't wanna be a sex doctor. I just wanna write and think.

Have you heard the news about the prostitutes in Bologna, Italy? Well, the Associated Press says that eight hundred high school students marched through downtown Bologna to protest cancellation of a sex-education lecture by a prostitute. Teachers had invited her to speak on "relations between men and women in society."

The Education Ministry in Rome vetoed it.

Confessions of a Priestesstute

Donna Marie Niles

When I was nineteen years old, I made what seemed like a conscious decision to become a prostitute. Having experienced sexual harassment on the job, in the streets, and in virtually every area of life, it was not a particularly fantastic leap to take. It was a very easy transition, raised as I was to be a female. I'm always surprised to find that more women don't choose to enter the life, especially those with extensive "dating" herstories. Any woman who has ever been on a date, who knows what it is to exchange affections or sex for dinner, or kindness, or survival, is quite prepared to be a hooker. Learning to serve, please and appease men is something that binds all women together. It's why secretaries, nurses, waitresses, wives, sales clerks, etc. are on the low paying end of the very same stick. To separate our experiences too much, or to believe that the ways we get by in this woman-hating world are so different, is a mistake. Women as either virgin or whore is one of the greatest lies that men ever created about us.

I took up working as profitably as I could within a structure that basically offered me either one man in marriage or many men for cash. As a white, educated, feminist hooker, I made more money than I ever expected to see again in life. Because I was an independent contractor, I had a lot of time left over to live my life in. These were two of the reasons why it was quite difficult to leave.

I'll never forget the depression I experienced in my first straight job out of the business. I was a secretary. As a prostitute, I had to keep moving, life was rarely predictable, and many people were interested in who and where I was: police, hotel security, tricks, cab drivers.

As a secretary, I was invisible, treated with either disregard or patronizing contempt. My credibility (i.e., getting heard or listened to) took a skydive as I changed from hooker to radical lesbian feminist. On top of this, I worked a regimented forty hour work week for ridiculously low pay. I was literally earning in two weeks what I had previously made in an evening, and paying taxes! It was a shocking welcome back to respectability.

But I have endured, and have not returned for many reasons. One of them is the exhaustion of the constant threat of arrest. It wears you out worrying about going to jail all the time. However, the major reason I left was I simply could no longer could justify working in an industry that profited from the sexual objectification of women. Since I felt I could no longer be in collusion with the men who make billions from our suffering, I had a lot of good-byes to work on. I said good-bye to the diet, fashion and the industries, and other institutions that tell me I am ugly and smelly and in need of alteration because I was born a woman.

When men sell women's bodies, or images of women's bodies, it is called pornography and it is legal, its right to exist vehemently defended with the first amendment. But when women sell their own bodies, it is called prostitution, and we can see what an imperative it's been to protect the rights of prostitutes in our society.

I began to get a glimmer of the magnitude, the enormity, behind the expression, "It's a man's world." I saw who was profiting from our blood, our loving, our bodies, and for whose profit and convenience every institution on planet earth was set up.

Ironically, I still expected them to give it all up. I can truly grasp the reformist feminist notion that by simply explaining, repeating the litany over and over, by holding enough demonstrations and writing enough letters, men will finally get it and abdicate. I spent years talking to men, trying to educate them as to the injustice of it all, explaining how feminism would save them, too. It was the only angle on feminism I was able to sustain their attention with.

Ultimately, I have come to realize that it is women who deserve that kind of loving, devoted patience, that passion and tenderness. We can't go around begging for their time, or attention, or power any longer. Men have no reason to surrender and no intention of handing over a system designed to nurture only themselves. We need to take back not just the night, but our lives if we are to have them.

When Colleen Needed a Job

Tracy Lea Landis

When Colleen needed a job, Alicia talked us into letting her work with us. One of our full-time girls had just left town, we had four shifts open and Alicia knew her friend would want the work.

We girls pretty much ran the parlor. The owner didn't know much about the business. He'd stop by in the morning to pick up his take, before any of us came to work. We rarely saw him. Most of the decisions were made on a seniority basis by the girls who operated the place.

Although last hired, Colleen immediately took the role of elder in our little work group. She'd grown up in the business and had worked the parlors before the rest of us. Jacque was at least seven years older, but was new to the business. She'd started working as a prostitute after her divorce because she couldn't raise a child on the salary of a department store clerk.

Alicia had also grown up in the business. She was the youngest in the group. After working in the streets for a couple of years, she was old enough to get a massage license and had gone to work in a parlor. That's where she met Colleen.

When you work in the business, you're lucky if you can find a man at all, and you adore his ass if he can manage to be at home when you need him. If he don't call you names when he gets pissed or drunk, well, that's nice, too. If he's never gonna be good for a steady job. . . well, that's a hassle, but it's pretty much what you can expect.

Something strange happens to most of the men who stay with a prostitute. They lose respect for themselves, somehow. They lose their ambition, if they ever had any, and they start letting their old lady take care of everything. If they have any trouble getting a job, pretty soon they just give up. Sure, they don't like it that their old

150

lady's a hooker, but somehow they can never do anything about it.

A lot of times, they'll get into running around while their woman is at work, playing games on her and with her money. Acting like a big shot, the man of leisure. Maybe they're just feeling guilty.

Colleen's man was never going to do much, but he was reliable. "He's always been there for me." Colleen once said. Jacque and I were in a bar with her after work and she started saying how all us girls had men who didn't do nothin'. "Hey, Will cooks, cleans, takes care of my kids; all the things I'd be doing if he worked. But he doesn't like me doing this, he hates that I'm doing this."

With all the other hassles Colleen had to deal with, having a man who was reliable was a great deal of comfort to her. She loved him very much for it. She said there was a time when Will had stepped out on her, but he had regretted it and never let it happen again.

She had two sons. The eldest came from her husband's previous marriage, but she always referred to him as her son. Colleen had provided her family with a big suburban home in one of the outlying districts of the city. It had all the nice things, a big freezer and a double garage, and a big boat on a trailer and a couple of cars in front. The living room was a huge family gathering spot, with a great big fish tank by the door and a nice color television next to the fireplace.

Like most of the girls we worked with, Colleen didn't have much to do with the neighbors. There were too many things that she wouldn't want to talk about with casual visitors. So Colleen and her husband raised the two boys quietly, amongst the comings and goings of a few relatives and friends in their average suburban home.

In that home was the sum of all Colleen had worked for, except, of course, what had been spent on drugs. Her man kept a good grade of drugs traveling through their house and they partied a bit. Whenever she and I worked together, she would always have a joint to share or have Will deliver one. There we'd sit, smoking, watching television, brushing our hair, fussing with make-up or nail polish, and talking.

Since Colleen had been in the business longer than any of us, and had worked at almost every parlor in town, she had plenty of stories to tell. Once, after she'd gotten to know us well enough to talk freely, we got on the subject of runaways who work in the business. Colleen told me the story of a young runaway she'd met at the last joint she worked. Colleen had been working for a dyke who owned, and also worked in, her own parlor. This dyke, Rita, had found a runaway girl who was as lost as they come, and had turned her on to the pleasures of lesbian love. She had also turned the little girl out and was successfully exploiting her confused little ass off.

Rita's parlor was a major competitor of ours because it was on the same well-traveled street, just six blocks away. Customers would often say that they had been to Rita's and girls who knew Rita could find out whether one of her customers was okay by giving her a call.

The girls at Rita's, and Rita herself, did a lot of drugs at work. Colleen used to get aggravated, and nervous as hell, when she'd find people's needles and shit hidden away in the bathroom cabinets. "If I can find 'em, damn it, so can the cops," she had warned.

Rita, in displays of lavish affection, provided drugs to the little runaway. It was very easy for the chick to get all strung out, with her very own never-ending stash; the bottomless baggie, the limitless gram.

Sometimes Rita would even go out shopping and bring new clothes for her little runaway lover. "Rita would bring her all these frilly little working clothes from discount places. Just trashy stuff." Colleen shook her head, "And this little girl was just thrilled like it was Christmas time or something."

Of course, Colleen tried to help the kid. "I shouldn'ta gotten involved," she said, "But I did."

Colleen had seen enough of this type of thing going on that she was very careful about how she tried to help. Stepping into Rita's crazy shit, she knew, could be dangerous for everybody, let alone possibly costing Colleen a job she felt she needed at the time.

This little runaway chick didn't know how to take care of her female stuff at all. She didn't know how to protect herself at work and she didn't know how to keep herself clean. Colleen tried to help her pull all that together.

"You know," Colleen said, "the basics."

She also tried to convince the kid that she shouldn't let Rita bank her money, that she oughta be holding her own money, not letting somebody else take care of it.

"I tried to get her to start thinking about how much money she had made for Rita," Colleen told me. "I tried to get her to see that the little presents from K-Mart were nothin' compared to the money she'd brought in."

The kid just kept insisting that Rita was taking care of her. She had been so messed up before she found her way to Rita and into prostitution that she felt taken care of, she felt loved. Colleen was able to find out a little about the home the kid had run away from, and it really would have been hard to tell which situation was worse.

The little girl kept insisting that she was being taken care of, until a couple months went by and her dyke momma accused her of stealing and pulled a gun on her.

Then the little runaway ran away again.

All the biker chicks who worked at Rita's were constantly doing heavy drugs. When Colleen was around that for very long, it reactivated a bad habit that she'd acquired along the way, an addition to crank. When it got out of control, her taste for uppers could turn her into an anemic scarecrow in a few short weeks.

When Colleen saw that working at Rita's was leading her down that self-destructive path, she came to work with us. As soon as she changed parlors, her regular customers quit going up to Rita's and came looking for her at our place.

Because Colleen was a genuinely friendly and caring person, she had a lot of regulars. The loss of Colleen's regular business pissed Rita off. She made excuses instead of telling us which customers were cool when we called.

Colleen's family knew what she did for a living. Even her eldest son, Colleen told me, knew where his momma got the bacon to put on the table. She didn't tell me any details about how he knew, how much he knew, or how he handled it. She only said that he knew.

Colleen's openness was a far cry from what Jacque and her friend, Laura, who also worked with us, enjoyed. Jacque and Laura would still, occasionally, after many years in the business, dust themselves with bathtub cleanser and perfume their bodies with ammonia cleaner before going home. They maintained an elaborate lie to their children, Jacque's live-in and long-time jobless lover, and their few neighborhood friends. As far as anyone who knew them was aware, the two made a living cleaning houses for people.

Jacque's daughter, Jenny, was in her early teens and once, during the summer, we had a series of crank phone calls at the work place from a couple of young girls. The girls who were working that day insisted the two voices sounded like those of Jenny and her best girlfriend, and that they had asked a bunch of curious questions, seemingly trying to find out what the place was about.

Jacque was terrified when she was told and refused to answer the phone on the job for weeks. We encouraged her to be honest with Jenny, to tell her the awful truth so that Jenny wouldn't get the mistaken impression that her mother thought it was all right to be a hooker as long as you could hide it, which of course was not how Jacque felt about it. But Jacque couldn't bring herself to face Jenny. She couldn't tell her.

Laura, who was very tight with Jacque and lived in the house right next door to her, had been left by the father of her son just before the baby was born. Shortly after Jacque had started working the parlors, Laura got work at the same parlor. Though Laura was fearful by nature and terrified of the idea, she allowed Jacque to get her the job, managed to survive her introduction to the world of prostitution and, eventually, got used to the standard of living the money provided.

For four years Laura kept up the lie that she and Jacque worked on a contract basis, cleaning houses for a living. She raised, and spoiled, her son on her own. The only family she had, all the while, was her best friend, Jacque, though they fought all the time.

Then, all out of the blue, the son's father, now a truck driver with a house of his own in another state, started coming to visit his son every couple of months and on holidays. Pretty soon he asked Laura to marry him and she, overjoyed and barely able to believe what was happening to her, accepted.

No one ever heard from Laura much after she left. She sent a couple of letters to Jacque. But we figure she just couldn't risk it. She would have to spend the rest of her life carefully pretending that the whole thing hadn't happened.

Laura would find a way, we all hoped, to fit into the suburban community she had married into. We hoped she would be able to make friends, learn new things and talk about everything that was happening in her present, never mentioning what had happened in her past. Most of all, we hoped that it would work for her, that she would be happy. We even envied her a bit — marrying out of the life.

It's been three years since I saw Colleen. I heard she had a parlor of her own for a while, but then it was an election year and the heat got bad, so she sold the place and moved her family to another town, intending to go straight.

I called Alicia the other day. She said Colleen had a straight job for a while, doing some kind of repair work on machines. But it hadn't worked out and she'd gone back to the parlors.

"You remember Harvey, don't you?" Alicia asked. "That trick friend of mine, the little Oriental guy? He said he'd been up to see Colleen the other day and when I asked him how she looked he told me, 'Don't ask. You don't want to know.'

"She's living with Rita, man. Do you remember how she used to hate Rita? I've got a little postcard here that she sent me and it sounds just like Colleen always did — warm, caring. But I just can't call her up. I've been kinda bummed out myself and I'm just afraid that if I talked to her right now. . ." Alicia, who came into the parlors to find a wise and caring Colleen to look after her, who was unable now to do anything to help, left the sentence unfinished.

Alicia said that Will had taken legal custody away from Colleen. He took both her boys.

The Madame

Phyllis Luman Metal

Oh God, girl, am I ever glad to see you. You're late, and I was afraid you wouldn't show up. Hurry and get your glamour on. Old what's his name from the Islands is in town. He'll be here in about fifteen minutes. You know who I mean, Old Pineapple. That old fart is loaded. I took his old lady for a massage this morning — she'd shit a bucket if she knew her old man came in for you-know-what. Ugly old bag, but she had the money. She got him started. Her folks had all that land in the islands. Hurry up now. . . No, not that wig, put on the red one, and, here, use some of this eye shadow I just bought. Yeah, that dress looks good. They'd sure never guess what you do the way you look when you come in here. Just as well, makin' those pots of yours all day. Here, lift up your skirt and let me give you a squirt of perfume where it counts. Here he comes. Now hide and go up and surprise him. . . and remember, everything you do is extra. Start with a hundred, and if he wants to take you in the shower and piss on you, that's fifty extra. I have to clean up the mess. And tell him how great his dick is; he loves to hear about it.

***

Well, Mr. Phillips, if you aren't a sight for sore eyes. I've missed you. You get younger looking every time I see you. Wish I could take you myself. But I've got a surprise for you today. She'll see that you have a good time. . . I try to make all the boys happy, but you're my special. God, we go back a long ways. I got nobody scheduled for over an hour, so take your time. . . go on up now, and she'll be right there. . .

***

Okay, now listen: the old fart is loaded, and he wants to spend it, so take your time with him. He's hungry. And be sure not to comment on that funny nick out of his dick. He says it happened during the war, but I think somebody took a bite out of it. He likes his asshole tickled with a feather; I just pulled one out of a bird's tail for you...

＊

Well, you did take a long time...almost an hour and fifteen minutes. What did he give you? Four hundred...that's good, he can afford it. He likes to eat pussy until he wears it out...Well, relax now. I brought us some good sandwiches with bean sprouts today. My soap is about to come on — John's about to catch his wife. She's been cheating on him. Have an olive.

The Continuing Saga
of Scarlot Harlot IX

Carol Leigh

. . . The pressure is on. When we last left Scarlot, she was emerging from her nest of cash and condoms to heed the call of duty and help organize a Hookers' Convention just before the Democratic Convention.

"I'm afraid," she confessed. "Our potential astounds me, but the fact that prostitution is illegal almost paralyzes me. Am I allowed to organize with other prostitutes? I don't think I'm allowed to talk to another prostitute. That might be conspiracy."

But here I am, in the midst of it. Two or three times a week I descend from my brothel-pad to meet with a variety of outlaws and deviants. (Deviants? No, we are the norm.) We band together to share our secrets of survival, celebrate our triumphs and exorcise abuse. We are the whores. We are the dykes. We are the working class women. We are the black women. We are big fat women. We are the incest survivors. We are the academics. We are the experts. We are the activists. We toss our tales into the circles. I squirm in my seat at the potential.

Will we affect the world? Is this the birth of a movement? Scarlot pleads for vows of faith and solidarity. "This is the revolution!" she cries, lurching to the edge of her metal folding chair. Fat women smile. Black women smile. Some women nod their heads. Other women stare into the center absorbed in private dramas. I wonder what will come of this puddle. I extract metaphors of frogs from tadpoles. I'm impatient.

Do you want to join an organization? You can buy t-shirts and carry a membership card. We'll call it FLOP — Friends and Lovers of Prostitutes. Good idea, huh? I bet all my pals would be proud to wear that on their chests.

Destroying Condoms

Gloria Lockett

In 1977, we were working on the street in Berkeley. I had just come from the drug store where I had purchased six dozen condoms to use in our work. The police stopped me and searched my car. They found the condoms. They said, "Oh, what have we here?" They took each condom out of its package, and using their penknives, cut holes in each one. They laughed, and one officer said, "Now go use these."

Another time, in San Jose, I had just purchased twelve dozen condoms. I was stopped by the police and they did something very similar. After they made holes in every condom and gave them back to me, useless, they said "Happy hunting!"

Prostitutes use condoms for various reasons, including a desire to retain a sense of privacy. We used condoms because we were trying to protect ourselves and our customers from venereal diseases. With AIDS, it is even more important, and yet police continue to do things like this. Sometimes, if they can't find condoms in your purse, they will search socks, coat pockets, pants pockets, bras and wigs to see if you have any, and if they find them, they destroy them. If they arrest you, however, they often will just confiscate them, supposedly to use as evidence in the trial. However, since few women arrested for prostitution ever go to trial, they are not needed as evidence. The police never return the condoms. As a result, most women only buy a few condoms at a time, at inflated prices. If they are arrested and released after the drug stores are closed, sometimes they can't get any more. If they need to continue working to make up for lost time, say if they desperately need the money, they then have to work without condoms, which is dangerous, especially with AIDS.

A Most Useful Tool

Sunny Carter

For five days my infant son lay in an oxygen tent flushed with fever. He was not responding to antibiotics. His pneumonia seemed determined to not go away. A nurse hurried briskly into our room carrying yet another tray holding several syringes. She squirted them into Brennan's tiny mouth one by one. Too weak to resist, he swallowed the medicines, his baby face wrinkling at the bad taste. Then he turned his little head wearily and vomited the stuff back up, the pinkish mixture puddling on the white hospital sheet.

The nurse clicked her tongue in exasperation. "Now look what you've done. We'll have to take these all over again." Brennan began to cry. I pulled back the plastic tent and picked him up, rocking him against my breast.

"No, goddammit, just leave him alone." Exhausted from worry and very little sleep, I began to cry, too. "Why can't you just leave him alone?"

She stared at me with cold indignity and turned on her heel to leave the room. Dr. Dannon stood in the doorway. "Never mind the oral medicines," he said. "We're starting him on IV's. That will be all."

She hurried past him, leaving us alone.

"You look worn out," he said.

"Yeah. So do you," I replied, seeing his drawn, kind face.

"I have some bad news. Brennan has cystic fibrosis."

I was a medical technician. I remembered vaguely studying the various genetic illnesses of children. Cystic fibrosis. Cystic fibrosis. "My God," I said, the knowledge dawning. "That's fatal."

He nodded, sorrow in his eyes. "He won't die now. Now that we know what's going on, he'll respond to the IV drugs. The average life expectancy is twelve years. Some live longer. I'm sorry."

I held my baby against me, numb with fear and exhaustion. I couldn't believe it. My son was going to die.

Later, after I had slept and eaten, Dr. Dannon came back. Calmer now, I had many questions, and I turned to him for answers.

Cystic fibrosis is a disease which primarily affects the lungs and the digestive system. Pneumonia occurs frequently. CF children produce copious amount of thick, sticky mucus which clogs the tiny airways in the lungs, creating a perfect breeding ground for invading bacteria.

"This is a very expensive disease," Dr. Dannon said. "During the years when he's relatively well, the average cost per child per year is ten thousand dollars. Can you come up with that kind of money?"

My yearly salary in 1976 was nine thousand dollars. Now I would need another ten thousand each year to keep my son alive. How in God's name was I going to get that money?

"Sure I can," I replied.

***

Brennan was released from the hospital a week later. I learned to do the chest percussion treatments he would need three times daily for the rest of his life. Every day I turned him head down on my lap and literally pounded the mucus loose so that he could cough it up and out of his lungs. How could I go back to work and still be there to give him treatments? How could I be at work during the times when he would be hospitalized? And how the hell was I going to come up with ten thousand extra dollars a year?

While Brennan slept, my mind raced. I could sell drugs. No, that wouldn't work. Drug dealers get arrested, then who would take care of my boy? I could rob banks or 7-11 stores. No, they get busted sooner or later, too. Well, I thought, I could learn to be a hooker. Even if they get busted, they usually just pay a fine. Hmmmm. Yeah, that was it. I'd learn to hook.

The decision made, I wondered exactly how one went about becoming a prostitute. I had two friends who were cab drivers. Didn't cab drivers traditionally know where to find whores?

I asked.

Sure enough, Norman knew a working girl named Linda whom he occasionally drove to her various assignments. He said he'd have her call me.

She did. We met for lunch and she answered my questions. She'd met her clients through a woman who had once been a centerfold model. The model's name was Marty, and she ran ads in the local newspaper advertising herself as a photographic model. For fifty dollars you could to to Marty's house and take nude pictures of her for an hour. At some point, the client might ask if she would have sex with him for money. Marty would explain that she only modeled, however, she had a few friends who might be interested. She would give the john three phone numbers, explaining that the first time he saw these ladies, the fee would be seventy-five dollars, twenty-five of which would go to Marty. After the first visit, the fee would be fifty bucks. Not a bad deal in those days. Fifty dollars an hour was top of the line stuff. . .

So, after a phone call and a meeting with Marty, I became one of her "friends."

I went shopping for what I imagined to be proper "hooker clothes": a long, flowing dressing gown, garter belts and stockings, ridiculously high heels. I practiced walking the length of my apartment until I felt confident that I could wear the damn things without falling down. I felt I had to call attention to my only good feature — my legs. The rest of me was twenty pounds overweight, I had no waist at all, my breasts were big, but droopy. My face was passing, but nothing to write home about. Still, nobody had ever kicked me out of bed, so, as I waited for my very first client, a fellow named Harold, I walked back and forth to make sure I had the shoes down pat, smoked one cigarette after another and made several trips to the john to check my make-up and hair.

The apartment was spotlessly clean, fresh sheets on my bed. I lit the candles I had bought, figuring the less he could see, the better off we both would be. Incense? Should I light incense? What the hell. . .

God the whole place stank of cigarette smoke. Didn't I have some Lysol spray somewhere? In the john? No, under the kitchen sink. Where was Harold? What if he didn't show up? Can of Lysol in one hand, a cigarette in the other, my dressing gown flapping behind me, I dashed through the place spraying madly.

My goddamned feet were killing me and the son of a bitch was twenty minutes late. I kicked off my shoes. He wasn't coming. I collapsed to the couch, a frenzy of nerves, excitement, disappointment.

It was just as well. He probably would have hated me on the spot. Better for him not to come at all than take one look at me and leave. It was a stupid idea in the first place and I should have known better than to think I could really. . .

The doorbell.

My God, he was here. What to do with the Lysol? Under the couch.

Where were my shoes? Oh, Jesus, there, in the middle of the floor, get them on, quick. . .the doorbell again, Jesus, don't wake the baby up, that's all I need, "Just a minute! I'm coming. . ."

I drew a breath, pulled my face into a smile. I opened the door.

There stood Harold Wong. All five feet three inches of him. All one-hundred-twenty-pounds of him. At five-feet-nine, not to mention four more inches of high heels, I towered over him as we stood in the doorway. I had a good thirty-five pounds on him. Stricken suddenly with the ludicrous picture we made, I began to laugh. Harold's face broke into a broad smile.

"Ah! So glad to see you so happy! And so big! I love big blonde woman!"

It was over before I knew it.

Twenty minutes had passed from the time he walked in until the moment he left, bowing and thanking me for a lovely time.

I sat on my bed, holding the hundred-dollar bill. He had actually *tipped* me. It was that easy. He had literally come and gone, and I was one hundred dollars richer in just twenty minutes.

I went into the bathroom and looked and looked at my reflection. I didn't look different, just happier. And I felt. . .well. . .*just fine*. No pangs of guilt, no remorse, no shame. What I felt was smug, joyous elation. By God, I was on to something here *and I knew it*.

Over the next few weeks I saw many of Marty's clients. Brennan was very well, and the future looked rosy enough to use some of the incredible money that was stacking up to move to a better, more centrally located apartment. I found a place that actually had a nursery right on the block. I could schedule several appointments in the afternoon and drop my son off at the nursery, come home and deal with my clients, then pick him up by dinner time.

I loved it. I made a solemn vow that I would save half of every dollar I earned toward the day Brennan would need to be hospitalized again. I also started a hobby — some people collect stamps, some model airplanes. I began to collect fifty- and one-hundred dollar bills. Every time someone gave me a bill, into an envelope it would go. In no time my "hobby" had mounted to four thousand dollars.

One afternoon my mother came to visit. There was no way to hide the fact that I no longer worked in a doctor's office, so I figured I might as well let her in on my new-found occupation. I handed her the envelope. She looked inside, amazed, then horror spread across her face.

"My God, honey, there's more than four thousand dollars in here! You didn't steal this, or do something..."

"Mom, I guess you could say I've become something of a, well, professional mistress to a couple of very well off, very nice people . . . It's really not too bad, and I don't want you to worry or . . ."

"How long have you been doing this?"

"A couple of months."

She began to re-count the money, her eyes wide.

"A couple of *months*?"

"Yeah."

"My God, I wish I had thought of doing this when *I* was your age." That's my mom.

As the months rolled on, I started to advertise in a local newspaper, in the personals column. Every week my post office box was stuffed with mail. Many of the letters went directly into my trash basket; those poorly-written with bad spelling on lined paper didn't have a chance. But a well-written letter on good linen paper, or better yet, typed with a company letterhead, got my immediate response.

I screened new clients by insisting that they give me their work phone number. Sometime in the next few days, I called that number and asked for Mr. Jones, or whoever. If the secretary connected me, I knew I had the man's real name and place of employment, so I felt fairly sure he was neither a knife-wielding psycho or a cop.

I soon learned not to deal with very young men. They want to impress you with their prowess, then usually try to talk you out of taking the money.

Still, on one occasion, I broke my rule.

He sounded so sweet, and he passed my clearance tests, so I gave him my address and waited for him to come.

Twenty-four years old, blonde and blue eyed, he sat, perched, on the edge of my couch as we chatted. I always made it a point to chat for a while, using all my senses to ascertain the safety of the situation before getting to the business at hand. I never saw a person more nervous, more afraid to look me in the eyes than this kid.

He excused himself to go to the bathroom, and I, thinking if I had ever seen a potential psycho this was it, went to the kitchen and got my hammer. Holding it close to my side, hidden in the folds of my dressing gown, I tried to sneak past the bathroom door to hide it close to the bed. Just as I approached the bathroom door, he came out, startled to see me there.

I was just as startled, and for a moment we stared at each other, both of us in shock.

"Oh my God, where are you going with that hammer!" He was pale with fright.

"Uh, nowhere...that is, you see, it was in *there*, and it belongs in *there*, so I was just moving it..."

"Oh, God. For a minute I thought you were some kind of crazy and you were going to kill me with the hammer. Look, I might as well just tell you...I'm a virgin."

His sweet face flamed with shame. "I know you've never met anyone as old as me who's still a virgin, but I just get so nervous every time I get close to sex with a real girl, not that you're not a real girl, I mean, but, but..."

I put my hand on his arm. "Yes I have," I said. "Almost every week I get a letter from someone, some even older than you, who are still virgins. It's okay, really. It's okay."

I led him gently by the hand into my room, and very gently, very slowly, we made love. I taught him how to touch me, how to handle a woman's body.

Some months later, he called to tell me he was engaged.

Once a psychologist called me. He was treating a young man who had a particular fetish. He couldn't maintain an erection unless he was wearing women's panties. And they had to be pink, no less.

The first time I saw "Pinky," we had sex while he wore his panties. The second time, I had him pull them down to his knees. The third time, I had him leave them around one knee, and *imagine* he was actually wearing them. Finally he was able to have sex with the panties lying on the bed beside me, where he could see and touch them.

Then, one day I put the panties under my pillow. He had to imagine them, see them in his mind. Within a short time, he was able to just think about his lovely panties to achieve an erection and orgasm. He still had his fetish, but at least he didn't have to be embarrassed by the presence of his little lacy drawers.

By and large, my clients became my friends. I refused to deal with men who held me in low regard, those who wanted my services, yet still looked down on hookers. I didn't need them. There seemed to be an endless supply of very nice men whose company I enjoyed, men who enriched my life (as well as my pocketbook) in many ways.

Prostitution, in itself, is neither good nor bad. Each woman brings to it what she will. How else can a woman without the years of education necessary to become a doctor or lawyer still earn the kind of money a lawyer or doctor earns? In fewer hours? How else could I have had so much time to spend with my son, when time was so precious?

My earnings enabled us to travel, gave him an opportunity to see more than would have otherwise been possible. By the time my son was seven, he had flown in an airplane more than many people do in a lifetime. We lived in New York for a year, where he saw dinosaurs and whales at the Natural History museum. We lived on an island in the U.S. Virgin Islands for several years, where he learned to snorkel the incredible coral reef, seeing the splendor of the underwater world. He collected hundreds of hermit crabs and built them an intricate home in an aquarium which he called Crab Condo. He learned to strip the outer edge of coconut fronds away, leaving only the long, fibrous center which he tied into a slip knot, the perfect way to sneak up on a fat lizard, slip the loose not around its neck and with a flick of his wrist, capture it. Together we caught whole jars full of lizards, picked a favorite, then let them go from the center of a huge chalk-drawn circle, cheering for our favorite as the lizards raced away.

I provided as full a life for my son as I could, and money was the key. Prostitution provided that money, and, even more importantly, it gave me the spare time I wouldn't have had with any nine-to-five "real" job. It provided the best private schooling, the chance to travel, the best medical care.

On October the first, 1985, my son died. He would have been ten years old that December.

Now, I am "retired," I became involved with a Prostitution and AIDS study funded by the government, interviewing prostitutes and drawing blood samples anonymously to see what percentage of prostitutes in my home city are infected with the AIDS virus. The experience led to my expanded interest in AIDS, and now I work with AIDS patients in many capacities.

Prostitution served me very well, indeed. It was a most useful tool.

I have no regrets, no shame, no remorse. Indeed, I look back on my prostitution experience with a sense of pride and accomplishment. I did it, I'm glad I did it, and I applaud those who do it now.

Here's to the Ladies of the Night — Carry on! Save your money, make wise investments, and above all else — *love yourself*.

Interview with Barbara

Carole

*Barbara is a thirty-nine year old woman. She's worked with prosti-
tutes' rights groups and lives in Richmond, California. I interviewed
her in her home, which she shares with her daughter, mother and
sister.*

Carole: How long have you worked as a prostitute?

Barbara: I've been a prostitute for seventeen or eighteen years.

Carole: Where have you worked?

Barbara: Basically California. I've also worked in Alaska,
Washington, Hawaii and Nevada. I've worked on the streets and in
the casinos in Nevada. But I don't work the streets anymore. What I
do now is really not prostitution, it's domination. I still charge for it
and I still like doing it. If I could work on the streets I would, but the
police make it too dangerous. They arrest you a lot so that you have
to spend all your earnings to get out of jail. And then, they make you
work in dark corners; you can't work out in the open for any amount
of time. They come along and say, "Move on, move on." Basically,
that's why I don't work the streets anymore. I'm older, too, but I think
if the police didn't bother me and if it was legal, I'd be working the
streets still. It's much easier and you don't have to play the boyfriend-
girlfriend routine, you know, and it's quicker! *(She laughs.)* If you get
a guy off the streets, it usually lasts about twenty minutes. The whole
date, from there to the apartment and back.

Carole: What are your experiences with police arrests? Are tricks
ever arrested?

Barbara: They never arrest johns. One time, I can remember in
particular when they arrested me and four other women in San Francisco. There were five guys there and instead of arresting them, they
made them testify in the trial against us.

Carole: Is that typical?

Barbara: That's typical, yes. If they catch you with the guy, no matter what the guy says, they won't arrest him. One time I can remember I was arrested and I was with a guy when the police pulled up behind us. I told him, "Look, don't say nothing, you know, just tell them, hey, I'm talking to you because as long as you don't say anything, I won't." Well, he freaked out and told the police, "Yeah, she solicited me for X amount of money," and they let him go. They wanted him to testify against me, but he didn't. The guy was into domination. At that time I didn't know what domination was, but he wanted me to whip him and beat him, and he wanted me to put him under a table and just do my commands, do whatever I told him to do. I thought he was crazy, but I also didn't know it was domination. *(She laughs.)* I knew he wasn't going to go to court, because if he'd come to trial, I would have told everything. They finally dismissed the case, but I had to go to court at least five times.

And the case was not a case. I mean, the guy had actively solicited me. But I had to pay the cost. I had to bail out of jail and make five court appearances.

Carole: How many times have you been arrested?

Barbara: To be honest, I don't know. At least thirty, probably closer to fifty.

Carole: What kind of violent experiences have taken place in your work?

Barbara: Well, I don't know if this is violent or not. To me, it was. It was the first time I was arrested in San Francisco. I was with a girl. I didn't know her. She had two guys with her. She said they wanted to date her, so we walked around to the place that we were supposed to date at, and we find out that the guys were policemen. So the police said, "You're under arrest," and he said, "Bitch, if you make a move, I'll knock you down in the streets right now. Do you hear me?" I said, "I'm not going to do anything," and he said, "Did you hear me, bitch?" You know, he screamed and hollered at me.

Carole: This was in San Francisco?

Barbara: Yes, the San Francisco police.

Carole: Have you been raped while working?

Barbara: Yes. The first year. I was working in Oakland. This guy pulled up to me. He was a young black guy, and he told me that he had a friend who had fifty dollars, but who was too ashamed to come in the area. He said he would take me to the guy. At the time, I didn't know any better, and I was loaded on reds, so I went with him. He was supposed to take me to this hotel, but he pulled up in this remote area. And when he pulled off, he grabbed my purse and told me, "Bitch, give me all your money." I told him I wasn't going to give him

167

anything. Okay, since then I've learned that you don't fight back. But I fought back that night. He wound up taking my purse and my coat. I wore wigs then, and he took my wig. He took everything. That was the only time something like that really happened...and I don't blame the guy. I blame myself for it because I was loaded on reds, because I should have known better in the first place, and, believe me, after that I have. That's about the most violent thing that has happened to me.

Carole: So, he didn't rape you?

Barbara: Well, yes, he did. He raped me. But the rape part was nothing. I mean, the devastating part to me was him taking everything I had. He did rape me. ∴ the rape was nothing. You know, he screwed for about twenty minutes, not even that long, maybe about fifteen. That part doesn't really stick with me because that wasn't the devastating part. Everything after that was.

Carole: When that happened, you didn't want to go to the police?

Barbara: I didn't even think about going to the police at all, you know. At that time I was so young. I was twenty-one. I had just started working. I thought beause I was a prostitute, how dare I go to the police...

Carole: Was it because you didn't want them to know you were a prostitute?

Barbara: Well, yes. But at that time I didn't think I had any rights. And, I was loaded, too. I figured I'd be in just as much trouble as this guy would be.

Carole: Were you ever raped again while working?

Barbara: I've had them try. It's just that that's the only time anyone's succeeded. I had this guy one time. I was in Emeryville. He pulled up to me and told me he wanted to date me.

I got in his car and we drove like we were going to my apartment. All of a sudden, he pulled over and said, "I don't have any money and you're going to fuck me right now." I said, "In the front seat?" He had a small knife, it was real small, like a pen knife, and he said, "Get in the back seat." So I got in the back seat. And I said, "Look, whatever you want to do, just do it. I won't fight at all, there won't be any trouble." He started dating me and I kept on being so nice. I'd say, "Oh, and you have to put on a rubber." *(She laughs.)* I was just real sweet. He couldn't stand it. He started dating me, he started screwing me and he pushed me out of the car. I think he really wanted me to fight and jump with him. And I wasn't violent at all — "Okay, you want some, fine I understand, just don't mess up my dress, don't mess up my hair." *(She laughs.)* He didn't want anything to do with me because I wouldn't fight him.

One time I was in Alaska. This guy pulled up and when he pulled up I knew that it wasn't someone I should go with, but it was cold. We were in Anchorage, and in Anchorage you have to work on the streets. They won't let you work in any of the hotels or bars. They harass you some on the streets, but you can still work. It was freezing that night and this guy pulled up and he looked wrong, but I went with him anyway. So I'm on my way to the apartment and two blocks before we get there he grabs me. Well, I had some hair spray, those little aqua-net hair sprays, they make good mace. I took it and sprayed it in his face and it sort of blinded him. Then I just got out of the car.

Carole: From your experience, how do the police respond to the rape of a prostitute?

Barbara: I've heard them say many times that you couldn't rape a prostitute. Once my girlfriends were attacked by some guys. They were in Berkeley and called the police. The police just said, "That's the price you pay, it comes with the trade...so why bitch and scream, you're a prostitute." Which is totally ridiculous.

Carole: Have you heard about the murders of prostitutes in the East Bay which have taken place over the last few months?

Barbara: I've heard about them, but not very much.

Carole: What about the Los Angeles and Seattle murders?

Barbara: Yeah, the Green River murders. Most of the girls he's killed have been prostitutes. He went from Seattle to Oregon and I think maybe to Los Angeles and then back to Seattle. The feds didn't want to get involved because even though it's interstate, they say it's not their territory. Why? Because they're only prostitutes. Their age range is thirteen to thirty-five or thirty-eight. I think that if the FBI got involved, they could stop it. And the parents, apparently they don't want to speak up because their daughters are prostitutes. But it's so low-key that I've barely heard about it, let alone other people hearing about it.

Carole: Back to the issue of rape. Barbara, I've asked some district attorneys about rape cases of prostitutes and several of them have told me that they think prostitutes report rapes when actually they've been robbed of their money. What do you think of that?

Barbara: That's ridiculous! If she goes to the trouble of reporting it, she's definitely been raped. Lots of times the women blame themselves if they get robbed or don't get their money.

Carole: You've said several times that you feel it's your responsibility to not get hurt. But after all, no one has the right to attack you.

Barbara: Oh, no, nobody has the right, but I do have the right to protect myself, and if I know how to protect myself and I'm not doing it, then I don't feel that I can blame them. Yeah, they're invading my territory, and they don't give a damn, but I'm saying that if I protect myself, nothing can happen. I'm pretty strong mentally and physically, not physically enough to fight a man, but basically, if I keep my head and think right, you know, if I'm not loaded, which most of the time I'm not. That one time I was. But if I'm working, I don't do drugs, and I mean nothing. I barely drink. Even though I do blame the person, I know that if I'd done what I needed to do, I wouldn't have been in that mess.

Carole: Have police officers tried to get sexual favors from you?

Barbara: Several times. But not as bad as the other girls. Once two other girls and I were sharing an apartment and the landlord decided to call the police and tell them we were working out of it. He flagged down this police. Well, I knew the guy he flagged down and he was really good. One time, he'd seen me turning a car date, doing a blow job in a car, and he didn't do anything on that occasion. And there were a couple of other times, too. Then after about four times, he told me that I owed him a date. He told me if I didn't want to go to jail, I should give him something. I said, "Well, I can't do that, I'm a prostitute, and if I do that you're gonna pay me." He wound up giving me a dollar and seventy cents. I didn't mind because I would much rather have dated him for a dollar and seventy cents than go to jail.

I've heard that happening many times. With vice officers, too. Most of the times I hear about it they're trying to scare the girls into something, you know. It's like, if you date me then I'll keep all the rest of the policemen away from you, or I'll tell you who all the police are.

Carole: Do you think it's better for the prostitutes not to give them anything?

Barbara: For me it was always better if I didn't date them. It's like dating a bartender. If you're in a place and he wants you then he'll keep letting you be there until he gets you. Then after he gets you, he won't want to see you anymore And so that's what I did with the bartenders and cops, too. I'd tease them and play like I was going to — "I can't do it right now, you remind me of a trick; you're too nice a guy." But I've dated a lot of police. Lots of them. I didn't know until afterwards.

Carole: It was during their off-hours?

Barbara: I don't know if it was or not. They said they weren't working, but they showed me their badges and stuff afterwards. One cop said he wanted his money back. I said, "Bull." I wasn't afraid of him. I knew that if he told people he'd get in more trouble than I would.

Carole: I've also heard that more black prostitutes are arrested than white prostitutes, and that black prostitutes are kept in jail longer. Is that true?

Barbara: That's true. I can barely remember any white girls who were in jail with me in Oakland. The black girl has a much harder time on everything. She'll get kicked out of the hotel much faster than a white girl. A white girl, if she's got any kind of class about her, can work anywhere. Whereas if you're black, if you do anything wrong at all, like getting up to go to a guy in a bar when he calls you over instead of making him come over to you, they can kick you. If you're black, they kick you out faster. In Las Vegas, they arrested a lot of white prostitutes, but at first there *were* only white prostitutes.

Carole: A San Francisco study by Mimi Silbert, PhD, of the Delancey Street Foundation, of two hundred street prostitutes revealed that two-thirds had been raped or forced to do things they didn't want to do. What do you think of those numbers?

Barbara: It sounds too high, and I've known quite a few prostitutes. See, people want to downgrade prostitutes and they think that guys can just take advantage of them. But most of the time the prostitutes set the rules. Johns go where we want them to go. We run everything. They pay you first, they come to your place, they wash, they must use a rubber. People think that the tricks call out the rules but I don't know what girls they talked to. Now junkies work totally differently from prostitutes who are not junkies. And they get hurt more.

Carole: Barbara, why did you first get into prostitution?

Barbara: I did it for the money. That was the only reason I got into it. I couldn't find a job that paid more than minimum wage, whatever it was at the time, two dollars and thirty-five cents. I had two children. I had no way of supporting them besides being on welfare. I was always working two jobs but with the one or two jobs I could still barely pay rent.

Carole: At this point, how difficult would it be for you to leave prostitution if you wanted to?

Barbara: It would be hard. I'm not into prostitution right now. I'm into domination. But if I wanted to leave both of them alone it would be very difficult because my mother stays here with me, and my sister and my daughter. My sister and my daughter have jobs that don't pay much and my mother is on social security, so I'm the breadwinner. I have to pay the rent, help take care of them. And I have to take care of myself, too.

Carole: What kinds of things would you change about prostitution if you could?

Barbara: First, I'd make it legal. Lots of prostitutes feel they're guilty when they're arrested and that they don't have any rights. I'd like prostitutes to train prostitutes to change that so they don't think that they have to have pimps. If a woman wants a pimp, that's her business, she should be allowed one. But if she doesn't want one, I don't think that she should have one. I'd make it so that prostitutes had a place where they could work. If they wanted to work the streets I'd make it so that they could. I'd make it so the police would do other things besides bother prostitutes. So many times I was harassed by policemen and they'd say: "It's much easier coming here and talking with you because you're not going to do anything to me."

I was in Amsterdam last year. We had a Forum. A lot of the girls were telling me how bad it was even though they have places to work out of. At first, you know, I went along with them and said, "Yeah, I understand," but then I went down to the red light district, and if I had had a red light district when I was a prostitute, I would have loved it. They have little store fronts, and they sit in the window. Some girls wear hardly anything, some are dressed regular. The guy comes up and if he wants you, he knocks on the door. You've got your bodyguard in there in case anybody wants to go off or anybody's drunk or whatever. Now, I don't think we'd have to be limited that way. The women in Amsterdam complained that this was the only place they could work. I think that women should be able to work where they want to. They also complained that if they got a regular job in additon to the prostitution, they had to tell people that they were prostitutes. I think that's totally wrong. I don't think that I should be stigmatized if I want to sell my body.

Carole: So, that was their main complaint, that they had to stay in one area?

Barbara: Yeah. And that the landlords charged them an arm and a quarter. That if they wanted to get out of it, or just take a part-time job, they had to say they were prostitutes. Still, if we had that much! Some of the women who were with us said, "Yeah, but that's horrible — they're standing there like cows and they're taking them out like cattle." Well, fine, but I'd much rather have guys come to me than go to them. *(She laughs.)* And most prostitutes would.

Carole: To change the subject a little, what have your experiences been with the courts?

Barbara: Juries have been fantastic for me. Not all, but most of them. I've taken most of my cases to jury trials. I've won most, and if I didn't, it was like a hung jury or they dismissed it before it went to trial. The group of women I dealt with, we all knew that we had the right to take it to court and trial and that we could win if we took it to trial. But, see, a lot of women don't know that. I had a public defender once, a woman, who told me: "Look Barbara, they want to give you a year's probation," and she said, "You know that you solicited the guy, go ahead and take the year." I said, "But, I didn't solicit him and I'm not pleading guilty — I don't want your year's probation, I didn't do anything, and I don't want anything." I wound up firing her and I paid a lawyer. And I won the case. Prostitutes need to know they can win.

Carole: Where did you get your legal advice?

Barbara: We read a lot. We went to court and we listened. We read the laws. We knew what was solicitation and what was not.

Carole: Can you tell me a little about your experiences in jail?

Barbara: The first time I went in it was horrible. In San Francisco. The matrons were horrible sometimes. I cried the whole time, I was scared to death. They'd arrested thirty or forty girls on prostitution. All the beds were lined up and the latrines were against the walls. If you had to use the bathroom you had to use it in front of all the girls. And the toilets were filthy.

Jail is no rehabilitation. If anything you get worse by being in jail. When I was crying that first time, one of the girls came up to me and said, "Honey, you better be quiet or else these girls are going to come out and they're gonna tease you and they're gonna get mad. You can't be crying in here." Well, I said fuck it, and I didn't care and I went ahead and cried anyway 'cause I was real uptight. But they're real hard and cold.

When they give you a sentence they tell you that you're going to go to Santa Rita for rehabilitation. But there's no real rehabilitation. They don't give you nothing. No counseling, no anything. And I don't know any jail that does. So, to be locked up bcause you don't want to take a two dollar and thirty-five cents job, I think that's horrible. Most of the prostitutes I know are not thieves. They're not people who would do anything to you. Now, I grant you I don't know a lot of junkies 'cause I stay away from them. They'd steal from their own parents. But a lot of girls just want to make a living and be left alone, you know.

Carole: Why do you think that prostitution is kept illegal in the United States?

Barbara: Because they're stupid and lazy. The politicians don't want to figure out a way to get the money, they're afraid that prostitutes will cheat and they won't get enough tax money. And men don't want women to have control over anything. Men want to run everything.

Especially white middle class businessmen. They can get away with anything and they know they can.

Carole: What other things would you do if prostitution was decriminalized?

Barbara: Well, a lot of violence would not happen if it wasn't a crime. Men take advantage of women, true enough, but if the girls were more organized and knew more, then they wouldn't let the guys take advantage of them. Beatings and robbings might not be if women would just stick together. There are so many things I could tell prostitutes so that they'd be protected but if I did that now, I'd be commmitting a felony because I'd be training a prostitute. It's also conspiracy to tell a girl that someone is a policeman. There are so many laws they can use on you. It's completely sickening to me. Just sitting on this bed could probably be illegal. *(Laughter)*

Carole: Prostitutes don't often go to rape crisis centers, why is that?

Barbara: They don't use them because I don't think they know they can use them. A lot of prostitutes think they're going to be looked down on; they're looked down on by so many people. They don't think they'll find a nice person who is willing to listen to them. They don't know if they're working with the police. Most of the time a girl doesn't go anywhere when she's been raped. Prostitutes need to know that they can go to these places. For example, I'm working for a project where I interview prostitutes. I interviewed two women, and when I told them that I was an ex-prostitute, one said: "You're just telling me that to make me feel good." My point is, if prostitutes knew they could talk to ex-prostitutes or that they didn't have to worry about being judged, it would make a big difference. For all they know, the rape crisis centers might be working with the police. Police are always there. . . .

Carole: If you could have other work options that paid better than the minimum wage, might you leave prostitution?

Barbara: Prostitution is something that I'd like to do on my own terms when I felt like doing it. What I mean is that I wouldn't want to do it all the time. I'd go out maybe twice a week instead of five, six times. I think I'd continue because I like the power that I have with men. I like making them do whatever I want them to do. But it gets stressful too. You have to be on your toes. But there's so much money in it. And there's a power thing in making them pay for it and in deciding whether or not I'm going to date them. If I want to be nice to you, that's my choice, and if I want to be a straight up bitch, I can do that too. That's my choice.

Stripper

Debi Sundahl

For the last five years, I have been working full-time as an erotic performer in San Francisco. I love being a stripper. I consider the theater where I work to be a model of what all sexual entertainment theaters should be. Because of the money I make, the wonderful women I work with, and the standards of quality at the theater, I have come to enjoy the art of burlesque and have passed that knowledge on to others.

Before moving to San Francisco and becoming a stripper, I was a student at the University of Minnesota with a double major in Women's Studies and History. I was active in both feminist and Marxist politics. Also, I worked as an advocate at the Harriet Tubman Shelter for Battered Women in Minneapolis, and for two years I worked with Women Against Violence Against Women (WAVAW), where I helped organize Minnesota's annual Take Back the Night March. At that time, feminism most actively focused on issues of violence against women. Many times, I presented an educational slide show which focused on degrading and/or violent images of women in the media. The show, initially produced by Women Against Pornography in Los Angeles, dealt mainly with rape, battering and incest, making only occasional anti-pornography references.

It was through feminism, and through my involvement with WAVAW, that I came out as a lesbian and met my lover, with whom I am still living. Coming out was the beginning of exploring my sexuality and sex in general. The first time I slept with a woman, I had physical feelings I did not know my body could have. It was an awakening, and I did not want to stop there. I wanted to explore all the taboo areas of sex.

I was well aware, through feminism, of the theory of oppression, and the lies, secrets, and silences that oppressed groups live with. It was obvious to me that sex workers were an oppressed group, suffering from stereotypes and social oppression, much the same as lesbians. Having just come out as a lesbian, I was not afraid to enter yet another unknown territory, and so, when I arrived in San Francisco, I answered an ad in the *San Francisco Chronicle*: "Dancers Wanted. Must be over 18. Part-time job for students and homemakers." Here was an indication that sex workers were not who society at large thought they were.

My suspicions proved true. The owners of the Lusty Lady Theater were involved in founding the Venusian Church in Seattle as well as the Institute for the Advanced Study of Human Sexuality in San Francisco. They were decidedly interested in the positive expression of human sexuality. The institute provided the education. The church expressed that education in an entertainment form the public could enjoy. The Church staged erotic performances and masturbation fantasies in a sensual place where people could feel comfortable. The managers of the Lusty Lady Theater, mostly women, kept a clean theater, paid their performers well, and were very supportive of both the dancers' and the clientele's expressing their sexuality. Alcohol and drugs were not permitted in the theater, the management was well organized, and I liked the other dancers, who were primarily young college students or struggling artists.

The hardest part of the job was dealing with my feminist principles concerning the objectification of women. Dancing nude is the epitomy of woman as sex object. As the weeks passed, I found I liked being a sex object, because the context was appropriate. I resent being treated as a sex object on the street or at the office. But as an erotic dancer, that is my purpose. I perform to turn you on, and if I fail, I feel I've done a poor job. Women who work in the sex industry are not responsible for, nor do they in any way perpetuate, the sexual oppression of women. In fact, to any enlightened observer, our very existence provides a distinction and a choice as to when a woman should be treated like a sex object and when she should not be. At the theater, yes; on the street, no. Having the distinction so obviously played out at work, I felt more personal power on the street. I was far less inclined to put up with harassment than I was before, even when I had taken self-defense training. Therefore, I did not feel exploited personally, either outside of my job or in it. I was no more the personal intimate sexual partner of the men for whom I performed than an actress is the character she portrays in a film or play. When people ask me, as they often do, "How does your lover deal with your being a stripper?" I respond by saying I'm a stripper not because I'm looking for other lovers but because it's my job. For the first time I felt I could express my sexuality in a safe environment. I was in control. Understanding that is was perfectly okay for a women to be a sex object in the appropriate context, and distinguishing what those contexts *were* allowed me to get on with the business of learning and enjoying my craft.

After I had worked at the Lusty Lady's peep show for two years, I was ready to move on. Fortunately, I lived in a city that has one of the best erotic entertainment theaters in the world. At the Mitchell Brothers' O'Farrell Street Theater, I was introduced to the art of burlesque in its traditional form. Burlesque has a long history and plays an important sexual role in society. A true art form, it has had its great artists and changes in style and form over the years. It is an insulting misconception about burlesque that anyone in a drunken, uninhibited state can strip. It takes practice and talent to be able to pull off an entertaining and truly erotic performance. To create good art, an artist must have a sophisticated and sensitive knowledge of her subject. Of the many strippers I have known, the best were those who had explored and were accepting of their sexuality. The pool of knowledge and emotions from which these women drew their creativity was sophisticated and deep. They liked themselves sexually and they held their profession in high regard.

The Mitchell Brothers' theater has a large stage and a superb lighting and sound system, and a beautiful, comfortable theater indicated the owners' respect for sexual entertainment. It was a big step for me to go from a small peep show, with its private booths, to a full-blown theater environment. My wages tripled, and so did my self-respect as an erotic dancer. The first time I saw the show, I cried because it was so beautiful, and because it is so difficult to *find* this beauty. Here was erotic entertainment as it should be, and it was here that I became committed to a career in the sex industry.

Of the crew of sixty performers (some of the best strippers in the country), half were, and still are, lesbians. We lamented the fact that very few women would come to the theater to watch us perform. The sex industry, and the institutions of the sex industry — the theaters, bookstores, and publications — have all been created by men, for men, and are the last great boys' club left totally untouched by feminism. It is a rare stripper who is not a feminist, and so we decided it was time to demand equal access to sexual entertainment.

I started the first women-only strip show at a lesbian bar in San

Francisco in July 1984. The weekly shows were an instant success. The dancers loved performing for the all-female audiences because they had more freedom of expression. They were not limited to ultra-feminine acts only; they could be butch, they could dress in masculine attire. They adored the audience feedback, which was enthusiastic, verbal, and supportive. Judging by the response and by the crowds, women were (and are) hungry for sexual entertainment and enthralled by the fact that, for the first time in modern history, they could have sexual entertainment to call their own. Since the vast majority of these women had never seen a strip show before, it was a safe place to explore the meaning of sexual entertainment. It was interesting to see the effect on the strippers as well: before the show, some felt cautious about letting other lesbians know what they did for a living. Now, they are treated with respect and awe in their communities. It has also been gratifying to see changes taking place in the lesbian community around sexual expression. Not once were we picketed by anti-porn groups. Instead, the response was overwhelmingly positive. We were excited to be participating in the new phenomenon of women creating erotica for women. The issues of the anti-porn movement were not our issues.

We are fortunate to have a new ground, and it's exhilarating. During this time, and in this spirit, I published the first issue of *On Our Backs*, a lesbian sexual entertainment magazine. I also began to make adult or X-rated videos for lesbians under the name of Fatale, which is from the name I had chosen for myself as a stripper, Fanny Fatale.

I am aware that I have been fortunate to have had a positive experience as an erotic dancer. It is because of this experience that I am strongly in favor of sexual entertainment. But stripping is traditional women's work as much as waitressing, teaching and secretarial work is. Consequently, it suffers from the same low pay. Considering the high demand for erotic performers and the low supply, and the fact that the service they provide is a rare commodity, most erotic performers are vastly underpaid. The working conditions, overall, are also poor; many theaters are run on a quasi-legitimate financial basis, and are not clean or safe. Often, the basic tools necessary for the job — like adequate sound and light systems, ample dressing room space, and equipment (like washers, dryers and irons) to care for costumes — are not provided. Even though most dancers work more than forty hours a week, no vacation or overtime pay is provided, nor are there any health benefits. Many dancers fear becoming ill because missing one day of work will put their jobs in jeopardy.

The social hypocrisy under which most dancers perform creates a high stress situation. On the one hand, social demand for their services is high, but on the other hand, they are stigmatized by society for working in the sex industry. It is difficult to be a stripper and resist internalizing negative stereotypes of strippers, i.e., they are abused, come from broken homes, abuse drugs and alcohol, lead violent lives, and are forced into or turn to the sex industry out of desperation. The stereotypes leave little room for self-respect. Fear of rejection by family and friends forces the stripper to lie about her occupation, especially when she is trying to obtain basic civil rights or legal assistance. The possibility that her children can be taken from her because of the nature of her employment makes living in the closet essential. Significant others in her life often cannot come to terms with her work, which can lead to emotional problems. In short, being a stripper means having to live with hostility; it means constantly struggling for self-esteem.

The sex industry suffers from sexist attitudes as much as any other area. Women have traditionally been bottom-level workers while men have held management and ownership positions. Only in the past few years have women begun to hold positions of power in the sex industry. The ramifications of women controlling the means of production of erotic entertainment materials will be revolutionary. The fact that women have had virtually no erotica created by them, for them is intrinsically tied to the sexist attitude that a woman's role in society is to be housewife/mother/sexual servant. In response to the anti-porn movement, women sex workers have had to take a stand and have begun to create erotica in their own interests.

The future looks promising and challenging. Women are opening vibrator stores, publishing erotic materials for other women, making adult videos with women in mind, and producing erotic entertainment. These women remember the early days of sixties feminism, when the right to control your body meant the right to be sexual as well. Crawling out from under the oppressive, anti-sex attitudes of the anti-porn movement, women are demanding the right to explore their sexual identity, defining the many possible ways of being sexual, and encouraging tolerance for *all* sexual expression.

I for one am tired of being the moral guardian of male sexuality and of suffering ostracism and condemnation if I choose to be sexually active or sexually autonomous. Sex education and the ability to communicate about all aspects of sex is essential to fostering social respect for sex workers as well as respect for personal sexual choice and expression. Like many oppressed minorities, we have suffered under the assumption that we must be protected from ourselves. The quasi-illegal and illegal nature of our work robs us of the power to define and control the conditions under which we are employed. We know better than anyone what is healthy and what is not healthy about our work.

These last five years, I have lived a rewarding and rich life as a stripper. Like most artists, I feel I have something special to say and something of interest to offer them. I see a bright and lively future for those on the progressive edge of sexual entertainment, and feel fortunate to be numbered among its outspoken participants. I know how good it can be, and am committed to sharing with others the wonderful realities of my job and the potential for the industry in general.

The Continuing Saga
of Scarlot Harlot X

Carol Leigh

Roaches and Ruminations

. . . I live in a posh, modern apartment with rustic wood paneling, a push-button fireplace and a panoramic view stretching from San Francisco to San Mateo. The gall to defy taboo, a series of risks and an inclination towards sexual experimentation have provided me with this aesthetic environment where I entertain clients, poke at my typewriter and recline on my queen-size bed, pondering.

The comfort and luxury of my solitary brothel is in sharp contrast to the fear which haunts me. Often I dwell upon my worst fears. Uncontrollable paranoia grips me as I gaze into the starry night. Men who hate prostitutes will rape and kill me. The Moral Majority will conspire with the Mafia against me. I will be arrested for everything. No man will ever really love and accept me. My whole family will find out and confront me with their disapproval. Prostitution is not okay. I am deluding myself and I will go crazy avoiding that revelation.

Food! I need food. I will become obese. I need to eat. I lift my head from velvet pillows, rolling off the queen size blue satin and head for my kitchen. Tomorrow I will go on a diet. I flick on the fluorescents.

There they are. A tiny tribe of enemies, scampering across my private moment. The truth, the truth and a irritating lack of perfection. And I pay so much rent. But I will never be safe.

I confess, I am to blame. I don't use Raid. I don't squash them. There are no vacancies in my Roach Motels — in fact, they've become symbols. There is no solution.

This whole issue reminds me of something. Birth control. Did you know that there is no good form of birth control? Foams and jellies are poison. I.U.D.s puncture the womb. Birth control pills are a crime against women. All that's left is rhythm and prophylactics. The rubbers bust and my cycles are obtuse.

Never mind, I'm just making excuses. I should go out and buy some boric acid. That works fine. I confess, I just practice avoidance, telling myself the roaches don't really multiply that fast. They'll die of old age, so I'll never have to fight. But I know the truth. I'll make a list. I'll go to the store. I'll use rubbers and rhythm and Roachproof...

I guess paralysis is a common affliction. I guess most people wrestle with apathy, pessimism, and confusion, not just prostitutes. So why should I be ashamed?

I'm not ashamed. I'm proud. I'm proud that . . .I'm not ashamed.

I have only one thing left to say. I'm a prostitute and if you don't like it, you're stupid. . .

PART II:
CONNECTIONS

Prostitution: A Difficult Issue for Feminists

Priscilla Alexander

Prostitution has been a difficult issue for feminists both in the current wave of the feminist movement, which began in the late 1960s, and in the earlier wave which began in the 1860s. As feminists, we abhor the exploitation of women's sexuality by profiteers, and some of us feel, instinctively, that prostitution supports an objectification of women's sexuality and of women, that is somehow related to the pervasive violence against us. In addition, we are defined, by ourselves and others, by our place in the age-old whore/madonna dichotomy. However, there is a growing realization among many feminists that the laws against prostitution, and the stigma imposed on sex work, keep all women from determining their own sexuality.

Few women reach puberty without being aware of prostitution. Many women have at some point thought about engaging in prostitution to pay their bills or to get out of serious debt, although for most it is only a fleeting thought. Many women have prostitution fantasies in which they equate sexual pleasure with depravity and "badness," on the one hand, or with power on the other hand. Many women equate prostitution with negative feelings about their own sexual encounters with men — for example, when the men are interested in quick, rather anonymous, casual sexual encounters, and the women are interested in more long-term, caring, sexual relationships. The result of such conflicting demands is that many women, at least some of the time, feel sexually used.

At the same time, the message beamed at young girls by parents, advice columnists, teachers, clergy, and others is that they should protect their virginity, save their sexuality for marriage, or at least for a significant relationship. While there may be good medical reasons for the delay of sexual intercourse (e.g., the greater risk of cervical cancer in women who become sexually active before the age of eighteen or twenty), such messages are generally "moral" in tone rather than "medical." Although the percentage of adolescent girls who are sexually active increases every year, so that being sexual has become the norm rather than the exception, the behavior is still condemned. For example, court decisions have ended the practice of expelling girls who become pregnant from school; instead they are now channeled into special, inferior programs, outside of the regular school curriculum. As a result, many girls still drop out, which effectively ends their education and sentences them to a lifetime of low-level, low-paying jobs, or dependence on welfare. Teenage women who become pregnant are blamed for it, while the biological fathers-to-be are neither blamed nor channeled to the side, there being no obvious indication of their sexual activity. At the same time, there is extraordinary resistance to providing comprehensive sex education in the schools, allegedly because sex education increases promiscuity.

Another factor that interferes with a dispassionate view of prostitution is that approximately one out of three women report that they were sexually "abused" by an adult male before they reached the age of eighteen. In addition, as adults, women face a one in four risk of being raped (or even one in three, according to some recent studies) by acquaintances or by strangers. If marital rape were to be included in those statistics, the percentage would be higher. Compounding this abuse is the persistent blaming of the victim with which we are all familiar. An incestuously assaulted five year old is described by a judge as "sexually precocious." When a high school girl, wearing dungarees, a turtle-neck and a loose shirt is raped, her rapist is described by the judge as responding "normally" to provocation. A standard defense to rape is that the woman was a prostitute, and in 1986 a judge in Pasadena, California dismissed a rape charge because the survivor was a prostitute, saying "a whore is a whore is a whore," and that he was not going to "enforce an illegal contract." In the same year, a district attorney in Fresno, California dropped all but three of thirty-two charges of forcible sex crimes against a man accused of raping six women, because at least four of the women he raped were prostitutes. This bias is carried into the home as well, particularly in the case of domestic violence: many battering husbands call their wives "whore" before they hit them, as though the label justifies the act. Although the laws against adultery and fornication have been repealed in many states, the stigma still remains. Women who are sexually active outside of traditional marriage are vulnerable to custody fights, and judges are still, in 1986, granting custody to fathers on those grounds. This is particularly true for lesbians and prostitutes, who are seen as being far outside of the norm, but it is also a problem for women who are in long-term, monogamous relationships with men outside of marriage.

In addition to the restrictions and negative experiences that make it difficult for women to view prostitution objectively, prostitution itself is shrouded in layer upon layer of mystique. The male-controlled media, which includes classic literature as well as modern television, movies, novels, and magazines, have largely created an unreal image of the prostitute. On the one hand, the media presents the "whore with the heart of gold" and the "sex goddess"; on the other hand, it presents the depraved, degraded prisoner, the sexual slave. Modern pornography has further confused the issue, by misrepresenting women's sexuality, including prostitution. Only recently have prostitutes themselves begun to write about their experiences, or to tell their experiences to other writers (Millett, 1973; Jaget, 1980; Perkins, 1985; Roberts, 1986; this book). In addition, some feminists have begun to write about prostitution, looking at the patriarchal structures that historically surround prostitution and the role that prostitution plays in contemporary society. (Macmillan, 1977; Perry, 1978; Barry, 1979; Walkowitz, 1980; Goldman, 1981; Rosen, 1982; Wells, 1982; Otis, 1985; Barnhardt, 1986.)

Prevalence of Prostitution

Prostitution has existed in every society for which there are written records (Bullough, 1978; Tannahill, 1980; Murphy, 1983; Otis, 1985; Lerner, 1986). For a long period in history, women had only three options for economic survival: getting married, becoming a nun (earlier, a priestess), or becoming a prostitute. The invention of the spinning wheel, around the 13th Century, enabled a woman working alone to produce enough thread to support herself, for the first time, as a spinster.

Prostitution has tended to increase in times of social change, particularly as women's roles changed. In medieval France, for example, as small towns grew into cities, and as the feudal system developed into a more diversified societal structure, the number of prostitutes increased and the forms of prostitution changed substantially. Thus, in 13th century France, prostitution was essentially a cottage industry, with a few women apparently working independently in a few small towns. In the 14th century, as the towns grew larger, prostitutes were confined to certain streets. In the late 14th and early 15th centuries, after the population had been decimated by the Plague, prostitutes were required to work in brothels, and then the brothels were "municipalized," with the city "farming" out the management of the brothels. With each step, the control of prostitution passed increasingly into the hands of men. Increasing pressure was put on the women to repent, however, and in the 16th century, with the growth of the Protestant Reformation and the adoption of a single official sexual standard for all men (as opposed to one for married men and monks, and another for priests and single men), prostitution was outlawed for a time (Otis, 1985). The Industrial Revolution in the 19th century was accompanied by a marked increase in prostitution. This was due, in part, to the migration of large numbers of women from rural, agricultural communities to urban, industrial cities. When they could not obtain jobs in the new factories, or when they could not subsist on the low factory wages, significant numbers turned to prostitution. A contributing factor was that women who left their families to work in factories were considered immoral and were subject to intense sexual harassment on the job. Once they were stigmatized for leaving home, the barriers to involvement in prostitution declined (Madeleine, 1919/1986; Longstreet, 1970; Rosen, 1977). A similar pattern can be seen in the newly industrializing nations today in Africa, Latin America, and Southeast Asia.

For most of history, prostitution has been a stigmatized profession, although it has rarely been prohibited outright. The status of prostitutes seems to have been tied directly to the general status of women: the more that women, as a class, have been confined and treated as chattel, the freer prostitute women have been to work without official harassment. As non-prostitute women have achieved increasing independence, however, prostitutes have been more restricted and condemned, often confined to segregated districts, or required to wear special clothing, for example. Similarly, when there were few women in a community, as on the American and Australian "frontiers," or in the gold rush mining towns, prostitutes had high status and could move freely in the community (Barnhard, 1986; Brown, 1958; Jeffrey, 1979).

At the present time, prostitution exists in every country in the world. Although the forms vary somewhat from place to place — due to differences in culture, economics and law — the institution itself is strikingly similar. A few countries, including Cuba, the USSR, and

China, have undertaken large-scale projects to "rehabilitate" prostitutes, and thereby eliminate prostitution. However, some women in all of those countries continue to work as prostitutes, especially in the large urban centers, and especially following an increase in tourism from other countries. Many countries rely on prostitution to provide foreign currency necessary for trade with the technological west.

Why Prostitution?

Prostitution exists, at least in part, because of the subordination of women in most societies. This subordination is reflected in the double standard of sexual behavior for men and women, and is carried out in the discrepancy between women's and men's earning power, which results in women in the United States earning sixty-seven cents for every dollar men earn, and even less in most other countries. This economic discrepancy has not changed much from the days of the Old Testament, at which time women earned about sixty shekels for every one hundred shekels earned by men.

The specific reasons that prostitutes have given for choosing their work, as revealed in the studies of Dr. Jennifer James in Seattle, have included money, excitement, independence, and flexibility, in roughly that order. First person accounts by women in the sex industry often mention economics as a major factor, coupled with rebellion at the restricted and tedious jobs available to them (Jaget, 1980; Perkins, 1985; Roberts, 1986). Studies by Dr. James and others have also revealed a high incidence of child sexual abuse in the life histories of prostitutes: around fifty percent for adult prostitutes; seventy-five to eighty percent for juvenile prostitutes (James, 1977; Silbert, 1979; Rush 1980; Sanford, 1980). The traditional psychoanalytic explanation for the relationship between childhood sexual abuse and later involvement in prostitution is that the child has come to view sex as a commodity, and that she is masochistic. The connection many prostitutes report, however, is that the involvement in prostitution is a way of taking back control of a situation in which, as children, they had none. Specifically, many have reported that the first time they ever felt powerful was the first time they "turned a trick." (Millett, 1973; Jaget, 1980; Perkins, 1985.) As painful as these statistics are, it is important to remember that many women with no history of sexual assault become prostitutes (and many survivors of child sexual abuse never work as prostitutes), so the relationship between prostitution and early sexual trauma is far from clear.

A number of authors have also looked at the fact that men and women do not appear to view sex in the same way and that men as a class seem to view sex as power, with rape being the most extreme form of the use of sex as power. Women as a class tend to see sex as nurture, and this generalization is subject to great individual differences. Prostitution also involves an equation of sex with power: for the man/customer, the power consists of his ability to "buy" access to any number of women; for the woman/prostitute, the power consists of her ability to set the terms of her sexuality, and to demand substantial payment for her time and skills. Thus, prostitution is one area in which women have traditionally and openly viewed sex as power.

Although prostitution is considered to be a uniquely human profession, there is some evidence to the contrary from both field and laboratory studies of non-human primates. Chimpanzees have been observed in the wild engaging in sexual activity in exchange for food, and in a laboratory study in which tokens were given to chimps for specific behaviors, observers suddenly noticed that a few female chimps had all the tokens. Further observation revealed a form of prostitution (Bullough, 1978).

Basic Categories of Prostitution

Street Prostitution: The most familiar form of prostitution, and the one that draws the most attention, is street prostitution. In the United States, about ten to twenty percent of prostitution involves street solicitation. The traditional pimp/prostitute relationship is most likely to occur in this setting, although about forty percent of street prostitutes work independently.

Massage Parlors: The next form of prostitution takes place off the street, but is still obvious to the general public. This includes massage parlors, encounter studios, and other euphemistic businesses. These businesses are generally clearly identifiable from the street; owners and managers are legally defined as pimps and panderers. Men are as likely to manage massage parlors as women, and are also as likely to demand that prostitutes engage in sexual activity with them, without pay — which, if prostitution were legal, would be considered sexual harassment on the job. In many U.S. cities, massage parlors and their employees are required to obtain licenses from the police department (see discussion of *de facto* legalization).

Bar and Cafe Prostitution: Less obvious to the general public is bar or cafe prostitution, in which women meet clients in the bar and take them to rooms above the bar (more common in Europe and Southeast

Asia) or go with the client to his hotel room. This form of prostitution sometimes is pimp-controlled, as when the women take their clients to a room connected with the bar or cafe, but can also involve independent women who meet clients in the bar or cafe and go back to the client's hotel. In the latter case, the prostitutes often give large "tips" to the bartenders and/or the owners of the establishment, but they do not actually work for them.

Brothels: Next is the brothel or bordello, which is an enclosed building, not open to the general public, in which prostitution takes place. In countries with "legalized" brothel systems, the brothel district is often completely separated from the rest of the city, sometimes surrounded by a wall or fence. Illegal brothels are generally well hidden from public view, to avoid police action against them. Whether the brothel is owned by a man or a woman, in most cases it is managed by a woman, who is known as a "madam."

Women who work in legal brothel systems are usually restricted in their movements outside of the brothel district. In Nevada, for example, the rural counties that have either legalized or tolerated brothel systems have imposed a large number of restrictions on the movements of the women who work in them. They are not allowed to be in a gambling casino or a bar at all, or to be in the company of a man on the street or in a restaurant. They are also not allowed to reside in the same community in which they work (they generally work a three-week shift in the brothel, after which they are "off" for a week or more). They are tested weekly for venereal diseases and monthly for antibodies to the AIDS virus. Since the women are required to register with the sheriff as prostitutes, these restrictions are easy to enforce. In some brothel systems, all legal prostitution is restricted to districts, as in the walled brothel cities in pre-Ayatollah Iran; in others, only "visible" prostitution is restricted to districts, as in the red-light districts in Holland.

Outcall: A large number of prostitutes, perhaps the majority, work outside of "houses." The traditional "call girl" worked independently, with a "book" of clients. In the last few years, a system of "escort services" has developed (originally as an "outcall" service offered by massage parlors), which works like a dating service in that the service connects clients and prostitutes, who then meet elsewhere. Whether they work through an escort service, or completely on their own, the prostitutes who work in this way are the most independent, and the most in control of their lives on and off the job. The owner of an escort service is legally a pimp, but the relationship is strictly a business one, and there is often little or no personal contact between the prostitute and her agent. However, in some cases, the agency provides a place for the women to rest and get to know each other between dates. (Barrows, 1986).

De Facto Legalization of Third-Party Controlled Prostitution in the U.S.

Although prostitution is illegal in most of the United States, a quasi-legalized brothel system has developed in many cities under the auspices of police department. San Francisco is a good example. In the early seventies, the San Francisco Board of Supervisors passed an ordinance regulating massage parlors, and requiring that both the owners of the massage parlors and the workers they employed obtain licenses from the Police Department's Permit Bureau. A conviction on a prostitution-related offense in the previous three years is grounds for denial of the license. Similarly, a conviction subsequent to getting the license is grounds for revocation. In 1981, the Board of Supervisors passed a similar ordinance regulating escort services.

On the face of it, it would seem that the legislation is designed to prevent prostitution; however, according to police testimony at the time the escort service bill was introduced, it is really designed to "regulate and control" prostitution, not prevent it. In reality, however, it guarantees a turnover of new employees because the police periodically raid the parlors and escort services, and revoke the permits of the women they arrest. The Board of Permit Appeals in San Francisco usually upholds the revocation, even when the charges have been dropped or a judge has dismissed them for lack of evidence (i.e., there was no "conviction"). After one such raid, I noticed an ad for a massage parlor that promised "all new staff."

Interestingly, the same massage license is required, whether the work is "legitimate" or sexual massage. When a woman applies for the license, the police assume she is a prostitute, and treat her accordingly. When the police raid massage parlors and escort services, and arrest all the women working there, they may not even charge them with prostitution. Instead, they arrest them for minor infractions of the massage parlor licensing code, such as failing to wear an ID badge on the outside of their clothes. Such cases are often dismissed the next morning by a judge who thinks such arrests are a waste of the taxpayers' money and the court's time. Even though there have been no convictions, the women who were arrested lose their licenses and, as a consequence, their jobs. The women who have been arrested do not stop working as prostitutes, however. Perhaps they work in the isolation of their own apartments, advertising in the local sex paper. Perhaps they go out on the street, exposing themselves to much greater risks of dangerous clients and cops. Or they may move to another city, where they don't have an arrest record, or any friends, to apply for another massage license, so the cycle begins again.

Pornography as a Form of Third-Party Controlled Prostitution

Another version of third-party controlled prostitution has developed as a result of court decisions which, in effect, decriminalize pornography. The proliferation of magazines, books, films, videotapes, and "adult" bookstores has been matched by the growth of the live pornography show, in which the line between pornography and prostitution is extremely thin. The legal definition of prostitution in California is "a lewd act in exchange for money or other consideration." The courts have held that sex acts for which all participants are being paid by a third party (viewer, pornographic film-maker, etc.), and in which there is no direct physical contact between payer and payee, are legitimate, while continuing to uphold the laws which prohibit the same actions if one participant is paying the other directly. In live pornography shows, including peep shows — where women perform in booths or on a stage separated from their customers by plexiglass windows or coin-operated shutters — as well as more conventional theatrical presentations, the line has all but disappeared. The main consumers of live pornography shows are tourists, and tour buses leave regularly from the major hotels in every city, taking visitors to pornography districts.

New case law is being developed as police charge that the live shows are, in fact, prostitution, while the pornographers contend that they are not, and that the sexual activity involved is covered by the First Amendment. Until recently, I thought there was a strong possibility that the legal struggle surrounding live pornography would result in prostitution laws being struck down, because some producers of live pornography would like very much to be able to become legally involved in prostitution. However, the current political climate in the United States makes such a court decision unlikely.

Moreover, the agitation by anti-pornography feminists, such as New York's Women Against Pornography, has already increased the enforcement of prostitution laws against pornography performers, and the pimping and pandering laws against the producers. The recommendations of the Attorney General's Commission on Pornography (the Meese Commission), which has taken up some of the language of the anti-porn feminists as a smokescreen to cover its real intention of broadening the scope of obscenity prosecutions, are also likely to increase the harassment of prostitutes.

Hotel Involvement in Prostitution

Although hotels are often prime movers in efforts to get police to "crack down" on prostitution, they also depend on the availability of large numbers of prostitutes for their business clients. This is especially true in large urban areas which, because of a decline in blue-collar industry, have become dependent on tourism as a major source of tax revenue. The convention industry is large in this country and, because of the continued discrimination against women in employment, particularly at the management level, convention attendees are overwhelmingly male. Many travel without their families. A significant number of those men feel that a visit to a strange city is not complete without a visit to a prostitute. In response to this, the massage parlor and escort service industry developed in this country, and the "sex tour" industry developed internationally.

Hotels use their security staff to screen prostitutes, to keep out those deemed unacceptable. According to a former security guard for a major hotel in downtown San Francisco, prostitutes who plan to visit a client in a first-class hotel are expected to check in at the main desk and announce their intention by saying they are there to give the client a massage, or to provide some other service. If the woman has a massage license, she is expected to show it to the desk clerk. Once she is on an upper floor, she is likely to be stopped by hotel security, who calls down to the main desk to see if she has checked in. If she has not, she will be taken to a room in the hotel, often in the basement, where she will be photographed, warned not to come back to the hotel, and told that her photograph will be circulated to other area hotels. If she is black, garishly dressed, or "too noisy," or drunk, she is more likely to be stopped than if she is elegantly dressed. Several years ago, the San Francisco Hilton Hotel was sued by a black woman who had been harassed in this way while attending a feminist conference. The Hilton settled out of court for fifty thousand dollars. More recently, a friend of mine, who was visiting a client in a hotel on perfectly legal business, and was dressed in a suit jacket and pants, was stopped and hassled by security guards in the same hotel.

A man checking into a hotel who wishes to find a prostitute has only to ask the bell captain for referrals. He can also ask most taxi drivers. Should he be diffident, he can check the *Yellow Pages* of the phone book for massage parlors or escort services, or the classified ads in the daily newspaper under the heading of massage, escorts, introductions, dating services, and/or personals. New headings appear from time to time. Occasionally, the free hand-out magazines found in hotels include ads for escort services and massage parlors, as was the case when I attended a National NOW Board of Directors meeting at the Hotel Statler in New York some years ago. Like the producers of pornography, hotel owners could derive great financial benefit from a tightly controlled brothel system.

The Law

Historically, prostitution issues have been addressed in a number of ways by by civil and religious governmental bodies. During periods of history in which "good" women were severely restricted (e.g., veiled, chaperoned, or confined to special quarters), prostitutes have been tolerated and allowed to work with few restrictions. In contrast, times in which women have been fighting for and achieving greater independence have also been times of greater restrictions and prohibitions against prostitutes. During the Renaissance, a period in which women achieved some measure of independence, prostitutes were often required to wear special clothing, and/or were confined to special districts. Interestingly, they were required to live in the same districts with Jews, who had to similarly mark their clothing. Again, in the 19th century, when women demanded the right to vote, England passed the Contagious Diseases Acts under which any woman suspected of being a prostitute could be arrested and taken to a "lock ward" in a hospital for examination and treatment for venereal disease. Many "innocent" women were arrested. Moreover, many women who did not have sexually transmitted diseases when they were arrested got them from the unsterile, newly invented speculums used to examine them (Walkowitz, 1980). The United States' laws prohibiting prostitution were enacted in this century just prior to ratification of the suffrage amendment in 1920 (Connelly, 1980; Rosen, 1982; Brandt, 1985).

In 1949, the United Nations passed a convention paper that called for the decriminalization of prostitution and the enforcement of laws against those who exploit women and children in prostitution. The paper, which was read to the United Nations General Assembly by Eleanor Roosevelt, has been ratified by more than fifty countries, but not the United States. Most European countries have "decriminalized" prostitution by removing laws which prohibit "engaging" in an act of prostitution; although most have retained the laws against "soliciting," "pimping," "pandering," "running a disorderly house," and "transporting a woman across national boundaries for the purposes of prostitution." The United States, on the other hand, has retained the laws prohibiting the act of prostitution as well (except in rural counties in the state of Nevada with populations less than 250,000, which have the option of allowing legal, regulated brothels). Prostitution is also prohibited outright in Japan, and in many Asian countries, including those in which "sex tourism" is a major industry. It is decriminalized in the Soviet Union, but women who work as prostitutes there are arrested for violating the law against being a parasite (i.e., not having a legally-recognized job).

In addition to laws prohibiting soliciting or engaging in an act of prostitution, and the related issues of pimping and pandering, or procuring, the United States has laws that bar anyone who has ever been a prostitute from entering this country, remaining in this country as a resident, or becoming a citizen. Deportation proceedings on those grounds were instituted in the early 1980s against a French woman who managed a brothel in Nevada, even though the business was perfectly legal.

West Germany, in addition to decriminalizing the act itself, has developed a variety of approaches ranging from a tightly controlled, single-zone brothel system in Hamburg, to a laissez-faire, open-zone system in West Berlin. Denmark has repealed most of the laws restricting the right of prostitutes to work, and has passed laws designed to help women who want to get out of prostitution.

In Holland, after a prostitute was murdered a few years ago, the government decided it might be a good idea to examine the laws and to see if there weren't ways to reduce the isolation of prostitutes. The government has been working closely with the feminist prostitutes' rights movement — the Red Thread, an organization of prostitutes and ex-prostitutes, and the Pink Thread, a feminist solidarity group. In late 1986, the Dutch government allocated funds to provide the Red Thread with three employees and an office.

The countries with the most restrictive legal systems, including the United States and many countries in Southeast Asia, have the most problems with violence against prostitutes (and women perceived to be *like* prostitutes), thefts associated with prostitution, pimping (especially brutal pimping), and the involvement of juveniles. Conversely, the countries with the least restrictive measures, including the Netherlands, West Germany, Sweden and Denmark, have the least problems. No country, however, is totally safe for prostitutes. The stigma still isolates the women, and the remaining laws still serve to perpetuate that stigma, rather than to dispell it and truly legitimize the women who work as prostitutes.

Discriminatory Enforcement of the Law

In 1983, 126,500* people were arrested for prostitution in the United States (U.S. Department of Justice, 1985). This is a 148.4 percent increase over the number arrested in 1973, the year that the prostitutes' rights movement began in this country with the founding of COYOTE. In comparison, arrests for all crimes increased only 35.6 percent. Although the law makes no distinction between men and women and, in most states, prohibits both sides of the transaction, the percentage of women arrested generally hovers around seventy percent. In 1979 it dropped to sixty-seven percent, probably as a result of feminist pressure on police departments to arrest customers as well as prostitutes, but in 1983, it was back up to seventy-three percent. About ten percent of those arrested are customers (usually arrested in a series of raids over a period of a couple of weeks, and then ignored the rest of the year). The remainder of the arrests are of transvestite and pre-operative transsexual prostitutes (i.e., men who, in the eyes of the police, look like women).

Enforcement practices similarly discriminate on the basis of race and class. Eighty-five to ninety percent of the prostitutes who are arrested work on the street, although only ten to twenty percent of all

---

*In 1984, the total number of arrests declined, for the first time since COYOTE began keeping track in 1973, to 112,200. There are many possible explanations: unemployment reached its peak in 1982, and has been declining ever since; heavy crackdowns in most cities have encouraged those who could to move their business off the street or, to retire; fear of AIDS may be discouraging new women from beginning to work as prostitutes. Gloria Lockett, Co-Director of COYOTE, who worked on the street for many of the seventeen years she was a prostitute, says that the percentage of street prostitutes in San Francisco who use IV drugs has increased sharply, which may mean that it is the women who don't use drugs who have been able to leave the street or to change their occupation.

prostitutes are street workers. While approximately forty percent of street prostitutes are women of color, fifty-five percent of those arrested are. The racism becomes even more apparent when you look at the figures on who gets jailed: eighty-five percent of prostitutes sentenced to do jail time are women of color. One student of street prostitution in New York City (Cohen, 1980) hypothesized that the reason for the disproportionate number of minority women being arrested was that there was more police activity in the neighborhood of ethnic minorities, where they were more likely to work. What he found, however, was that police were, in fact, more active in white neighborhoods, where most of the prostitutes were also white. He then hypothesized that the racial bias of the mostly white police officers was to blame. My own hunch is that the women of color are mostly likely to be arrested when they drift towards and/or into the white districts. Certainly, prostitution in New York's Times Square did not become a major issue until black prostitutes moved from Harlem to the theatre district as white customers stopped going to Harlem during the racially tense 1960s.

The enforcement practices in Las Vegas, Nevada, where all prostitution is illegal, also supports this latter hypothesis. In recent years, the casinos have increasingly relied on sex, or the implication of sex, to draw customers to their stage shows, and then to the gaming tables. Elegant prostitutes who look like the stereotype of a Las Vegas showgirl are allowed to work with impunity, so long as they don't draw customers away from the gambling tables. Black prostitutes, however, are not allowed to work in the casinos and hotels (blacks have been admitted as customers only since 1962). As a result, the percentage of street prostitutes who are black is high. The laws against prostitution are rigidly enforced against street prostitutes, and a large number of black women are arrested each night. For a few years, the city ran a mandatory "counseling" program for prostitutes, which operated from 8:00 p.m. to midnight. The poor, black prostitutes were in the counseling program, while the middle- and upper-class white prostitutes made money working the casinos.

Enforcement practices vary from city to city, and from time to time. According to a report from the California Attorney General's Office, in 1980, the San Francisco Police Department arrested more prostitutes annually than the police department in Los Angeles, a city more than ten times its size, and with far more visible prostitution on clearly defined strips.

In all cities, there are periods of intense enforcement, followed by periods of relative calm, often seemingly without any clear logic to the pattern. Traditional analysts claim that pre-election politics always demand raids, although since a majority of the population supports a change in the law, it is difficult to see how the crackdowns would help incumbents.

If law enforcement is designed to reduce the amount of prostitution, it has failed miserably. Moreover, crackdowns are generally initiated with a fanfare about how the police are going to rid the streets of violent crime, but crackdowns are actually often followed by an increase in robberies, many of which involve some form of violence, as well as burglaries and other real property crime, as the people who have been dependent on the now-jailed prostitutes seek to replace lost income.

Crackdowns, and arrests in general, tend to reinforce the dependence of prostitutes on pimps, who are often their only friends outside of jail who can arrange for bail, an attorney, child care, etc. Many women who have worked independently before their first arrest are, moreover, recruited into working for pimps by other prostitutes in jail who convince them of the need to have someone outside to take care of business.

Crackdowns also pressure many women to move on to other cities, cutting off their connections with local friends and networks of support, including agencies that could help them leave prostitution if they wanted to. Their isolation in new cities further increases their dependence on pimps, and effectively entraps them in "the life."

Pimps

The legal definition of pimping is "living off the earnings of a prostitute." By that definition, those who profit from prostitution include not only the stereotyped pimp with a stable of women, who beats them with coat hangers if they fail to bring in enough money, but lovers who shop for groceries and do the laundry, taxi drivers, bell captains, the business-like owners and managers of massage parlors and escort services, madams, and others who personally and directly receive money from prostitutes and/or provide connections between prostitutes and customers. Also included would have to be the publishers of the *Yellow Pages*, newspapers and some magazines, the banks that offer credit cards, travel agents who book sex tours, and a host of corporate entities that are never charged with violating prostitution laws.

When most people think of pimping, of course, they think of bad

pimps who lure unsuspecting women into prostitution and physically abuse them when they resist or don't bring in enough money.
Most people do not view such violent relationships in the context of
relational violence in general, such as violence in marriage. If you
consider that about fifty percent of adult prostitutes were either
physically or sexually abused in childhood, often by their fathers, it is
not surprising that many would find themselves in violent relationships as adults. This is not to condone such relationships, merely to
put them into context. Many prostitutes I know say that while they
have known some prostitutes who seem to be perpetually victimized,
they have known at least as many others who are rarely, if ever,
injured or abused.

The battered women's movement has had a profound effect on the
consciousness of prostitutes and, increasingly, battered prostitutes
are turning to battered women's programs for help. They are often
even more frightened to pursue the matter in court than battered
wives, but they are beginning to realize that they can, perhaps, have
help getting out of the situation. At least some of the time, that is,
because too many battered women's programs routinely refuse to
serve prostitutes, or if they do, assume that "prostitution" is the
problem, not "battering." They refuse, for example, to allow the
women to continue to work as prostitutes outside of the shelter, even
when other women are expected to continue to work. Some of this
may have to do with legal concerns, but in states where homosexual
acts are a crime, shelters do not expect battered lesbians to go
"straight" because of the law.

Forced Prostitution

The issue of forced prostitution is often used to obscure the issue of
the right of women to work as prostitutes. Therefore, it is important
to discuss this issue separately. At the same time, I want to make a
distinction between being forced by a third party (e.g., a "pimp") to
work as a prostitute, particularly where violence or deceit is used,
and being forced by economic reality. Most people who work for
compensation do so because they need the money — for themselves,
for their children. In any society, people make decisions about work
based on some kind of evaluation of the options open to them. And
most people choose what they perceive to the the best-paying job for
their skills. It is easy for other people to judge the nature of the work,
but it is up to the individual to make her or his own decision about

what work to do. That being said, in the technological western countries, where most women are at least functionally literate and there is a significant array of occupational choice, about ten percent of women who work as prostitutes are coerced into prostitution by third parties through a combination of trickery and violence. This figure appears to be relatively constant in the United States, as reflected in studies done at the turn of the century and current estimates of COYOTE and some other prostitutes' rights organizations (Rosen, 1982). At the other extreme, in India, where there is massive poverty with large numbers of people dying in the streets, and where there are few occupations open to women, seventy to eighty percent of the women who work as prostitutes are forced into the life.

In the Philippines, women's rights advocates estimate that there are approximately 300,000 prostitutes, a large majority of whom work in the vicinity of American military bases, some voluntarily, but many under duress (including being sold into prostitution). Some leave the Philippines to look for other work, or to be married, only to find that the work in the new country is still prostitution. Their isolation is compounded by the fact that, in many cases, they do not have legal immigration papers. At the Second World Whores' Congress, held in Brussels in 1986, a woman from the Philippines reported being offered a job in a hotel in Europe by a high government official at home. She was not a prostitute at the time, and no mention was made of sex. After much indecision, she decided to go. When she arrived, she found that the job was in fact prostitution, and that she had no choice in the matter. She was able to escape with the help of a concerned customer, and she is now trying to get the government official prosecuted, although without much hope of success. She is also afraid for her life due to the continued power of the official even since Aquino's election.

In India, young girls are sometimes sold by their parents to traders, allegedly for service to the "goddess," but actually for work in brothels in the major cities. Bombay, a city with eight million inhabitants, has anywhere from 100,000 to 200,000 prostitutes and 50,000 brothels. Again, the prostitutes are rarely able to escape.

The prohibition of prostitution, as common in countries with the highest percentage of forced prostitution as it is in countries with the least amount, does not begin to address the problem. Laws against "traffic" in women, which are supposed to prevent the forced movement of women and girls across national or state boundaries for the purposes of prostitution are, instead, used to keep voluntary prostitutes from traveling. Forced prostitution cannot be addressed until voluntary prostitution is legitimate. Feminist attempts to simply stop it, and to "rescue" the women who have been so badly abused, are doomed to fail until the laws that punish prostitutes are abolished and businesses that employ them are regulated in ways discussed elsewhere in this essay. Organizations likely to have the greatest impact are those that seek to empower prostitute women to make decisions about their lives, and give them the skills to do so, without making judgments — moral or otherwise — about the work they do.

Violence Against Prostitutes

The danger of violence to prostitutes comes not only from pimps, but from customers and police. A study of street prostitutes and sexual assault found that seventy percent of the women interviewed had been raped on the job, and that those who had been raped had been victimized an average of eight to ten times a year. Only seven percent had sought any kind of help, and only four percent had reported any of the rapes to the police (Silbert, 1981).

Murder is a serious danger to prostitutes, particularly since serial murders of prostitutes are rarely investigated thoroughly by police until at least ten or more women have been killed or until the killer, emboldened by his "success," begins to kill "square" or "innocent" women. The Hillside Strangler and the Southside Slayer, in Los Angeles, the Leeds Ripper, in England, and the Green River Killer, in Seattle, are only four examples.

The police, who are sworn to protect people from violence, are largely negligent when it comes to people who are seen as powerless, and that includes prostitutes. Because prostitutes are seen as having few supporters in the outside world, police — particularly under-cover vice officers — feel free to insult and roughly handle the prostitutes they arrest. Police handcuff their victims from behind, then roughly pull their arms. They demand sex before or during the arrest; and inflict beatings and kickings. They issue specific insults about the individual prostitute's body, and taunts about the how the police officer could get a free blow job with no one the wiser. The arresting officer may suggest that the prostitute give the sheriff a blow job to get out of jail. Few prostitutes file complaints, unfortunately, feeling they have no choice but to accept this abuse as part of the job, and so the few accounts that surface must be seen as symptoms of a much larger problem.

When the law prohibits only soliciting or engaging in prostitution, prostitutes feel that they have some ability to avoid police entrapment — they can try to evaluate the potential client and avoid police. However, in twenty-five states, including California and Washington, recent revisions to the law have made it a crime to "agree," or even "manifest agreement" to engage in prostitution. This means that the customer can initiate all mention of sex and money; if the prostitute merely smiles, the police can say she has agreed.

The police in Everett, Washington set up a phony escort service a few years ago; they placed ads in the paper recruiting employees and customers. The ads to recruit prostitutes merely offered a high-paying job. Women who answered the ads — many of whom had never worked as prostitutes before — were asked if they would be willing to engage in prostitution. When they agreed, they were arrested. Undercover officers were also used to entrap male customers. When the case came before the court, all of the charges were dismissed (presumably because of the outrageousness of the sting operation). However, all of the women now have permanent records of a prostitution arrest and are, in fact, described as 'known prostitutes.' One officer actually had sex with one of the women, justifying it in court by saying he didn't "come."

Drugs

Prostitution is hard work, both in physical and emotional terms. Therefore, it is not surprising that a significant number of prostitutes use drugs of one kind or another to make the work easier. These drugs can include heroin and other downers, but also include such generally popular drugs as marijuana and cocaine (until recently, the favorite of some attorneys and and even some legislators). A study of prostitutes and drugs found that while one hundred percent of street prostitutes had used heroin at one time, eighty-four percent were addicted. At the same time, while twenty-two percent of "high-class" prostitutes had tried heroin, none were addicted (Goldstein, 1979). A second study found that of addicted prostitutes, forty-eight percent were addicted before prostitution (James, 1975). A more recent study found that one third to one half of jailed prostitutes in New York City were IV users (Des Jarlais, 1986). Gloria Lockett, Co-Director of San Francisco COYOTE, says that when she was working on the street, IV use was rare, but it appears that the percentage of street prostitutes in some parts of the Bay Area who use IV drugs is quite high. As suggested above, this may have to do with the non-IV using women changing their work locations to avoid police harassment.

Sexually Transmitted Diseases

One excuse often given for the illegality of prostitution is the supposed responsibility of prostitutes for the veneral disease epidemic in this country. Countries that have legalized and regulated prostitution often require regular check-ups for venereal and other sexually transmitted diseases. Such programs have had a minimal effect because prostitutes are generally implicated in only a small proportion of venereal disease, at least in affluent, western countries where condoms are easily obtainable. Although one study of prostitutes (done at venereal disease clinics) found that twenty to thirty percent of the women had some venereal disease, a study of Nevada's legal prostitutes found less than two percent to be positive. When Chicken Ranch, the Fayette County, Texas brothel of "The Best Little Whorehouse in Texas," was closed, the number of gonorrhea cases rose substantially. This is consistent with the rise in venereal disease following the closing of brothels from 1917-1920. The U.S. Department of Public Health has consistently reported that only about five percent of the sexually transmitted disease in this country is related to prostitution, compared with thirty to thirty-five percent among teenagers. (Conrad, 1981; Rosen, 1982; Brandt, 1985).

The studies cited in this section were all done prior to the AIDS epidemic. There have been a number of studies on the rate of infection with the AIDS virus among prostitutes, and it appears that about four or five percent of the prostitutes in the United States, most of them IV drug users or lovers of IV users, have antibodies to the virus. For a more thorough discussion of AIDS and prostitutes, see the article on the scapegoating of prostitutes for AIDS, later in this volume.

Prostitutes have always been quite concerned about sexually transmitted diseases. They know, for example, that gonorrhea is asymptomatic among women eighty percent of the time, and that if untreated, it can lead to a life-threatening condition known as pelvic inflammatory disease (PID). Therefore, prostitutes have tended to be quite responsible about being checked for disease to protect themselves, as well as to protect others. They quickly learn to recognize the symptoms of sexually transmitted diseases in men and refuse to have sexual contact with men they believe to be infected. Prostitutes have always made use of any prophylactic measures that have been available, including barrier methods of birth control, such as condoms and diaphragms, and spermicidal jellies and foams. This caution has only increased since the outbreak of AIDS. Even brothel managers, who in the past encouraged women not to demand condoms, by charging more for unprotected sex, are beginning to change to an all-condom policy.

The prostitutes least likely to protect themselves from venereal disease are those who are seriously addicted to heroin and too financially desperate to insist on such precautions. The prohibition of prostitution has not served in any way to solve this problem. What is probably needed, particularly with AIDS, is to educate the customer class, i.e., all heterosexual men, of the need for condoms so they will no longer argue against them.

Juvenile Prostitution

The primary focus of this essay is adult prostitution. However, since some sources estimate that five hundred thousand to one million juveniles are involved in prostitution and pornography in this country, it is important to assess the severity of the problem.

About 128,900 juveniles were arrested in 1983 for status offenses such as running away from home or avoiding school, a sixty percent decline since 1973.* Seventy-seven percent were girls. Because most status offenders are runaways, they are unlikely to have any conventional marketable skills; they turn to prostitution in order to survive. In 1983, thirty-three hundred people under the age of eighteen were arrested for prostitution. One study of street prostitutes found that the average age of entry into the life was thirteen (Silbert, 1979), although it is COYOTE's experience that most women who work off the streets, and many who work on the streets, as well, began working in their twenties and thirties.

Various studies of juveniles who are runaways, drug and alcohol abusers, and/or prostitutes have revealed that a high percentage (from thirty-five to eighty-five percent) are survivors of incest. Stereotypically, these young people become involved in prostitution when they arrive in a big city bus station where they are picked up by a sweet-talking pimp, treated well for a while, and then coerced into working as a prostitute to "repay the debt." While this obviously does occur, in some cases young girls deliberately go to big cities to find pimps to turn them out. These young women are also likely to leave pimps they don't like, either for another pimp, or to be independent, or sometimes to return to their families.

*This figure increased again, to 147,000, in 1984.

On the other hand, workers in shelters for runaways and other programs for juvenile prostitutes find that at least some juvenile prostitutes are independent of pimps. They are more likely to live together as a group, pooling their money, and to go out and work as prostitutes only when the money runs out.

Whatever the path of recruitment into prostitution, once there, most juveniles find the work devastating. It is dangerous and emotionally draining, and they are ill equipped physically or experientially to protect themselves. There are shelters in most major cities, but since each houses only a few clients at a time, the vast majority of juveniles must fend for themselves. In San Francisco, it has been estimated that each year there are about five thousand juvenile prostitutes working in the city, but the shelters have only enough bed space for a few hundred.

The police use loitering and prostitution laws, as well as laws against being a runaway, to pick up these young people. Typically, they will take the arrested juvenile to a facility for offenders who are under eighteen. The facility is then required, by law, to inform the parents of the juvenile that she or he is in custody. If the juvenile has been arrested for a status offense, she or he is usually sent back to the parents. Since most of them have run from incest and/or other child abuse and neglect, they are likely to run again, this time to a different city. The voluntary shelters are similarly required to notify the parents, which keeps many runaways from going to shelters in the first place.

Current laws treat the juvenile prostitute as the criminal. They could easily focus, instead, on the pimps and customers of juvenile prostitutes, who are clearly guilty of child abuse. The customers of juvenile prostitutes, like the customers of adult prostitutes, are middle-aged, middle-class, married white businessmen. In one study of juvenile prostitution in Minneapolis, the authors found that some customers look specifically for prostitutes the age of their children (Baizerman, 1979).

Juvenile street prostitutes see an average of three hundred customers a year (far less than the fifteen hundred that the average adult street prostitute sees). If it is true that there are about 500,000 adolescents working as prostitutes in this country, juvenile prostitution accounts for about one hundred and fifty *million* cases of sexual abuse of juveniles that are both undetected and uncared about in this society. Even those who write about sexual abuse of children and try to give a sense of its prevalence often omit the number of violations by customers of juvenile prostitutes, even though it would only strengthen their case that sexual abuse of children is a national dilemma of monumental proportions.

As serious as the problem of juvenile prostitution is, however, a police crackdown on their customers would not solve the problem. If their customers were rounded up, these young prostitutes would have no source of income, and would be in a worse economic position. The solutions must be found elsewhere.

The Need for Alternatives

This country spends an inordinate amount of money to arrest, prosecute, and incarcerate women and men involved in prostitution. In 1977, the cost of arresting one prostitute in New York and keeping her in jail for two weeks was three thousand dollars. In that same year, San Francisco spent an average of two thousand dollars to arrest and prosecute one prostitute. At the same time, virtually no money is allocated by government or private foundations for programs that would help prostitutes who want to change their occupations or their lives.

Within the criminal justice system, little is spent on rehabilitative programs in women's jails, even relative to the small amount spent for men. There are a few programs for adult prostitutes outside of the criminal justice system in this country (e.g., Mary Magdalene Project in Southern California and Genesis House in Chicago), but not nearly enough. There are also a growing number of programs for juvenile prostitutes, particularly in Minneapolis, Seattle, San Francisco, and New York, but again, not nearly enough.

Any programs set up to help people involved in prostitution must acknowledge and deal with the positive attractions of prostitution. First and foremost is the economic incentive: the average prostitute in this country can gross from about one hundred to two hundred dollars a day, or more, with a great deal of flexibility about hours and days of work. Programs that try to help prostitutes make a transition into low-paid, boring jobs tend to fail.

Transition programs should have ex-prostitutes on their staffs to help deal with sexual stigmatization, and the amount of sexual and physical abuse tolerated in prohibited prostitution.

Shelters for battered women are inconsistent in the way they deal with prostitutes. A few take them in without question, but many would rather not. They might say, for example, that they don't have enough well-trained staff to deal effectively with pimps finding the shelter and demanding "their" women back. Those shelters that do accept prostitutes as clients, on the other hand, say that "pimps" are no more tenacious about finding the shelter than "husbands" or "boyfriends" of other women. A second concern is that prostitutes "act out" and need specially-trained staff. A third, flippant, response several shelter workers have given me is that they would be glad to accept prostitutes as long as they didn't "work out of the house," the assumption being that prostitutes would be more likely to violate house rules than other women. As more information comes out about the desperate plight of some battered prostitutes, I hope more shelters will take them in. At the present time there is little refuge for prostitutes trying to leave abusive situations.

Who Benefits from the System

It is difficult to see how anyone benefits from the present system. At the time the United States prohibition was enacted, it was at least partly in response to feminist concerns about the abuse of women and children involved in prostitution. After an extensive muckraking campaign in the press, exposing the "horrors" of brothel prostitution (romanticized in the film "Pretty Baby" a few years ago), there was much pressure to close the brothels (Longstreet, 1970; Madeleine, 1919/1986). There was also a presumption that white women were being kidnapped and sold into slavery in foreign lands (not Europe, of course), so that there was pressure to do something to stop "traffic" across national borders. In fact, Chinese women had been imported wholesale, and sold into brothels on the west coast, while there was little or no traffic in the other direction. Prostitution was also an occupation filled by immigrant women from all countries because it required little command of English. A significant number of the prostitutes who worked in Virginia City, during the days of the Comstock Lode, were immigrants, as were many prostitutes in San Francisco during the gold rush (Goldman, 1981; Barnhardt, 1986).

While the enactment of laws before World War I prohibiting prostitution, pimping, running brothels, transporting women across state lines for "immoral" purposes, etc., did nothing to reduce prostitution, it did have other effects. Before prohibition, most brothels were owned and managed by women, most of whom had been prostitutes themselves. After the legal brothels were closed, the brothel business went underground and was headed by a male, criminal hierarchy that continues. Most massage parlors and escort services today are owned by men. Closing the brothels also forced many women to work on the streets, subjecting them to greater risks of violence. The basic conditions of women's lives, which caused some of them to choose to work as prostitutes, did not change.

For most of recorded history, prostitution has been set up for the benefit of the customer, no matter what system was in place. The stigma enforced by the prohibition in this country is also enforced by systems of regulation that require prostitutes to dress differently or to live and work in special districts, or deny them the right to relationships. The health schemes that require prostitutes to have weekly checks for sexually transmitted diseases are similarly designed to benefit the customer, since there is no equivalent requirement that customers be checked to protect the prostitute, or regulation requiring brothels to provide condoms, disability insurance, workers' compensation, or health insurance. What constantly amazes me is that there is so little variation in the way nations deal with prostitution, under the law, even where there is enormous variation in just about every other aspect of society.

The current system of de facto legalization, in which the workers in massage parlors and other prostitution businesses are licensed by the police, does not reduce the number of women working as prostitutes, it merely registers them as prostitutes with the police, forever.

The number of prostitution arrests increased every year from the time the prohibition was enacted until 1983, which presumably means the number of women working as prostitutes increased accordingly. At the same time, the average age of prostitutes has been dropping in this country. In Europe, which has less oppressive systems, the average age is twenty-five, while here it is eighteen. Again, in our youth oriented culture, the system seems designed to benefit (if you can call it that) the customer.

Options for Change

In 1949, the United Nations called for the decriminalization of the specific transaction between prostitute and customer that is prostitution, while it recommended keeping all related activities a crime. In those countries that have adopted most of the provisions of the convention (most of the Northern European countries), the problems that so plague the prohibited system in this country are less severe. However, the continued prohibition of related activities, such as pimping (living off the earnings of a prostitute), pandering and procuring (bringing prostitutes and customers together, recruiting prostitutes), renting a premises for the purpose of prostitution, keeping a disorderly house, advertising, and soliciting, makes it almost impossible to find a place to work legally, or to engage in the kind of activity that is necessary to contact prospective clients. This leaves the prostitute subject to the exploitation of criminal third parties, landlords, bar owners, bell captains, etc. The pimping and pandering laws are even used to arrest women who work together for safety, even when no money changes hands.

The criminalization of pimping and pandering in this country makes no distinction between a coercive relationship and one that is mutually voluntary, or between a lover relationship in which one person supports another by working as a prostitute, and an employer-employee relationship in which several prostitutes turn over some or all of their earnings to a third party. This makes it difficult for prostitutes to lead normal lives outside of their work, and fails to protect them from abusive exploitation. When prostitutes who have been beaten and/or raped by pimps report the crime to the police, all too often the police and district attorneys refuse to prosecute the real crime, and instead press charges of pimping or pandering, to which the prostitutes may have no objection. In a way, it is like arresting a man who rapes his wife for marrying her, not for the rape. Prostitutes in countries that have decriminalized prostitution but left pimping a crime feel the prohibition reinforces their dependence on abusive men, and they are working to change those laws.

There are two main alternatives to prohibition, generally termed decriminalization and legalization. In Europe, decriminalization is sometimes referred to as abolition, and refers to the abolition or repeal of the prostitution laws. However, the term abolition is also used by some activists, including Kathleen Barry in the United States, and The Abolitionist Society in Europe, to refer to the long-term goal of eliminating all prostitution.

Ideally, decriminalization would mean the repeal of all existing criminal codes regarding voluntary prostitution, per se, between consenting adults, including mutually voluntary relationships between prostitutes and agents or managers (pimp/prostitute relationships), and non-coercive pandering (serving as a go-between). It could involve no new legislation to deal specifically with prostitution, but merely leave the businesses which surround prostitution subject to general civil, business, and professional codes that exist to cover all businesses. Such problems as fraud, theft, negligence, collusion, and force would be covered by existing penal code provisions. Alternatively, existing sections of the penal code could be modified to specifically address the issue of coercion, and business codes could be enacted to require management to provide sick leave and vacation, as well as disability, workers' compensation, and health insurance. Decriminalization of prostitution and the regulation of pimping and pandering, it seems to me, offers the best chance for women who are involved in prostitution to gain some measure of control over their work. It would make it easier to prosecute those who abuse prostitutes, either physically or economically, because the voluntary, non-abusive situations would be left alone.

Decriminalization allows for the possiblity that the lives of prostitutes can become less dangerous. For one thing, under a comprehensive decriminalization scheme, it would be possible for prostitutes to join unions and engage in collective bargaining in order to improve their working conditions. It would also be possible for prostitutes to form professional associations, and develop codes of ethics and behavior designed to reduce the problems involved in prostitution as it now exists. Finally, it would be possible for experienced prostitutes to train new prostitutes, so that their first experiences would be less dangerous.

Legalization, on the other hand, has generally meant a system of control of the *prostitute*, with the state regulating, taxing, and/or licensing whatever form of prostitution is legalized, leaving all other forms illegal, without any concern for the prostitute herself. Traditional regulation has often involved the establishment of special government agencies to deal with prostitution.

The brothels in Nevada, for example, are licensed and regulated by the government, and the women who work in them are registered as prostitutes with the sheriff. As discussed earlier, they are severely restricted in their movements outside of the brothel. Independent prostitution is illegal, as is prostitution in massage parlors, for escort services, and of course, street prostitution. The women generally work fourteen-hour shifts, on three-week (seven days a week) tours of duty, during which they may see ten or fifteen customers a day, or more. They have little or no right to refuse a customer (although the management tries to keep out potentially dangerous customers), and they have not been allowed to protect themselves from sexually transmitted diseases by using condoms (although at least two houses in Nevada are now all-condom houses, to prevent AIDS). Because of the grueling aspects of the long work shifts, many of the women use drugs (to help them stay awake and alert or to help them sleep) supplied by the same doctor who performs regular health checks.

Before much can be done to help prostitutes, the laws must be changed. The transaction between prostitute and client must be removed from the purview of the law, and the other laws dealing with prostitution must be reevaluated, and repealed or changed as necessary. Since street prostitution is singled out as "the problem," it is important for residents, business people, and prostitutes to get together to iron out compromises that take into consideration the right of prostitutes to work without harassment, and the right of other residents and businesses to go about their lives and work without harassment.

In the meantime, until prostitution has been decriminalized, the non-coercive managers regulated, and those who use fraud and force prosecuted, pressure must be put on police and sheriff's departments, district attorneys, public defenders, bail bondspeople, judges, and pretrial diversion and probation programs to improve the treatment of persons arrested under these archaic and oppressive laws.

Should the laws in this country be changed as a result of pressure from men, including well-intentioned civil liberties attorneys, or pornographers with their own motives, there is a good chance that a brothel system will be imposed or that high-class prostitution will be decriminalized and working class prostitution (i.e., street prostitution) will remain a crime, as was proposed by the New York Bar Association in 1985. Unless there is a strong voice pointing out the oppressiveness of brothel systems, both to the women in such a system and to their sisters outside, most people in this country will assume that such a system works to the benefit of all concerned. In a brothel system, prostitution will be kept off the street, and out of the sight of children, they assume, and all in all, it would just be better, safer, and cleaner. The problem is that none of those assumptions are correct, and in exchange for a false sense of security, we would get a punitive system.

Whatever you or I think of prostitution, women have the right to make up their own minds about whether or not to work as prostitutes, and under what terms. They have the right to work as free-lance workers, as do nurses, typists, writers, doctors, and so on. They also have the right to work for an employer, a third party who can take care of administration and management problems. They have the right to relationships outside of work, including relationships in which they are the sole support of the other person, so long as the arrangement is acceptable to both parties. They have the right to raise children. They have the right to a full, human existence. As feminists, we have to make that clear. We have to end the separation of women into whores and madonnas.

Our experience with the Equal Rights Amendment and with abortion — not to mention sexual assault, domestic violence, sexual harassment, sex discrimination, lesbian/gay rights, and the rest of the issues on our agenda — should tell us that if we leave the issues up to male legislators and pressure groups, the resulting legislation will not be in our interests. The same is true with prostitution.

Finally, the onus for the abuses that co-exist with illegal prostitution must be put on the system that perpetuates those abuses, and no longer on the prostitutes who are abused. If we ensure that prostitution remains under the control of the prostitutes — and not in the hands of pimps, customers, and police — then we will have given the prostitutes the power, and the support, to change that institution. We will all benefit.

Notes:

Baizerman, Michael, et al, "Adolescent Prostitution." *Children Today*, September/October 1979.

Barnhardt, Jacqueline Baker, *The Fair but Frail: Prostitution in San Francisco, 1849-1900*. Reno, NV: University of Nevada Press, 1986.

Barrows, Sydney and William Novak, *The Mayflower Madam: The Secret Life of Sydney Biddle Barrows*. New York: Arbor House, 1986.

Brown, Dee, "Some Ladies of Easy Virtue" and "Pink Tights and Red Velvet Skirts" in *The Gentle Tamers: Women of the Old Wild West*. Lincoln, NE: University of Nebraska Press, 1958, reissued 1981.

Bullough, Vern and Bonnie Bullough, *Prostitution: An Illustrated Social History*. New York: Crown Publishers, Inc., 1978.

Cohen, Bernard, *Deviant Street Networks: Prostitution in New York City*. Lexington, MA: Lexington Books, 1980.

Connelly, Mark Thomas, *The Response to Prostitution in the Progressive Era*. Chapel Hill, NC: The University of North Carolina Press, 1980.

Conrad, Gary L., et al, "Sexually Transmitted Diseases among Prostitutes and Other Sexual Offenders," in *Sexually Transmitted Diseases*, October-December 1981, pp. 241-244.

Darrow, William W., "Prostitution and Sexually Transmitted Diseases," in K.K. Holmes, et al, *Sexually Transmitted Diseases*. New York: McGraw-Hill, 1984.

Des Jarlais, Don, in private conversations with the author in 1985 and 1986.

Goldstein, Paul J., *Prostitution and Drugs*. Lexington, MA: Lexington Books, 1979.

Jaget, Claude, *Prostitutes: Our Life*. Bristol, England: Falling Wall Press, 1980.

James, Jennifer, "Prostitutes and Prostitution," in *Deviants: Voluntary Actors in a Hostile World*, Edward Sagarin and Fred Montanino, eds. General Learning Press, Scott, Foresman & Co., 1977.

----, "Motivations for Entrance into Prostitution," in *The Female Offender*, Laura Crites, ed. Lexington, MA: Lexington Books, 1976.

----, "Prostitution and Addiction: An Interdisciplinary Approach," unpublished paper, 1975.

----, "Self-Destructive Behavior and Adaptive Strategies in Female Prostitutes," in Norman L. Farberow, ed., *The Many Faces of Suicide*. New York: McGraw-Hill, 1980.

----, "Women as Sexual Criminals and Victims," in *Sexual Scripts: The Social Construction of Female Sexuality*, Judith Long Laws and Pepper Schwartz, eds. Hinsdale, IL: The Dryden Press, 1977.

Jeffrey, Julie Roy, "The Rarest Commodity. . . Are Women," in *Frontier Women: The Trans-Missippi West 1840-1880*. New York: Hill and Wang, 1979.

Lerner, Gerder, *The Creation of Patriarchy*. New York: Oxford University Press, 1986. Especially the chapter, "The Origin of Prostitution in Mesopotamia."

Longstreet, Stephen, ed., *Nell Kimball: Her Life as an American Madam*. New York: The Macmillan Company, 1970.

Madeleine: An Autobiography. New York: Persea Books, 1986. Originally published by Harper & Brothers, 1919.

Millett, Kate, *The Prostitution Papers*. NY: Ballantine Books, 1973.

Murphy, Emmett, *Great Bordellos of the World: An Illustrated History*. London: Quartet Books Limited, 1983.

Otis, Leah Lydia, *Prostitution in Medieval Society: The History of an Urban Institution in Languedoc*. Chicago: The University of Chicago Press, 1985.

Perkins, Roberta and Garry Bennet, *Being a Prostitute*. Winchester, MA: Allen & Unwin, Inc., 1985.

Roberts, Nickie, *The Front Line: Women in the Sex Industry Speak*. London: Grafton Books, 1986.

Rosen, Ruth, *The Lost Sisterhood: Prostitution in America, 1900-1918*. Baltmore, MD: Johns Hopkins University Press, 1982.

Silbert, Mimi H., PhD, principal investigator, *Sexual Assault of Prostitutes*. San Francisco: Delancey Street Foundation, 1981.

Sourcebook of Criminal Justice Statistics. Washington, DC: U.S. Department of Justice, 1985. Published annually.

Tannahill, Reay, *The History of Sex*. New York: Stein and Day, 1980.

Walkowitz, Judith R., *Prostitution in Victorian Society: Women, Class, and the State*. Cambridge: Cambridge University Press, 1980.

The Social Consequences of Unchastity

Gail Pheterson

The prostitute is the prototype of the stigmatized woman. She is both named and dishonored by the word "whore." The word "whore" does not, however, refer only to prostitutes. It is also a label which can be applied to any woman. As an adjective, "whore" is defined as "unchaste."[1] Significantly, unchastity in a man does not make him a whore although it may determine his status in other ways. The whore stigma is specifically a female gender stigma which can be defined as "a mark of shame or disease on an unchaste woman."[2] This article provides a framework for understanding that stigma along two socially critical dimensions of unchastity, namely impurity and defilement. Those dimensions have been chosen because they expose social justifications for racial, ethnic, and class oppression (grounded in notions of impure identity) as well as for physical and sexual violence (grounded in notions of defilement through experience). Each dimension will be explored for both women and men with the help of research and interview citations.[3] Since one function of the whore stigma is to silence and degrade those it targets, this article is self-consciously committed to giving voice and respect to persons traditionally denied such legitimacy.

Impurity

One definition of unchaste is impure. Impure is defined as "dirty, mixed with foreign matter, adulterated, mixed with another colour." Unmistakably, such a definition activates associations of racial and ethnic diversity wherein only white, non-foreign people are chaste. People of color, foreigners (people of different origin than the ethnic norm), and Jewish people become the unchaste ones, the dirty ones. Pure is defined as "clean, white, and unadulterated." Often clean is used in the sense of clean hands; clean hands belong not only to white people but particularly to white middle- and upper-class people. Servants, workers, and childrearers "dirty their hands." An analysis of the impurity dimension of unchastity brings us directly to the links between the whore stigma and racism, anti-Semitism, and classism.

Women of color, Jewish women, and working-class women are vulnerable to the whore stigma as women *with a denigrated status*. Men who deviate from the white heterosexual male norm are also vulnerable, not to the whore stigma but to racial, sexual, or class stigmas. In fact, no one is immune to accusations of unchastity; it appears that no one can fit all norms and that "the dynamics of shameful differentness are . . . a general feature of social life."[4]

Racism and the Whore Stigma

Whores and blacks have traditionally been treated as slaves and criminals. They are considered the unclean ones. They are considered the sexy ones. Black women are often assumed to be whores. One black woman who is not a prostitute said, "When I stand waiting for a bus, especially in a white neighborhood, men passing assume that I'm working. My color means 'whore' to them." Black men are often assumed to be pimps. A white woman said, "Since I've had a black boyfriend, people look at me suspiciously, as if I was a whore and he was my pimp. One white man actually asked if my boyfriend was my (smirk) boss, although it sure seemed obvious to me that we were a couple. He even had the nerve to ask if I needed help to get away!"

Black women are assumed to be sexually available; they must prove their honor. Black men are assumed to be sexually predatory; they must prove their worthiness. White men traditionally accuse black men of raping white women, an accusation which has historically led to the murder of black men.[5] White men also traditionally rape black women, a transgression which is blamed on the sexual nature of black women. Both sex and race are seen as dark, mysterious, and dirty. Both are judged unchaste and thereby unfit for public life. Accusations of impurity are used to deny visibility, voice, and power to the "sexy ones" and to the "dark ones." Symbolically, sexy and dark have intertwined into one alluring taboo. People of color are considered mistresses (women) and monsters (men) regardless of their sexual behavior. In essence, the whore stigma together with the racial stigma dehumanizes people of color and transforms human sexuality into a beastial force.

Prostitutes are considered shady women regardless of their color. A black street prostitute, when asked about differences between black and white whores, said, "We're all standing on the same corner.

We're all sucking on the same dick. Sure, some white men won't take me, a black lady, into a hotel because they're afraid of being conspicuous, but in private or on the street a whore is a whore." It is true that in some countries (such as the United States), a higher percentage of black women than of white women are sent to jail for prostitution.[6] And, in many countries (such as the Netherlands, France, and Germany) third world women are more likely to be exploited in prostitution than native white women. Such racist mechanisms compound the stigmatization of whores of color but they do not minimize the "dark mark" branded on any prostitute.

Racial impurity is put forth as a justification for prohibition and segregation.[7] Prohibition refers to restrictions in particular about what enters the body. Segregation is an attempt to separate the chaste from bodily temptation and contamination. The impurity assigned to race is glued to the shame assigned to sex. Divisions into the pure and the impure, the madonna and the whore, the wife and the prostitute, or the white and the black mirror divisions of conscience from pleasure, belief from act, or segregation from sisterhood. Laws are made, cities are planned, and children are raised to ensure those divisions either officially or unofficially.

Although unchastity stigmatizes only women as whores, it does stigmatize certain groups of men in other ways. Like men who affiliate with prostitutes, homosexual men and men of color are deemed unworthy. Homosexual men are targeted with a gay or faggot stigma because they are regarded in dominant society as female men; men of color are targeted with a pimp stigma because they are regarded in dominant society as violent and irresponsible men. Stigmatization effectively denies heterosexual white male privilege to gays and men of color and, at the same time, absolves heterosexual white men of identification with sexual variations or of responsibility for sexual violations. One prostitute in Italy said, "Lots of married men prefer pre-operative transsexual prostitutes (men in the process of becoming women who have both breasts and a penis); they want gay sex without forfeiting heterosexual identity."

Anti-Semitism and the Whore Stigma

Jews, too, have been identified as unchaste. However, whereas black unchastity is primarily attached to mythologies about black women's sexual mysteries and black men's physical violence, Jewish unchastity is primarily attached to mythologies about Jewish women's sexual victimization and Jewish men's financial conspiracies. "The 'beautiful Jewess' is she whom the Cossacks under the czars dragged by her hair through the street of her burning village."[8] Or, perhaps closer to modern associations, the Jewess is she who underwent sexual experiments in Nazi concentration camps. One Dutch woman whose parents both survived Nazi camps said, "I don't know if it's because of my thick black hair which stands out in Holland (racial difference) or my parent's camp background (history of abuse), but my Gentile boyfriends always talk about their excitement in being with a Jewish lover and about feeling protective toward me and about my being different from other Dutch women. It sort of makes me feel like an orphan whore." On the male side, the Jewish man is he who wants money and has intelligence, both of which incite him "to do evil, not good."[9] One Jewish man said, "They wanted my ideas but, as soon as *I* profited from them, they accused me of taking over."

Frequently in contemporary societies, stereotypes about Jews are not specified by gender and both Jewish women and Jewish men are seen as victims and connivers. Jewish victimization is stigmatized as unchaste because of supposed racial impurity (used to justify persecution) and defilement (the condition of having been spoiled by abuse). Jewish intelligence is stigmatized as unchaste because it is supposedly deviant, manipulative, and financially self-serving. A portrait of the Jewess as whore and the Jew man as pimp emerges with little reference to sexuality. That portrait is ambiguous. Victimization and intelligence are stereotypes which elicit contradictory feelings of compassion, blame, resentment, guilt, respect, and jealousy. Unchastity in the case of Jews is therefore both enviable and suspect: Jews are, at least, *acknowledged* as sufferers and *validated* as survivors. On the other side, they are *suspected* both for their history of persecution and for their history of survival. "Why were they persecuted?" "How did they survive?" Those questions glare suspiciously at Jews. The historical link of Jewish survival to oppressive interests, be they tax collection in the past or Western imperialism in the present, is used to stain Jewish credibility. Anti-Semitism is essentially the blaming of Jews for society's ills and injustices. Jews are thereby accused of unchastity not only by the ruling class, but also and most painfully by other oppressed peoples.

Jewish oppression and prostitution oppression have many parallels. Like Jews, prostitutes are unchaste both according to conservative ideologies (for their sexual license) and according to radical ideologies (for their transactions with sexist and capitalist men). Both Jews and prostitutes are denigrated and idealized and blamed for basic social problems. Furthermore, the reality of their

218

persecution and daily abuse is frequently doubted or denied. Both Jews and whores are stigmatized for their past experiences, their non-conforming intelligence, their assumed quest for money, and their assumed sexuality. Historically, they have both been legally forced to identify (and isolate) themselves publicly by wearing certain clothes or symbols such as a strange hat or particular color.[10] They both have had to hide or "pass" or migrate in order to survive. And, they both are perceived as simultaneously passive victims and guilty agents (Jews for communism-or-capitalism, whores for disease-or-disorder).

Whether or not particular Jews are stigmatized as whores or as pimps, they are subject as Jews to the paradoxes of the whore stigma. One Jewish prostitute said, "Sex and money stigmas are nothing new for me and I learned about leading a double life from being a Jew in a community of Gentiles. I also learned as a Jew that it's good and necessary to build your own life regardless of what other people think of you. Besides, I know that people will respect exactly the same things in me that they envy or reject, so it's impossible to please. I've got no choice but to live my own life."

Classism and the Whore Stigma

Whereas a person of color is portrayed as *bad* and a Jew is por-trayed as *different*, a working-class person is portrayed as a *nobody*. It follows that dominant societies have set out to tame the colored, expel or exterminate the Jew, and ignore the worker. Chastity for the worker means invisible subserviance. Working-class people include, of course, people of color and Jews; however, in relation to white Gentile co-workers or certainly white Gentile bosses, people of color and Jews are urged to "know their place" and to "pass" as nobodies, or anybodies. Their position may be different from that of white Gentile workers, but in essence class oppression is a dynamic whereby all workers are pressured into conformity and obedience. Women fall under the same requirements as men within the public labor force; in addition, any woman without a maid to clean or a governess to care for children (the large majority, thus) becomes a worker in the private labor force. There, too, her chastity is measured by the invisibility of her labor.

The labor process is associated with dirt, money, feces, noise, muscle, sweat, tears, pain, and repetition. Workers are expected to dirty themselves in the interest of human reproduction and produc-tion. They are considered the work horses of society; as such, their own humanity is denied. They are relegated to the back room or the basement or the "bad side of town". They are excluded from opportunities, culture, public debate, and power. Classically, male workers are hired for their brawn not their brains and female workers are hired for their appearance not their performance. Essentially, the male worker's muscle and the female worker's smile are prostituted to middle- and upper-class demands.

The impurity attributed to women workers leads to sexual assumptions and requirements. A man on a beach in Chicago yelled to a woman: "If you weren't so rich, you'd be a whore!" He was crudely expressing the common assumption that poor women are whores and rich women would be whores if they needed money. In other words, women who work for money are called whores. It is true that the more access a woman has to money and privilege, the freer she is likely to be from selling her labor, especially labor sold at the cost of legitimacy. If a woman can separate herself from images of unchastity, then she can hope to gain immunity from the whore stigma. Even then, however, she remains a nobody. At best, the traditional woman can hope to take on the identity of her husband.

In former times, every woman who worked in a public job was "working-class." And, all working women were treated as prostitutes by higher-class men.[11] Women workers in professions of different classes are presently still in a battle against male sexual presumptions and harassments.[12] However, the struggle amongst women workers for rights is usually articulated as a struggle against being treated like whores, rather than as a struggle against the treatment of whores. Prostitutes serve as models of the stigmatized working woman. Women who work, regardless of their class, are vulnerable to the whore stigma. Especially in countries where cultural values weigh against public labor for women, such as the Netherlands, the whore stigma is firmly attached to the work needs and wishes of women.

Race oppression, Jewish oppression, and class oppression are distinct mechanisms of subordination and control. Impurities of blood, history, and status are attributed to the targeted group and used to justify social ostracism, physical mistreatment or persecution, denial of rights, and sexual abuse of women. Oppressed men are assumed to be mean or greedy or inhuman. Oppressed women are assumed to be whores or whorish unless they prove otherwise; there is, however, no proof of chastity for a self-identified or life-experienced woman. Even white skin, Gentile ancestry, and middle-class status are no guarantee of stigma immunity for women.

Defilement

Whereas unchastity as impurity refers to identity, unchastity as defilement refers to experience. Female virginity is commonly considered the opposite of defilement: the virgin is unspoiled and the defiled girl (or woman) is "spoiled." Non-virginity refers specifically to sexual experience; defilement refers to physical as well as sexual pollution or violation. Boys and men are not stigmatized by (hetero-sexual) non-virginity or defilement. In fact, the lost innocence which devalues girls is apt to raise the status of boys. Sex and violence dishonor women and honor men. Women are stigmatized with *The Scarlet Letter*; men are rewarded with *The Red Badge of Courage*.[13] Her shame is his honor.

Most traditionally, a girl is suppposed to remain a virgin until she marries at which time her husband "takes her." If she should engage in sexual relations before marriage, then she becomes unchaste and, in some cultures, uneligible for a marriage of standing. Whether the sex was voluntary or imposed is irrelevant to the social damage incurred through the loss of virginity. If the sex was imposed then, on the one hand, the girl can at least claim passivity; on the other hand, imposition implies the double damage of sex and abuse. In either case, girls are stigmatized as whores once they have been exposed to sex, by force or by choice. The anxiety with which parents protect their girls from sexual temptation or violation reflects their awareness of the whore stigma. Because the stigma is so devastating for the future of a girl, parents are socialized to protect their daughter's *reputation* even at the expense of her safety, development, or physical integrity. Such a distortion of values has led some fathers to pathologically "protect" their daughters from *other* men by interrogating them, beating them, and/or by sexually claiming them for themselves. One woman told: "I was daddy's little girl. When I hit high school, around age fifteen, I started screwing around a lot . . . As soon as my father found out, he would find an excuse to beat the crap out of me. It happened whenever I had a new boyfriend." Another woman recounted: "My father didn't physically violate me, although I remember I didn't want to wash dishes because then he would slobber all over me with 'affection,' but he held an inquisition every Sunday morning over exactly what I had done the night before. He also competed with my boyfriends, coming into the room where they were and showing off his muscles. He also told me: 1) he would find me a boyfriend when the time came; 2) I would end up walking the streets; 3) no man would marry a nonvirgin; and 4) if I got pregnant, I would not have to run away from home."[14] Another woman said,

"My father used me sexually since I was five. And then, when I started going on dates with boys, he would accuse me of being a whore. I asked him why I sudddenly became a whore once I had a boyfriend of my age when he'd been fucking me for years! He said that with him it was different because he loved me and it was in the family."

Child sexual abuse is the most classic scenario for the shaming of girls. Accusations of girlhood unchastity are then used to justify and pardon male sexual violation. In one striking example, a judge pronounced in a child molestation case: "I am satisfied we have an unusually sexually promiscuous young lady (a 5-year-old child). And he (the defendent) did not know enough to refuse. No way do I believe (the defendent) initiated sexual contact."[15] And, less extreme but essentially identical, a woman recalls telling her boyfriend about having been molested by a man at age eight: "It was like a ghost returning as the familiar grin came to his face and he said, 'You must have been a sexy little girl.'"[16] In the same vein, a lawyer said of a 14-year-old incest victim, "I can understand her father; she is a beautiful girl." Female beauty, also of a young girl, was thereby offered as a justification for sexual intrusion.

Unlike fathers, mothers rarely abuse their daughters sexually. However, they are socialized to guard their daughter's chastity, be it with warnings, accusations, or denials. Mothers are commonly known to worry if their daughter develops early physically or if she develops a conspicuously female body. One mother said to her daughter when she saw her modelling a new bathing suit: "You can't go out in that! Some man will rape you!" Implicitly, the girl is held responsible for preventing male sexual assault. And, if she should nonetheless fall victim to abuse, she may be blamed for having been provocative or her mother may blame herself for having given her daughter too much freedom. In other cases, the girl is not blamed for the abuse, but she is expected to act "as if nothing happened." One woman recalled complaining to her mother about "Uncle's messy kisses": "I thought she'd tell off my uncle but instead she slapped *me* across the face!" The tendency of mothers to suppress their daughter's sexuality and of fathers to possess their daughter's sexuality is a part of the gender socialization of women and men. Unintentionally, the "protections" of both parents can function more to stigmatize than to safeguard girl children.

Also therapists classically collude in blaming girls for sexual abuse. A male therapist responded in the following way to an incest victim: "From some of the details which she related of her relationship with her father, it was obvious that she was not all that innocent. But she was unable emotionally to accept her own sexual involvement with him."[17] Other therapists, especially of the classical Freudian tradition, are apt to deny the reality of sexual contact between father and daughter altogether.[18] In that case, sexual abuse is not attributed to the girl's seductiveness but to her wishful fantasies. Indeed, the first response to a child's disclosure of incest has often been to accuse the child of lying. Girls are thereby taught to hide their experiences of abuse and to silence their pain.

Once stigmatized as unchaste, girls may become sexually more active and may begin to identify more with harlot than housewife models of femininity. One woman who became a prostitute said, "I was already labelled a whore as a teenager so why not get paid for it?" Another young woman who had been carefully "saving herself" for marriage said, "I was the perfect 'good girl' and then I got raped. It never had been so great saving myself and, once it had happened, I started doing it a lot." And another woman declared, "I was born a whore. My father used to take me around and all his friends would say, 'Hey, who's your pretty date — give me a hug, honey'... Since I was young, I identified with harlot images in movies. I liked the glamor." Another woman who was sexually abused by her father said, "My father would call me all sorts of names and would storm around saying, 'You're no goddam good. You're a whore. You're a nothing. You're this and you're that. You're bad through and through.' They (father and mother) would turn even the most innocent relationship (with a man) into a really dirty thing...they're constantly calling me a whore — so therefore I am. So therefore I can go to bed with anybody. It's a vicious circle."[19]

The sexualization and vilification and molestation of girls constitute obvious violations of girlhood integrity. It is a cultural shock to realize the pervasive, even normative, occurrence of such adult invasion and abuse of children in society.[20] One woman who never suffered such violations said, "I was aghast to hear my father list the fact that he had never molested me as one of his accomplishments as a father." Apparently, respect for his daughter's sexual integrity did not come naturally. Unlike her father, the girl was not congratulated for her virginity. Only unchastity is significant for women, and then as a stigma rather than as an accomplishment.

The relation between sexual abuse and the whore stigma is especially important now that the incidence and effects of incest are being exposed (see footnote 20). Given the stigmatizing equation of whore with sexual unchastity with abuse with badness, the abused girl is forced to either bury her experience or relinquish legitimacy. Identifying abuse with female unchastity rather than with female oppression maintains the illusions which surround violence against women. One illusion is that female behavior causes male sexual violence. Another illusion is that male sexual violence causes irreparable damage to female personality. Women are thereby not only violated, but also blamed and stigmatized. They are expected to repent rather than to recover. One woman said, "People make all sorts of assumptions about me when they hear about my past. I had an awful childhood of beatings and rapes. Thank God it's over. But the burden goes on in people's judgment of me. It's as if I became a bad person by being treated badly."

For adult women, the criteria of chastity is not virginity, but monogamous marriage (or religious life). And, the keeper of female sexuality is not the father, but the husband (or God). Like children, adult women are shamed and blamed for abuse. It is interesting to note that sexuality and abuse brand girls as (unchaste) women and brand women as (bad) girls.

Within marriage, sexual and physical abuse of wives by husbands is even more acceptable than abuse of daughters by fathers within the nuclear family. One prosecutor in England referred to husband abuse of wives as "reasonable assault" in certain cases, in particular cases of sexual infidelity.[21] Indeed, sexual infidelity is commonly used by husbands as a justification to exercise control, domination, and/or physical abuse. Even close friends and family members are apt to excuse male violence within marriage. One woman repeated a conversation with her mother: "Mom, Chuck (her husband) has beaten me bloody. He has held a gun to my head and . . . he has forced me to have sex with women and other men. He is always threatening to kill me." The mother replied, "But, Linda, he's your *husband*."[22] Certainly not all officials or families are unsupportive, but the stigma attached to the battered or sexually abused woman is socially legitimized. A battered woman said, "I have learned that the doctors, the police, the clergy, and my friends will excuse my husband for distorting my face, but won't forgive me for looking bruised and broken."[23] Conspicuous mistreatment is taken as a sign of the woman's "misconduct," as if battering is a righteous punishment of female unchastity.

Outside of marriage, women are stigmatized as whores for any sexual encounter. Phyllis Schlafly, the most vocal of American antifeminist campaigners said, "Virtuous women are seldom accosted."[24] In other words, being accosted is evidence of a lack of virtue, or unchastity.[25] Furthermore, a woman victim is classically accused of

224

having provoked, invited, or not resisted sexual violation.[26] Prostitutes serve as models of female unchastity. As sexual solicitors, they are assumed to invite male violence. Supposedly, a whore cannot be violated because she already is in violation of chastity norms. In one case of a prostitute being raped, a Dutch officer of justice said in court that "given her profession, the sexual abuse could not have made a deep impression upon her."[27] A Dutch research study revealed that policemen ranked the rape of street prostitutes as the least serious of all possible rapes. Rape by many strange men was ranked as the most serious. Rape by a boyfriend or male acquaintance and rape of a drunk woman were ranked only slightly more seriously than the rape of a prostitute. The researcher asserts that rape is judged according to the risk taken by the woman in her behavior and whereabouts. Significantly, police judgment of the seriousness of a rape is the primary determinant of whether the case is brought to court.[28] Prostitutes know only too well how difficult it is for a whore to prove that she has been raped. Even the presence of a known prostitute in court is thought to jeopardize the credibility of a rape victim.[29] Identification or association with unchastity (be it sexually, racially, or professionally defined) is considered a sign of defilement and availability. That view of the "female as either pure or common to all"[30] works to condone male violence against so-called unchaste women and to blame those women for any abuse they suffer. Of course, those women could be any woman whose virtue is called into question.

Male unchastity is defined more by color, ethnicity, class, or homosexuality than is heterosexual behavior. Fortunately, those indicators are recognized as prejudices rather than proofs, at least in countries with strong traditions of tolerance, such as the Netherlands. For example, the association of rape with black men is a deeply engrained prejudice, but racial identity would not be acceptable as explicit legal evidence of guilt. A woman's sexual history, however, is frequently brought to bear upon the reliabilty of her testimony.[31] During the last few years, such information is changing status, thanks to feminist struggle, from proof to prejudice. Nonetheless, many courts in North America and West Europe are still likely to hold the rape victim responsible for the rapist's crime.[32]

The ultimate defilement is death by murder or disease. Then, too, unchastity is blamed for fatal corruption or pollution. In particular, the sexual unchastity assumed of prostitute women and homosexual men is perceived as a choice wraught with shame and vulnerability. Violence, illness, and most extremely, death are considered the punitive consequences of self-imposed danger. Revealingly, the murder of a whore or a gay man is considered a "prostitute murder" or a "homosexual murder." Both the whore and the gay man are seen as accomplices to their own demise. One such case was the murder of Pier Paolo Pasolini in Italy. The trial focused as much on the victim as on the murderer. Public scandal centered around Pasolini: Why did he involve himself in a gay scene? Why did he risk murder?[33] Similarly, the murder of a prostitute is as much an incrimination of her reputation as of the murderer's crime. Murder victims of the infamous Jack the Ripper were described in the press as prostitutes; in fact, some were and some were not. The sexual histories of the victims filled newspapers, as if to warn other women of the perils of sexual unchastity.[34] Significantly, concern was expressed only about the danger to non-prostitutes. Also more recently, whore murderers in Leeds, Los Angeles, and Seattle have not been considered a serious social menace until non-prostitutes have been killed. The murder of whores does not worry, grieve, or outrage dominant society. In fact, violence against prostitutes is likely to increase public dissociation from whores.

Disease, like violence, is often blamed on the unchaste. The whore stigma has been defined as *a mark of shame or disease on an unchaste woman*. Historically, even before sexual transmission of disease was understood, prostitution (the symbol of unchastity for women and men) was erroneously associated with epidemics such as the Plague.[35] Also today, the attribution of disease to prostitution is often more based upon assumption than fact.[36] Unchastity is assumed to begin with the whores and spread from them to chaste society via men. The triangle between "dishonorable whore" and "unworthy husband" and "chaste wife" is most clearly drawn by assumptions of sexual disease transmission. "An 'innocent' woman could only get venereal disease from a 'sinful' man. But the man could only get venereal disease from a 'fallen woman.'" That description is offered in an excellent social historical study of venereal disease which goes on to say that such a "uni-directional mode of transmission reflected prevailing attitudes (at the turn of the century) rather than any bacteriologic reality."[37] The same prejudicial attitudes which prevailed at the beginning of the century still justify the blaming of prostitutes for disease.[38]

Like prostitutes, homosexual men have historically been stigmatized as sexually diseased.[39] However, unlike prostitutes, homosexual men are assumed to be insulated from chaste heterosexual society. They are therefore blamed not for contaminating "sinful men" and "innocent women" but rather for causing their own demise through supposed perverse promiscuity. In reality, homosexual men are not insulated (nor truly distinguishable) from chaste society, as evidenced by the fact that male prostitutes cater primarily to publically heterosexual, married men. That fact illustrates the distortion and hypocrisy of privileging supposedly chaste society. On a practical level, it also illustrates the necessity of sexual education and examination for all sexually active persons rather than for only those publicly identified as unchaste.

Sexuality, abuse, and disease are often perceived as both causes and symptoms of unchastity. Whether those socially significant factors lead to pleasure, pain, or death, they are often interpreted as defilement and as justification for permanent stigmatization. Any woman is vulnerable to the whore stigma as a result of life experience, sexist abuse, or ill fortune. Homosexual men occupy a socially parallel position to prostitute women when it comes to violence and disease. Heterosexual men are likely to feel immune to stigmatization only when they publicly distance themselves from "the unchaste ones."

Conclusion

Unchastity is used to justify oppression and abuse. Women in general and deviant or subordinate men are especially subject to stigmatization as impure or defiled persons; dominant men may be subject to stigmatization on the basis of the unchastity of their associates (be they, for instance, prostitutes or homosexuals). The task of recognizing unchastity as a normal human reality and not as a peculiar condition of inferior humans calls for a profound transformation of values and attitudes.

Notes

1. See: *Collins Double Book Encyclopedia and Dictionary*. London: Collins, 1976. See also: Fowler and Fowler, (eds.) *The Concise Oxford Dictionary*. London: Oxford University Press, 1964, fifth edition in 1974, for this definition of "unchaste: indulging in unlawful or immoral sexual intercourse; lacking in purity, virginity, decency (of speech), restraint, and simplicity; defiled (i.e.polluted, corrupted)." The present article focuses upon two of the above definitions: "lacking in purity" and "defiled." All following definitions in the text are drawn from *The Concise Oxford Dictionary*.
2. This definition was derived by combining the definition of "whore" with the following definition of "stigma": "a brand marked on a slave or criminal; a stain on one's character; a mark of shame or discredit; a definite characteristic of some disease."

3. Much of the material for this analysis was drawn from the author's research on attitutes toward prostitutes, published in Dutch and English: Gail Pheterson, *The Whore Stigma: Female Dishonor and Male Unworthiness*. The Hague: Dutch Ministry for Social Affairs and Employment, 1986. All unreferenced citations throughout the present text were direct communications to the author in personal interviews.

4. Erving Goffman, *Stigma: Notes on the Management of Spoiled Identity* (New Jersey: Prentice-Hall, 1963), p.167.

5. Angela Y. Davis, *Women, Race and Class*. New York: Random House, 1981.

6. Freda Adler and Rita James Simon, *The Criminology of Deviant Women*. Boston: Houghton Mifflin Company, 1979, pp. 88-89.

7. This analysis was heavily influenced by Lillian Smith, *Killers of the Dream*. London: W.W. Norton and Co., 1949.

8. Jean-Paul Sartre (translated by George J. Becker), *Anti- Semite and Jew*. New York: Schocken, 1948, pp.48-49.

9. *Ibid*, p. 39.

10. See: Sietske Altink, *Huizen van Illusies, Bordelen en Prostitutie van Middeleeuwen tot Heden*. Utrecht: Veen, 1983, p.62-63, for a description of legal dress codes for prostitutes throughout history. See Max I. Dimont, *Jews, God and History*. New York: The New American Library, 1962, p. 230, for a description of legal dress codes for Jews between the sixteenth and eighteenth centuries. Among a host of prescriptions, both were required to wear peaked hats and forbidden to wear fine clothes.

11. An Huitzing, *Betaalde Liefde: Prostituees in Nederland, 1850-1900*. Bergen: OCTAVO, 1983, p.75.

12. Catharine MacKinnon, *Sexual Harrassment of Working Women*. New Haven, Connecticut: Yale University Press, 1979. Also: Elizabeth Stanko, *Intimate Intrusions, Women's Experience of Male Violence*. London: Routledge and Kegan Paul, 1985.

13. Both novels are American classics of the nineteenth century. *The Scarlet Letter*, written by Nathaniel Hawthorne, was first published in 1850; *The Red Badge of Courage*, written by Stephen Crane, was first published in 1895.

14. Judith Lewis Herman, *Father-Daughter Incest*. London: Harvard University Press, 1981, p. 117.

15. Elizabeth A. Stanko, *Intimate Intrusions*. London: Routledge and Kegan Paul, 1985, p. 95.

16. Ellen Bass and Louise Thornton, *I Never Told Anyone*. New York: Harper and Row, 1983, p. 181.

17. Judith Lewis Herman, *Father-Daughter Incest*. London: Harvard University Press, 1981, p. 185.

18. *Ibid*; Also: Florence Rush, *The Best Kept Secret: Sexual Abuse of Children*. Englewood Cliffs, NJ: Prentice-Hall, Inc., especially the chapter "A Freudian Cover-up." Also: Jeffrey Moussaieff Masson, *The Assault of Truth*. New York: Farrar, Straus and Giroux, 1984.

19. Stanko, p.30.

20. Judith Herman, *Father-Daughter Incest*. Cambridge, Massachusetts: Harvard University Press, 1981; Jennifer James, "Prostitutes and Prostitution." In: E. Sagarin and F. Montanino (eds.), *Deviants: Voluntary Actors in a Hostile World*. General Learning Press, 1977, pp. 368-428; Diana Russell, "The Incidence and Prevalence of Intrafamilial and Extrafamilial sexual abuse of female children." *Child Abuse and Neglect* (1983) 7, 2, 133-146; Mimi Silbert and Ayala Pines, "Victimization of Street Prostitutes," *Victimology: An International Journal*, vol. 7, no. 1-4, 1982, pp.122-133.

21. Stanko, p. 130.

22. Stanko, p. 53. Also see: Eileen Evason, *Hidden Violence: A Study of Battered Women in Northern Ireland*. Belfast: Farset Co-operative Press, 1982, for further elaboration on the theme of husband justifications for violence against wives.

23. Stanko, p. 48.

24. *Ibid*, p. 139.

25. It is irresistible to mention that the loss of honor incurred through sexual abuse has governed women's lives for hundreds of years. A study of prostitution in 15th century France gives the following description: "In the end, the consequences of rape were exactly the same as those of questionable or shameful conduct. The victim was almost always disgraced...even those who testified in her favor always considered her defiled by what had happened to her. She herself felt ashamed, guilty, and disgraced. In this respect her youthful assailants had attained their objective, for the raped woman realized that in the eyes of those around her, and indeed in her own mind, the distance separating her from the public prostitute had greatly diminished. Reduced to a state of psychological and physical weakness, she had little hope of regaining her honor as long as she stayed in town." Specific examples of such loss of honor through rape are plentiful. In one case, when a servant girl complained to her mistress about having been attacked and insulted by three bachelors, she was given notice, for "if she was accused of such bad things, (the mistress) was not about to keep her, unless she was given convincing proof indicating whether the girl was a respectable person or a nasty hussy." See: Jacques Rossiaud, "Prostitution, Youth, and Society in the Towns of Southeastern France in the 15th Century," *Selections from the Annales: Economies, Societes, Civilizations*, Volume IV (edited by Robert Forster and Orest Ranum). Baltimore: The John Hopkins University Press, 1978, pp. 17,41.

26. Nel Drayer, *Seksueel Geweld en Heteroseksualiteit*. The Hague: Ministerie van Sociale Zaken en Werkgelegenheid, 1984; Diana E.H. Russell, *Rape in Marriage*. New York: Macmillan, 1982; Stanko, 1985.

27. See: Leidsch Dagblad, "Buitenlust," "Officier: Verkrachting Doet Prostituee Minder." Diemen: October 9, 1985. (Dutch words of Mr. Franken van Bloemendaal, officier van justitie , Amsterdamse rechtbank: "Door het beroep dat zij uitoefent, zal het seksueel misbruikt worden wel geen diepe indruk op haar hebben gemaakt").

28. See: E. Ter Mors, "Zedenpolitie. Wie de Goede Zede Wil Verdedigen is Met de Wet Gebrekkig Gewapend." Eindscriptie Politie- Academie, 1978 (discussion of research in Nel Drayer, above). For a discouraging vivid description of nearly identical attitudes in the Middle Ages, see: Leah Lydia Otis, *Prostitution in Medieval Society, The History of an Urban Institution in Languedoc*. London: The University of Chicago Press, 1985, p. 68-69.

29. Specifically, the prosecuting attorney of a rape case in California asked a known prostitute not to be present throughout a rape trial because she thought it would reduce her client's credability. The prostitute was a close friend of the client, a non- prostitute, and had initially been asked by her traumatized friend to be present for emotional support.

30. See above: Jacques Rossiaud, p. 12.

31. See above footnote 26 (Nel Drayer; Diana Russell). Also Diana Russell, *The Politics of Rape*. New York: Macmillan, 1982.

32. For an analysis of court attitudes and judgments in 48 rape cases in the Netherlands from 1980-1984, see: Ed. Leuw, "Verkrachtingszaken voor de rechtbank: een kwalitatieve analyse van observatiegegevens." *Tijdschrift Voor Criminologie*. Boom Meppel: 27e jaargang, juli/oktober, 1985, pp.212-234. According to this study, the victim is assumed to be "purely innocent" (author's quotation marks) in a majority of cases when the rapist is considered "sick" (psychologically irresponsible) or "bad" (immoral). Gang rapes fall under the category "bad." In 25% of the cases, however, the rapist is considered "normal" (such as a "failed seductor") and co-responsibility is then often sought in the victim. Some Dutch lawyers also claim victim co-responsibility for rapes which are considered "normative" within the sub-culture in question (2 of the 48 cases). The characteristics of the rapist and the circumstances/cultural context of the rape are shown to affect court decisions. The Dutch author claims that courts in the Netherlands are far less likely than courts in other countries to claim victim co-responsibility for rape, p.226.

33. See: Guy Hocquenghem, "Niet iedereen kan in zijn bed sterven." *Tegenlicht of Pasolini*. Translated from the French article in *Liberation*, Paris, November, 1975.

34. Wendy Hollway, "I just wanted to kill a woman. Why? The Ripper and Male Sexuality," *Feminist Review*, no.9, October, 1981, p. 33-40.

35. See: Leah Lydia Otis, *Prostitution in Medieval Society, The History of an Urban Institution in Languedoc*. London: The University of Chicago Press, 1985, p. 41.

36. Allan M. Brandt, *No Magic Bullet: A Social History of Venereal Disease in the United States Since 1880*. New York: Oxford University Press, 1985.

37. *Ibid*, pp.31-32.

38. *Ibid*.

39. Jeffrey Weeks, *Sex, Politics and Society: The Regulation of Sexuality Since 1800*. London: Longman, 1981.

Lesbians and Prostitutes:
A Historical Sisterhood

Joan Nestle

The prevalence of lesbianism in brothels throughout the world has convinced me that prostitution, as a behavior deviation, attracts to a large extent women who have a very strong latent homosexual component. Through prostitution these women eventually overcome their homosexual repression. (from *Female Homosexuality: A Psychodynamic Study of Lesbianism*, by Frank Caprio, 1954.)

We're having the meeting during Lesbian/Gay Freedom Week because many prostitute women are lesbians — yet we have to fight to be visible in the women's and the gay movements. This is partly due to our illegality but also because being out about our profession, we face attitudes that suggest we're either 'traitors to the women's cause' or not 'real lesbians.' (A speaker at "Prostitutes: Our Life: Lesbian and Straight," San Francisco, June, 1982.)

These indoor prostitutes are on the rise. Captain Jerome Piazza of the Manhattan South Public Moral Division estimates that there are at least 10,000 inside 'pros' in the city. Women Against Pornography contends that there are 25,000 prostitutes working inside and outside the city, over 9,500 of them on the West Side alone. (*West Side Spirit*, June 17, 1985.)

To prepare for the United Nation's Conference on Women, the Kenyan government put new benches in the parks, filled in the potholes and swept the prostitutes off the streets. (*New York Times*, 1985.)

The original impulse behind this essay was to show how lesbians and prostitutes have always been connected, not just in the male imagination but in the actual histories of both. I hoped that by putting out the bits and pieces of this shared territory I would have some impact on the contemporary feminist position on prostitution as expressed by the feminist anti-pornography movement. But in doing my reading and listening for this work, a larger vision formed in me, the desire to give back to working women their own history, much as we have been trying to do in the grassroots lesbian and gay history projects around the country.

Whores, like queers, are society's dirty joke; to even suggest that they have a history, not as a map of pathology but as a record of a people, is to challenge sacrosanct boundaries. As I read of the complicated history of whores, I realized once again I was also reading women's history with all its contradictions of oppression and resistance, of sisterhood and betrayal. In this work I will try to honor both histories — that of the woman whore and the woman queer. First my own starting point. In the bars of the late fifties and early sixties where I learned my lesbian ways, whores were part of our world. We sat on barstools next to each other, we partied together and we made love together. The vice squad, the forerunners of the Moral Division with whom Women Against Pornography have no qualms collaborating, controlled our world, and we knew clearly that there was little difference between whore and queer when a raid was on. This shared territory broke apart, at least for me, when I entered the world of lesbian feminism. Whores, and women who looked like whores, became the enemy or, at best, misguided oppressed women who needed our help. Some early conferences on radical feminism and prostitution were marked by the total absence of working women in any part of the proceedings. The prostitute was once again the *other*, much as she was earlier, in the feminist purity movements of the late nineteenth century.

A much closer connection came home to me when I was reading through my mother's legacy, her scribbled writings, and discovered that at different times in her life, my mother had turned tricks to pay her rent. I had known this all along in some other part of me, particularly when I had shared her bed in the Hotel Dixie in the heart of Forty-Second Street during one of her out of work periods, but I had never let the truth of my mother's life sink in.

Finally, I have recently entered the domain of public sex. I write sex stories for lesbian magazines, I pose for explicit photographs for lesbian photographers, I do readings of sexually graphic materials dressed in sexually revealing clothes, and I have taken money from women for sexual acts. I am, depending on who is the accuser, a pornographer, a queer and a whore. Thus, both for political and personal reasons, it became clear to me that this work had to be done.

One of the oldest specific references that I found to the connection between lesbians and prostitutes was in the early pages of William W. Sanger's *History of Prostitution* (1859). Similar to the process of reading early historical references to lesbians, one must pry women loose from the judgmental language in which they are embedded. Prostitution, he tells us, "stains the earliest mythological records." (p. 2) He works his way through the Old Testament telling us that Tamar, the daughter of Judah, covered her face with her veil, the sign of a harlot. Many of the women "driven to the highways for refuge, lived in booths and tents, where they combined the trade of a peddler with the calling of a harlot." (pp. 3-7) Two important themes are set out here, the wearing of clothes as both an announcement and an expression of stigma, and the issue of women's work.

It is in Sanger's chapter on ancient Greece that we find the first concrete reference to lesbian history. Attached to the Athenian houses of prostitution, called dicteria, "were schools where young women were initiated into the most disgusting practices by females who had themselves acquired them in the same manner." (p. 48) Here is evidence of intergenerational same sex activity which is also used for the transmission of subculture survival skills. A more developed connection is revealed in his discussion of one of the four classes of Greek prostitutes — the flute players known as Auletrides. These gifted musicians were hired to play and dance at banquets, after which their sexual services could be bought. Once a year, these women gathered to honor Venus and to celebrate their calling. No men were allowed to attend these early rites, except through special dispensation.

> Their banquet lasted from dark till dawn with wines, perfumes, delicate foods, songs and music. Once a dispute broke out between two guests as to their respective beauty. A trial was demanded by the company and a long and graphic account is given of the exhibition (by the recording poet) but modern tastes will not allow us to transcribe the details. . .It has been suggested that these festivals were originated by or gave rise to those enormous aberrations of the Greek feminine mind known to the ancients as lesbian love. There is grave reason to believe something of the kind. Indeed, Lucius affirms that, while avarice prompted common pleasures, taste and feeling inclined the flute players toward their own sex. On such a repulsive theme it is unnecessary to enlarge. (Sanger, p. 50)

233

Oh how wrong the gentleman scholar is. This passage, far removed from the original, may be a mixture of some Greek history and much Victorian attitude, but it is provocative both in its tidbit of information and the language it uses to express it. In 1985, I attended my first Michigan Women's Music Festival and all during the festivities I kept thinking of those early flute players pleasuring each other; I wondered if it would change some of the themes of cultural feminism if this historical legacy was recognized.

Throughout the history of prostitution runs the primacy of dress codes. This drama of how prostitutes had to be socially marked to set them aside from the domesticated woman, and how the prostitute population responded to these state demands, led me to think many times of how lesbians have used clothes to announce themselves as a different kind of women. Prostitutes, even up to the turn of the century, were described as unnatural women, creatures who had no connection to wives and mothers, much as lesbians were called, years later, a third sex. In an 1830 test, we are told, "she (the prostitute) could serve men's needs because a great gulf separated her nature from that of other women. In the female character, there is no midway. It must exist in spotless innocence or hopeless vice." (Rosen, p. 6) This view of the prostitute as another species of woman is to continue through the years. In 1954, a popularizer of erotic subcultures will write: "The only thing I was sure about then was that the prostitute is no more like other women than a zebra is like a horse. She is a distinct breed, more different from her sisters under the skin that she — or the rest of society — could possibly realize. . .They have one common denominator, an essential quality that distinguishes them from other women — a profound contempt of the opposite sex." (Stern, p. 13, p. 15) Both dykes and whores have a historical heritage of redefining the concept of woman.

To make sure prostitutes did not pass into the population of true women, different states have set up regulations through the centuries controlling her self presentation and physical movements. In Greek times, all whores had to wear flowered or striped robes. At some time, even though no law decreed it, the prostitutes all dyed their hair blond in a common gesture of solidarity. In the Roman period, "the law prescribed with care the dress of prostitutes on the principle that they were to be distinguished in all things from honest women. Thus they were not allowed to wear the chaste sola which concealed the form or the fillet with which Roman women bound their hair or to wear shoes or jewels or purple robes. These were the insignia of virtue. Prostitutes wore the toga like men...some even went a one step further in a bold announcement of their trade and wore over the green toga a short white jacket, the badge of adultery." (Sanger, p. 75) A provocative point made throughout the history of the state regulations concerning prostitute dress is the inclusion of men's apparel as part of the stigmatizing process. For instance, in the late fourteenth century, "prostitutes were required to carry a mark on their left arm...whereas in Castres (1375) the statutory sign was a man's hat and a scarlet belt." (Otis, p. 80) Here, as in lesbian history, cross dressing signals the breaking of women's traditional erotic, and therefore social, territory.

For the next three hundred years, prostitutes will be marked by the state, both in being forced to wear a certain kind of clothes or mark like a red shoulder knot, a white scarf or, in a chilling prefiguring of history, a yellow cord on their sleeves. They will be controlled in the places they will be allowed to live and work. As I read of the demanded dress codes, I was reminded of the warning older lesbians gave me in the fifties as I prepared for a night out: *Always wear three pieces of women's clothing so the vice squad can't bust you for transvestism.* We dressed to answer two needs: to avoid the state's penalties for being women of difference and to announce our own cultural participation.

The states also drew up litanies of control defining the multitude of ways prostitutes lost their social freedoms. In fifteenth century France, a prostitute faced up to three months imprisonment if she was

1. to appear in forbidden places
2. to appear at forbidden hours
3. to walk through the streets in daylight in such a way as
to attract the notice of people passing (Sanger, 150)

Five centuries later, on another continent, the poetry of control will have the same purpose but be more elaborate in its requirements:

Rules for Reservation El Paso, Texas, 1921

Women must keep screen doors fastened on inside and keep curtain on lower half of screen door.

Must sit back from doors and windows and not sit with legs crossed in a vulgar manner and must keep skirts down.

Must remain in rooms until after twelve o'clock, and when they come out on the street they must not be loud or boisterous or be playing with each other or with men. They must not be hugging men or women around the street or be trying to pull men into their cribs.

Must not sit in windows with screens down or stand in doors at any time.

Must not cross the street in middle of block, but must go to

Second or Third Street and cross over.
Must not yell or scream from one room to the other or use
loud, vulgar language.
Must not wear gaudy clothes or commit any act of flirtation
or other act that will attract unusual attention on the streets.
Must not work with the lights out. (Woolston, pp. 336-337

I reproduce these decrees of control here because they are the
prostitutes' historical documents of oppression and few, I think,
realize how completely the police could infringe on a working
woman's life. They also prefigure the control the vice squad was to
have in lesbian bars in the fifties, when even our bathroom habits
were under surveillance.

Yet within these controlled borders some of the women turned
their social prisons into social freedoms, becoming the intellectual
free women of their day. The history of prostitution has its lumin-
aries, women who used the power of their stigmatized place to
become unusual women, women who lived outside of the domestic
restrictions that entrapped the vast majority of their sisters. Thus we
have the biographies of famous courtesans, extolling their wit and
depicting their involvement in literature and politics. Successful
prostitution accomplished what passing for men did for some
lesbians: it gave them freedom from the rigidly controlled world of
women.

A rich, untapped source of lesbian history is diaries and
biographies of courtesans, madams, strippers and other sex workers.
Of course, to take these documents seriously, as seriously as the
letters of female friends in the 19th century, is going to test the class
and attitude boundaries of many feminist scholars. Another problem
will be that often fact and fiction are intertwined in these works, but
both the fact and the more imaginative creations can be valuable
sources in piecing together a fuller lesbian history.

In Cora Pearl's *Grand Horizontal: The Erotic Memoirs of a
Passionate Lady*, written in 1873, several mentions are made of
female same sex activities. The first takes place in a French convent
school for poor girls in the year 1849. The narrator soon discovers
that her schoolmates had learned to please each other: ". . .the degree
of interest which my companions exhibited not only in their own but
in each other's bodies was something strange to me." The author then
goes on to describe at length a sexual initiation scene in a bathtub,
under the careful tutelage of Liane, an older student who brings both
of them to orgasm as the rest of the girls watch. At night, the courte-
san-to-be says, she "was taught the pleasures of the body which

236

within a year or two became so keen that I was convinced that anyone who neglected them was a dunce indeed. These pleasures were exclusively female." She carefully assures her reader that these pleasures were never forced on any girl too young or inexperienced to receive them. She goes on to tell how she discovered that the older women, the school mistresses, also enjoyed lesbian sex. "Suddenly going into one of the classrooms to fetch a set of needles I discovered Bette on her knees before Soeur Rose, one of the younger and prettier mistresses, her head thrust beneath her skirts. I had time to glimpse an expression on her face which was familiar to me as that on the faces of my friends at certain times of mutual pleasure." (Pearl, p. 22)

The narrator develops both a philosophy of pleasure and of female bonding based on these early sexual encounters. "Our nightly experiments in the dormitory can be imagined. Eugenie, my particular friend, hearing from Bette of the incident with Soeur Rose, determined to introduce me to the pleasure the lips and tongue can give, and I did not find that pleasure at all mitigated by distaste; then as since, I was keenly conscious that one of the greatest joys in life is experiencing the pleasure one can give to one's lovers. And now I was fully grown, and keen to experience myself the full extent of the pleasure I could give to others. For the most part we fell into pairs, and there grew up between many of us true and real devotion, unmatched since . . . our experiments were by no means without their effect on my later career, for I learned at that time to be wary of no activity which pleasure was the result of." (Pearl, p. 23)

Later on in the memoirs, Cora goes to bed with a lesbian wife of a male client, a woman described in what we call today butch terms. "She then invited me to warm her which being a guest I did. She was of a sturdy and muscular build, with breasts which were firm rather than full, indeed no more presenting the chest of a woman than of some men I have known." The wife asks Cora to share her bed, explaining that, "not long after marriage she discovered that men and their figures were if not entirely repugnant at least unexciting to me, whereas the female admiration for the female figure was what she could not but give vent to." (Pearl, p. 166) Cora muses as they make love, "another woman must more securely know through pleasuring herself how to give pleasure to a fellow of her sex." In the world of women's history research, we often hear the statement, but women did not talk about sex in those days. If we turn to different sources, however, like the writings and records of sexually defined women, we may discover that women of different social positions talked in all kinds of ways. The question is, do we really want to hear their voices, and how will we fit them into what Adrienne Rich calls the lesbian continuum.

In 1912, a lesbian prostitute anarchist named Almeda Sperry enters both histories by writing a love letter to Emma Goldman that uses a frankness of language we hunger for in our research. "Dearest it is a good thing that I came away when I did — in fact — I would have had to come away anyway. If I had only had the courage enough to kill myself when you reached the climax then — then I would have known happiness for at that moment I had complete possession of you...Satisfied, ah God no...At this moment I am listening to the rhythm of the pulse coming in your throat. I am surging along with your life blood, coursing in the secret places of your body. I cannot escape the rhythmic spurt of your love juices." (Falk, pp. 174-175) Emma Goldman, we learn from Candace Falk's new work, *Love, Anarchy and Emma Goldman*, was no stranger to frank depictions of desire, so it comes as no surprise that she inspired such a passionate response. Almeda Sperry, lesbian and prostitute, should be as much a part of our history as Natalie Barney or the Ladies of Llanglollen. Neither her language nor her profession is genteel; she may not fit easily into academic reading lists but the understanding of our history, of women's history, will be poorer for the exclusion of such voices.

In the memoirs of Nell Kimball, a heterosexual madam, many references are made to lesbians. One of the more famous madams of her times was Emma Flegel, born in 1867, a Jewish immigrant from Lubeck, Germany who came to America and worked as a cook's helper until circumstances forced her to marry and settle in St. Louis. There she opened a highly successful brothel and was known throughout the subculture for her love affairs with her girls. "Emma apparently always had a favorite among her girls, with whom she'd carry on a crush for a year or so before seeking a new favorite." (information sent to the Lesbian History Archives, New York). Here we see how ethnic lesbian history can interconnect with the general story of both lesbians and prostitutes, as long as shame does not get in the way. This does not mean a history without concepts or conflicts, but it does mean a commitment to opening up new territory, to the inclusion of women who may challenge prevailing lesbian feminist categories.

***

Besides recognizing the history of prostitutes as a valuable source for lesbian history, another connection that emerges is the lesbian customer and protector of prostitutes. In the wonderful and moving story of Jeanne Bonnet, a passing woman of San Francisco in the 1870s, which was given life by the work of the San Francisco Lesbian and Gay History Project and Allan Berube in particular, we meet a woman who first came to the Barbary Coast brothels as a customer but in 1876 decided to enlist some of the women she visited in her all women's gang. They ended their lives as prostitutes and survived by petty stealing. One of the women she won away from her pimp, Blanche Buneau, became her special friend. But the anger of the scorned man followed the two women into the privacy of their life. In the words of Allen Berube: "After dark, according to Blanche, Jeanne sat in a chair smoking her pipe and drinking a glass of cognac. She took off her male attire, got into their bed and with her head propped up on her elbow, waited for Blanche to join her. Blanche sat down on the edge of the bed and bent over to unlace her shoes when a shot was fired through the window hitting Jeanne, who cried, 'I join my sister,' and died." We are told that her funeral in the year of 1876 in San Francisco was attended by "many women of the wrong class. . .the tears washing little furrows through the paint on their cheeks." (Berube, LHA).

In Jonathan Katz's *Gay/Lesbian Almanac: A New Documentary*, we find a mention of a "female care, R., age thirty eight" who "proclaims her characteristics in the most flagrant way through her manner of dress which is always the most masculine, straight tailored hats and heavy shoes. She makes a living by prostituting herself homosexually to various women." (Katz, p. 339) Here, embedded in the language of Dr. Douglas C. McMurtrie, author of "Some Observations on the Psychology of Sexual Inversion in Women," we have another clue to lesbian history. Perhaps R. will seem more worthy of our attention when we are told by the doctor: "R. feels absolutely no shame or delicacy regarding her position. In the city. . .she frequents public places dressed in a manner to attract general notice. She is heaped with contempt and scorn by the normal and feminine women who see her. She seems, however, to rather glory in this attention and adverse criticism." (Katz, p. 339).

Homosexual women visiting lesbian prostitutes is also documented by Frank Caprio, a pop psychologist from the fifties who captures that decade's combination of prejudice and sensationalism perfectly. "In these brothels, which are referred to as 'Temples of Sappho,' lesbian practices consist of intercourse via the use of a penis substitute, mutual masturbation, tribadism and cunnilingus. While many of the clients are passively homosexual, they often assume an active role and in this way they find an outlet for their repressed homosexual cravings. One of these 'Temples of Sappho,' in Paris, catering to women clients, is lavishly furnished. A bar occupies a portion of the lower floor where alcoholic beverages may be obtained. The lesbian inmates are attired in transparent, sex appealing undergarments and stimulate their women clients with inviting gestures. Private rooms in an upper floor are devoted to sexual liasons which follow the preliminary acquaintanceship. . ." (Caprio, p. 93). It is the challenge of lesbian historians to sort out what is bona fide lesbian culture here and what is Caprio's imagination but we do know from oral histories that such places existed and not only in "exotic" Paris. Mabel Hampton, for example, a black eighty-four-year-old New York lesbian, tells about a brothel in Harlem during the thirties that catered only to women customers, and whose lesbian madam kept a shotgun by the door to scare away curious men. One important point I would like to make is the need to include questions about prostitution and prostitutes in any oral history done with older lesbian women. If the message is given that this is shameful territory, that the "feminist" interviewer would be appalled by fem whores or butch pimps, or by a myriad of cultural and personal overlappings of these two worlds, then this whole part of our women's history will again go underground. We will lose insight and understanding about how lesbians in particular, and women in general, who lived outside the pale of domestic arrangements organized their lives.

Lesbians have and still do turn to prostitutes for sexual comfort as well as work as prostitutes themselves. In 1984 in a small town in Tennessee the police set up an entrapment net using a policewoman posing as a prostitute. After the arrests for soliciting were made, the names of the arrested were to be published in the town's newspaper. In an article entitled, "Police Sex Sting Nets 127," we hear a woman's voice, one of the arrested would-be customers:

> . . . and many of them admitted they had made a mistake.
> "Some mistakes you can only make one time," said the only woman charged during the three day undercover operation. "My mother and grandmother are ministers in Missouri. I'm not a low-life."
> The woman, who turned twenty four today, sat in her car and wept after being given her citation. She was convinced she would be fired from her job, which she had only recently gained.
> "I do have some girlfriends, but things aren't great right now," she told the police decoy.
> She later told a reporter that she thought the undercover operation was unfair.

240

"I think the cops should have said, 'Hey, don't do it again,' and let me live my life.

"You're talking about a story. I'm talking about my career."

from *The Tennessean*, November 22, 1984

In the early decades of the twentieth century, lesbians and prostitutes were often confused in the popular and legal imagination. Mabel Hampton tells how she was arrested in 1920 at a white woman's house while waiting for a friend. Because of an anonymous tip that a wild party was going on, "three bulls" came crashing through the door, and even though Ms. Hampton clearly was a "woman's woman" she was arrested for prostitution and sent to Bedford Hills Reformatory for two years at the age of nineteen. According to Ms. Hampton, many of the girls arrested for prostitution were, in fact, lesbians. Ms. Hampton, who takes adversity as a challenge, sums up her Bedford Hills experience by commenting, "I sure had a good time with all those girls." Mabel's good time was not hers alone; Estelle Freedman has chronicled the scandal over blatant lesbianism that was going to hit Bedford Hills a few years later. Here we have another clue to a fuller lesbian history; we need to go back to prison records and start exploring the lives we will find summarized in the terse sentences of the state.

We know from Ruth Rosen's work, *The Lost Sisterhood*, that from 1900-1918, the background period to Ms. Hampton's arrest, prostitutes were becoming the victims of anti-vice campaigns, campaigns that established practices of harassment, surveillance and arrest that were later to be used against clearly defined lesbians and their gathering places. "The growth of special courts, vice squads, social workers and prisons to deal with prostitution," (Rosen, p. 19) became the lesbian legacy of the forties and fifties.

A police form used in interrogating arrested prostitutes from this period, the 1920s, lists the following categories under the heading of general health: Use liquor Drugs Perversion Homosexuality. (Woolston, p. 331) It is in this decade that police boast of the new methods they have developed to humiliate working women: "a spectacular method for striking terror into the heart of the wrong doers is the sudden and sometimes violent raid. A patrol wagon dashes up to the suspected house. Police scramble out and attack various entrances and exits and round up the inmates." (Woolston, p. 214). Fifty years later, a prostitute describes a bar raid with these words:

"You can feel them in the air, when you're in the bar, and sometimes they take the whole bar out, all of the girls sitting at the bar and put them in the wagon and take them downtown and put them through a

241

lot of hassles. They can just walk in and take you for I and D (idle and disorderly persons) if nothing else." (Turril, p. 8). Any lesbian who has been in a bar raid would recognize this description.

Another striking example of how the two worlds come together is shown in an excerpt from an oral history by Rikki Streicher, owner of a lesbian bar in San Francisco. The time is the forties but the incident has its roots in the early 1900s:

> I was working as a waitress at the Paper Doll. Somebody called up and said the cops were on the way. I sent everybody home and stayed. So I was the only one there, so they took me in. If you were a woman, their charges were usually 72 VD which meant they took you in for a venereal disease test and seventy-two hours is how long it took. They took me in but decided not to book me. So a friend came down and got me out. (Streicher, p. 5)

Here the lesbian is being policed with a procedure clearly growing out of the social view of the prostitute as a carrier of a social disease. In the medical records of the state, lesbian and prostitute history often become one. According to Dr. Virginia Livingston, a staff physician of the Brooklyn Hospital for Infectious Disease during WWI, "the hospital had a clinic for prostitutes and many of the prostitutes were lesbians." (WBAI interview, March 7, 1980). The connection between sex and disease which was to haunt prostitutes during the war years, causing many incarcerations, is once again, in the social air. And once again, whores and queers must be on the alert for the loss of civil liberties in the face of social panic.

Because prostitutes were the first policed community of outlaw women, they were forced to develop a subculture of survival and resistance. We have seen some details of this culture in the earlier discussion of clothes and women's gatherings. But to enter modern times, I suggest much unexplored lesbian history lies in the so-called dens of legalized vice that sprang up in the first decade of the twentieth century. In the famous red light districts of that time, in New Orlean's Storyville, in San Francisco's Barbary Coast, in New York's Five Points and Tenderloin districts, lesbian stories are waiting to be told. An ad from one of the famous blue books of the time included, in its listings of sexual services available, a reference to female homosexual entertainment. (Rosen, p. 82) From the prostitute subculture comes the phrase, "in the life," the way black lesbians will define their lesbian identities in the thirties and forties. From this world comes the use of a buzzer or light to signal the arrival of the police in the backroom of a lesbian bar, a tradition still strong in the lesbian fifties.

Rosen tells us that "these districts, although in a state of transition, still offered women a certain amount of protection, support and human validation...The process of adapting to the district, or 'the life' as it is called, involved a series of introductions to the new language...the humor and folklore of the subculture." (Rosen, p. 102). A prostitute in Kate Millet's *Prostitution Papers* will comment years later, "It's funny that the expression 'go straight' is the same expression for gay people. It's funny that both these worlds should use that expression." (Millet, p. 41)

***

The final, and perhaps most ironic, connection between these two worlds that I want to discuss is how lesbians and prostitutes are tied together in the psychology literature. One of the prevailing models for explaining the sickness of prostitutes in the fifties was that prostitutes were really lesbians in disguise who suffered from an Oedipus complex and therefore were hostile to men. As Caprio put it in his 1954 work, "While it seems paradoxical to think of...prostitutes having strong homosexual tendencies, psychoanalysts have demonstrated that prostitution represents a form of pseudoheterosexuality, a flight from homosexual repression." (Caprio, p. 93). Helen Deutsch saw the problem in another interesting light. Identification for the prostitute was with the masculine mother and she "has the need to deride social institutions, law and morality as well as the men who impose such authority." (Bullough, p. 89) Another type of prostitute, Deutsch continues, is "the woman who renounces tenderness and feminine gratification in favor of the aggressive masculinity she imitates," (Bullough, p. 89) thus making her a latent lesbian. Mixed in with the attempts to explain the sickness of the prostitute, are the stories of hundreds of women's lives. Caprio, for example, says he had done hundreds of interviews with lesbian prostitutes from around the world. I cannot bear to spend too many words on this connection because I have felt the weight of these theories in my own life. My mother took me to doctors in the early fifties to see who could cure her freak daughter. It is enough to say that prostitutes and lesbians have a shared history of struggle with the law, religion and medicine, all attempting to explain and control the "pathology" of these unusual women. Lesbian prostitutes have suffered the totality of their two histories as deviant women — they have been called sinful, sick, unnatural and a social pollution. In the decade of lesbian feminism, they have not been labeled because they are invisible. Even so astute and caring a gay historian as Jeffrey Weeks feels the need to deny their existence in the service of a patriarchy-free lesbian history. "Even Magnus Hirschfield, whose study of homosexuality aimed to treat both male and female alike, saw a tendency in lesbians to turn to prostitution. It was as if lesbians had to be explained and justified always in terms of a largely male phenomenon." (Weeks, 88). The existence of lesbian prostitutes is not a blemish on the story of our people; we will lose more than our history if they are judged not worthy of inclusion. In 1985, the lesbian feminist community profusely welcomed the world of lesbian nuns into the lesbian continuum with the publication of *Lesbian Nuns: Breaking Silence*. I see a close connection between these three groups of undomesticated women — the prostitute, the nun and the lesbian. And recent research done on prostitution in medieval society by Leah Lydia Otis bears out a profound connection between at least two of these groups. In the fifteenth century it was not unusual for whole houses of prostitutes, run by women, to turn themselves into a convent when they reached the age of retirement. Thus the sisterhood was preserved and the women could continue to live in one version of medieval separatism. As always, the same sex documentation is harder to find, but we do have a glimmer. "In Grasse in 1487 a prostitute was sentenced to pay a fine for having disobeyed the vicar's regulation forbidding prostitutes to dance with honest women." (Otis, 81)

Four centuries later, prostitutes and nuns will be joined once again by a historical tragedy that called for the highest acts of human courage. Vera Lasker in her passionate work, *Women in the Resistance and in the Holocaust: The Voices of Eyewitnesses*, tells us that some of the best safe houses for resistance fighters were brothels and convents. (Lasker, 6) She also asserts that some of the most daring women in the service of the resistance were prostitutes. The full story of the fate of prostitutes both in the resistance movement and in the concentration camps still has to be told and I hope the one who does it is a whore. I am sure that in the telling of this history, we will also find lesbian women who wore the black triangle of the asocials.

"Among the first women in Auschwitz were German prostitutes and Jewish girls from Slovaka. These women were issued evening gowns in which they were forced to help build Auschwitz in rain or snow. Of the hundreds, only a handful survived by 1944." (Lasker, 15) Nun, queer, whore — think of the challenge posed to the unrestricted feminist historian and to all of us in our imaginations.

***

Both lesbians and prostitutes were and are concerned with creating power and autonomy for themselves in seemingly powerless social interactions. As one interviewer of working women has said, "From the point of view of the prostitute, power and control must always be in her hands in order to survive." (Cohen, 97) A lesbian prostitute wrote in 1982, "I'll make sure I'm out of there in ten or fifteen minutes. I'm always keeping my eye on the time and I decide how long I'll stay depending on the amount of money and what the guy is like . . .They want more, but in the end we set the terms of the relationship and the Johns have to accept it." (Richards, LHA)

The class structure that exists for prostitutes also exists for lesbians. Call girls and professional lesbian women have things in common. They both have more protection than the street walker or the bar dyke, but coming on to the wrong people can deliver them both into the hands of the state. Both are often in a hurry to disconnect themselves from their sisters in the street in an effort to lighten their own feeling of difference.

The irony, at this point, is that lesbians have more legal protection than prostitutes because of the power of the gay rights movement. We have lesbian and gay elected public officials, but no politicians who clearly claim their public sex past. A spokesperson for Prostitutes of New York (PONY) said in 1980 if the hookers and the housewives and the homosexuals got together "we could rule the world." (Stout, 3) But in order to do this, we must face the challenge of our own history, the challenge to understand how the "lesbian" world stretches from the flute players of Greece to the Michigan festival of lesbian separatists. Why has this seemingly obvious connection between lesbians and prostitutes gone unspoken in our current lesbian communities? What impact has cultural feminism and classism had on this silence? And will a reunion of these two histories give us a stronger political grasp on how to protect both prostitutes and lesbians in this fearful time? If we can make any part of our society safer for these two groups of women, we will make the world safer for all women because whore and queer are the two accusations that symbolize lost womanhood — and a lost woman is open to direct control by the state.

The reclamation of one's history is a direct political act that forces the birth of a new consciousness; it is work that changes both the hearer and the speaker. I saw this very clearly when I attended the ground breaking conference in Toronto last year, "The Politics of Pornography, the Politics of Prostitution," and heard one of the keynote speakers, a stripper in Toronto's sex district, document the history of her art form in Toronto. Her telling created history as it communicated it. In her soft voice, she outlined the development of her profession and the oppression she and the others had to fight. It was a straight-forward history filled both with pride and problems; I was sitting with two other strippers, and as Debbie documented the changes and challenges in their work, they sat on the edge of their seats. They told me later they had never heard it put that way. Out of dirty jokes and scorn, a history was born. I hope that more and more women who perform or work in the worlds of public sex will choose to tell their people's story.

Final Note: The collage method used in this paper has certain dangers that I want my readers to be aware of. The first is that I may dilute the historical specific-ness of each instance of connection because both terms "lesbian" and "prostitute" have their own socially constructed legacies. Second, because I have culled the references from a wide variety of sources, and I am in no way an expert in any of the historical periods, I may over-simplify the resulting discoveries. However, I mean this work to be both factual an provocative, to break silences and to challenge assumptions and most of all, to provide the materials for us all — the lesbian, the prostitute and the feminist (who may be all three) — to have a more caring and complex understanding of each other so we can forge deeper and stronger bonds in the battles to come. *I want to thank Margo St. James, Priscilla Alexander and Gail Pheterson for their encouragement of my work and for their pioneer efforts in the prostitutes' rights movement.*

Bibliography

Berube, Allan. From a manuscript sent to the Lesbian Herstory Archives (LHA) Bullough, Vernon. "Prostitution, Psychiatry and History," in *The Frontiers of Sex Research*, ed. Vern Bullough. Buffalo: Prometheus Books, 1979.

Cario, Frank. *Female Homosexuality. A Psychodynamic Study of Lesbianism.* New York: Grove Press, 1954.

Cohen, Bernard. *Deviant Street Networks.* Lexington: Lexington Books, 1980.

Curb, Rosemary & Nancy Manahan. *Lesbian Nuns: Breaking Silence.* Tallahassee: Naiad Press, 1985.

Falk, Candace. *Love Anarchy and Emma Goldman.* New York: Holt, Rinehart and Winston, 1984.

Freedman, Estelle. *Their Sisters' Keepers: Women's Prison Reform in America 1830-1930.* Ann Arbor: The University of Michigan Press, 1981.

Hampton, Mabel. Tapes in possession of LHA.

Katz, Jonathan. *Gay/Lesbian Almanac A New Documentary*. New York: Harper and Row, 1983.

Laska, Vera. *Women in the Resistance and in the Holocaust: The Voices of Eyewitnesses*. Westport: Greenwood Press, 1983.

Maria. "Maria: A Prostitute Who Loves Women," *Proud Woman*, 11 (March-April 1972).

Millet, Kate. *The Prostitution Papers*. St. Albans: Paladin Books, 1975.

Otis, Leah Lydia. *Prostitution in Medieval Society*. Chicago: Univ. of Chicago Press, 1985.

Pearl, Cora. *Grand Horizontal*. New York: Stein and Day, 1983. First published in English, 1890.

Richards, Terri. From a statement read by the author, a lesbian prostitute, at "Prostitutes: Our Life: Lesbian and Straight," a meeting in San Francisco, June 22, 1982. Organized by the U.S. Prostitution Collective.

Rosen, Ruth. *The Lost Sisterhood: Prostitution in America 1900-1918*. Baltimore: Johns Hopkins Univ. Press, 1982.

Sanger, William. *History of Prostitution: Its Extent, Causes and Effect Throughout the World*. New York, 1876.

Stern, Jess. *Sisters of the Night*. New York: Gramercy Pub., 1956.

Streicher Rikki. Excerpt from interview that appeared in *In the Life*, no. 1, Fall 1982. Publication of the West Coast Lesbian Collection, available at LHA.

Stout, Ruth. "The Happier Hooker," *Daily News*, Sept 16, 1980.

Turrill, Barbara. "30 Minutes in the Life." Transcript of talk for WGBH radio, May 13, 1976. Available at LHA.

Weeks, Jeffrey. *Coming Out*. London: The Anchor Press, 1977. Woolston, H.B. Prostitution in the United States Prior to the Entrance of the United States into the World War. 1921. Reprinted- Montclair, New Jersey: Patterson-Smith, 1969.

Prostitutes Are Being Scapegoated for Heterosexual AIDS

Priscilla Alexander

The Statistics

Prostitutes are being blamed for transmitting AIDS to heterosexual men in this country, even though there is no evidence that such transmission has occurred. In the United States, as of December 22, 1986, five hundred fifty-seven men and five hundred thirty-three women, for whom the only known risk factor was heterosexual contact with a person who had AIDS or was at risk for AIDS, had been diagnosed with the disease. They total four percent of the 28,905 cases diagnosed since the Centers for Disease Control (CDC) began keeping weekly records (AIDS Weekly Surveillance Report, United States AIDS program, Center for Infectious Diseases, Centers for Disease Control) in June 1981. In 1986 alone, two hundred men and two hundred eighty-three women for whom the only known risk factor was heterosexual contact have reportedly come down with AIDS. Since 1981, the percentage of men who have gotten AIDS through heterosexual contact has remained constant at two percent of males cases, while the percentage of women who have gotten AIDS through sex with men is twenty-eight percent of female cases.*

If prostitutes were effectively transmitting the AIDS virus to their customers, there would be far more cases of white, heterosexual males diagnosed with AIDS than is reflected in the current statistics, because some IV users in New York have been infected with the AIDS virus since at least 1976, and a third to a half of street prostitutes use IV drugs. Some prostitutes have been diagnosed with the disease, others have tested positive for the antibodies, and a few have given birth to children who later came down with AIDS. The average street prostitute sees 1,500 customers a year.*

A simple calculation, taking as its basis that perhaps five percent of 20,000 prostitutes in New York were infected in 1978, follows: 4,000 prostitutes x 1,500 customers x 3 years [to allow some time for incubation] x 20 percent [one estimate of the rate of female to male transmission] = 360,000 diagnosed cases of AIDS among the client population. However, only approximately seventy men have been diagnosed with AIDS who claim contact with prostitutes as their only risk factor, again indicating that prostitutes are not passing the disease as quickly as is commonly believed. These men are being recorded as part of six hundred fifty men in the undetermined risk factor category.

No record of the number of prostitutes who have been diagnosed with AIDS is being kept by the Centers for Disease Control in Atlanta. If the results of various studies of the incidence of seropositivity among prostitutes and/or IV drug users described later in this essay are accurate, the likelihood is that any prostitutes who are diagnosed would be counted under the IV user category, which includes nine hundred eighty-eight women since 1981, and four hundred thirty-three women in 1986 alone. In fact, COYOTE only knows of five women thought to have AIDS who have been identified specifically as prostitutes, one in Hartford, Connecticut, three in San Diego, California, and one in San Francisco. And yet, according to the December 6, 1985 issue of the Centers for Disease Control *Morbidity and Mortality Weekly Report* (MMWR), in an article on perinatal transmission of the AIDS virus, the CDC identifies prostitutes as a high risk group, along with "women who have used drugs intravenously for non-medical purposes; women who were born in countries where heterosexual transmission is thought to play a major role...and women who are or have been sex partners of men who...are bisexual, have hemophilia," or who are members of high

---

*In this country, seventy percent of adult patients are gay or bisexual men (eight percent of whom are also IV users), seventeen percent are heterosexual IV users, two percent are recipients of whole blood transfusions or blood products, one percent are hemophiliacs, and three percent are heterosexuals with no identified risk factors. This last group, now referred to as "undetermined risk factors," includes a few men who claim contact with prostitutes as their only risk factor. In terms of contact tracing, there has not been a single documented case of a man getting AIDS from contact with a prostitute.

risk groups and/or have evidence of HIV infection. Before I discuss the evidence about prostitutes, per se, however, a few words about AIDS, itself, and how the virus is transmitted.

How AIDS is Transmitted

Most researchers believe that it is not easy to "catch" AIDS for a number of reasons. For one thing, the AIDS virus is not hardy; outside of the body it is easily killed by heat, chlorine bleach, some detergents, etc. Most researchers also believe that it takes repeated contact with the virus, or contact with a particularly large amount of the virus, to become infected.

Once the virus enters the blood stream, it attaches itself to what are called T helper (T4) cells that normally act as a kind of mastermind for the immune system, creating antibodies to fight foreign proteins that enter the body. The AIDS virus enters the nucleus of the T4 cells where, using genetic material in the host cell, it replicates itself over and over, finally destroying the host cell and moving on to other T4 cells. The destruction of the T4 cells leaves the immune system powerless to fight off certain kinds of "opportunistic" infections caused by bacteria, protozoa, and other infectious agents that are usually easily controlled by the human immune system. It is these opportunistic infections (e.g., toxoplasmosis, pneumo-cystic carinii pneumonia) that kill the patient. For an excellent discussion of the etiology of the disease, I recommend the articles by John Langone in the December 1985 and September 1986 issues of *Discover* magazine.

There are two efficient routes for transmission of the AIDS virus, direct blood to blood contact with an individual who is infected with the virus, and unprotected sexual contact with an infected partner. A third route of particular concern to women is perinatally, from infected women to their infants prior to or during childbirth.

The risk to users of intravenous (IV) drugs, especially heroin, is through sharing unsterilized needles, (a practice that is common in "shooting galleries" in some cities) because the virus is injected directly into the bloodstream. Likewise, hemophiliacs and others who, in the past, received blood transfusions or blood products containing the virus were at high risk of becoming infected because of the virus being directly transmitted into the bloodstream (all blood donations are now screened for the AIDS virus).

Sexual contact is the other major risk factor for AIDS. At first researchers thought that the *number* of sexual partners was the deciding factor, but more recent studies have suggested that the *kind* of sexual contact may be more important. Clearly, however, anyone who engages in casual sex with relative strangers is at a higher risk of coming into contact with a virus carrier than is someone who has been in a mutually monogamous relationship since before 1977, although the risk of becoming infected (as opposed to having sex with someone who is infected) will depend on the nature of the sexual activity.

Anal intercourse appears to be the most risky activity, particularly (although not exclusively) for the "receptive" partner. This is because the lining of the colon is very thin, designed for easy crossover of nutrients and wastes, and is easily torn, and also because blood vessels are extremely close to the surface. Fellatio appears not to be a particularly high-risk activity, as a longitudinal study of gay men, done by researchers at the University of California, San Francisco, found the same low seroconversion rate for men who were celibate and men who only engaged in oral sex. Very little of the virus is found in saliva, and it is thought that the enzymes in saliva and the acids in the digestive tract are effective in killing the virus contained in ejaculate. Vaginal intercourse is not thought to be as risky for either partner for two reasons; the vaginal walls are quite thick, and although researchers in San Francisco and Boston have been able to culture the virus from the vaginal secretions of some women with AIDS, it is difficult to do and the quantity of the virus appears to be small, in marked contrast to the amount of virus found in blood or semen. However, it may be that during menstruation the risk is greater because of the presence of blood and because the blood vessels are closer to the surface at that time. In any case, male-to-female transmission appears to be more efficient than female-to-male. Cunnilingus is thought to be a relatively low risk activity. Low risk does not, however, mean no risk, and all sexually active people should learn and practice safe sex.

Studies of Prostitutes

There have been a number of studies in this country to determine the prevalence of antibodies to the AIDS virus in prostitutes and intravenous drug users, including some tests of blood that had been stored since the late 1970s. There have also been a number of studies of prostitutes and their customers in several countries in Central

Africa where AIDS is almost exclusively a heterosexual disease.

On the East Coast, the seropositivity rates have been relatively high. In Miami, according to the New York Times, ten of twenty-five prostitutes (forty percent) who visited an AIDS screening clinic for testing were seropositive; eight of the ten admitted to intravenous drug use. A problem with this study is that it was done at an AIDS screening clinic, and generally, the only people to be examined and/or tested at AIDS screening clinics are people who already have symptoms suggestive of AIDS. Thus, the seropositivity rate might not be reflective of the whole prostitute population in Miami, but rather only of those who thought they had AIDS.[1]

In New York, in a voluntary study conducted by Don Des Jarlais, of the New York State Division of Substance Abuse Services, two-thirds of twenty women who used IV drugs were seropositive. In a companion study interviewing seventy-five women in jail for prostitution, one-third to one-half were IV users, of whom Des Jarlais assumes that two-thirds would be likely to be seropositive, although he did not test the women in jail for antibodies because of the invasive nature of the test. Thus, up to a third of street prostitutes in New York may have been infected through IV use. Tests of stored blood samples from IV users in New York City, dating back to the late seventies, showed that one out of eleven (nine percent) from 1978 was seropositive, while in 1979, fourteen out of forty-nine (twenty-nine percent) were seropositive. This study probably gives a good indication of the seropositivity rate among street prostitutes in New York City, since they are the ones who spend time in jail, but should not be construed to tell anything about the prostitute population as a whole. For one thing, while one-third to one-half of street prostitutes use IV drugs, very few prostitutes who work away from the streets use needles.[2]

The figures have been much lower on the West Coast. Mandatory testing in 1985 of ninety-two women arrested for prostitution in Seattle, using the ELISA test, found that only five (5.5 percent) were seropositive. Retesting at a later date with the more accurate Western Blot test found that none were seropositive. A 1986 study of thirty-five women, all but two of them prostitutes, found that none were seropositive. Participants were recruited in a clinic for sexually transmitted diseases, so it is likely that if the virus was prevalent in Seattle, it would have shown up in this group.[3]

A "voluntary" study of women in jail in Orange County, California, found that ten out of four hundred women (2.5 percent) were seropositive, almost all of them IV users. In addition to the fact that people in prison do not always believe they have the right to say no when asked to participate in a study, this study is again of street prostitutes, (among whom IV drug use is higher than it is among other prostitutes) as street prostitutes are likely to be the ones in jail.[4]

A voluntary, community study in San Francisco found that only nine (four percent) of two hundred twenty sexually active women in San Francisco were seropositive, and that the risk was the same for prostitutes and non-prostitute women. Some epidemiologists feel this study is skewed because all participants come to the study in response to either articles in the newspapers, flyers that are distributed in bars and on the street, and face-to-face outreach on the street. However, my impression from talking with the interviewers working on this study is that the prostitute population is a fairly decent cross-section.[5]

Interestingly enough, both the New York and San Francisco studies found that most of the prostitutes interviewed consistently used condoms. In contrast, the San Francisco study found that non-prostitute women were much less likely to use condoms.

A study at Sybil Brand Women's Prison in Los Angeles found that six percent of ninety women tested were seropositive. Fifty-two percent of the women, who ranged in age from eighteen to thirty-two, used IV drugs and thirty-two percent regularly engaged in anal intercourse. This study is skewed in the same way as the Orange County and New York City studies in that the participants were in jail.[6]

The difference between the East and West Coasts appears to be directly related to the different antibody prevalence in the IV user population. In New York City, it is estimated that forty to fifty percent of users of IV drugs are seropositive, while in San Francisco, the incidence is only about ten percent. In the United States, the use of IV drugs is more common among street prostitutes, who represent ten to twenty percent of all prostitutes, than among prostitutes who work off the street, who are more likely to use alcohol, non-injected drugs or no drugs at all.

In the United States, there have been no reported studies of seropositivity in heterosexual men who do not have AIDS or ARC (AIDS Related Complex) that includes data on their contact with prostitutes and/or their use or nonuse of condoms, although some data exists on heterosexual male AIDS patients. A study by Robert R. Redfield, M.D., et al, published in the *Journal of the American Medical Association*, found that of ten heterosexual men at Walter Reed Army Hospital who were diagnosed with AIDS or ARC, eight had had sexual contact with prostitutes in various parts of the world, one had multiple female sex partners in New York City, and one had sex with a woman from Haiti. Redfield, et al, believe these cases are evidence of female-to-male transmission. The study also reported on

253

five women diagnosed with AIDS or ARC, three of whom were married to men with AIDS, one of whom was a sex partner of a bisexual male in New York City, and one of whom was a sex partner of a New York City IV user. Since the publication of Redfield's article, however, a series of letters have been published in *JAMA* disputing his findings for a variety of reasons, including the consequences of admitting to homosexual activity and/or IV drug use in the military. Interestingly enough, when the United States Army tested fifteen prostitutes near a U.S. Air Force base in Honduras and found that six of the women were seropositive, and then claimed the study as proof that prostitutes were infecting GIs, Redfield disputed their claim. He said that the direction of transmission was more likely to be from the GIs to the prostitutes, because none of the women in the study used IV drugs.[7]

The Los Angeles Times reported, in December 1985, that eight heterosexual men in Los Angeles, all of whom had a history of promiscuity including visits with prostitutes, had recently been diagnosed with AIDS.[8] It is difficult to interpret any of these reports, however, because no reports on heterosexual male AIDS patients have included information on the use of condoms.

In Central Africa, the rate of seropositivity for prostitutes ("prostitute" being a term that is apparently applied to any woman who is sexually active outside of marriage, whether or not money is exchanged) is much higher. According to the *New York Times*, in Rwanda, thirty-three women identified as prostitutes were tested for the anti-bodies. Twenty-nine (eighty-eight percent) were seropositive. A second study in Rwanda found that eighty percent of eighty-four prostitutes were seropositive. However, a study of twenty-five men identified as customers found that only seven (twenty-eight percent) were seropositive. The twenty-five men reported a median of thirty-one sex partners each year, thirty of them prostitutes.[9]

In Kenya, a study of ninety women identified as prostitutes found that forty-nine (fifty-four percent) were seropositive, three-fourths of whom had symptoms of ARC. However, a study of thirty-five sexually active men found that only three (nine percent) had antibodies, compared to two (five percent) of forty-five medical personnel studied as controls.[10]

In Central Africa, the ratio of male to female AIDS cases is 1.1:1, in marked contrast to the picture in the United States and Western Europe. Nathan Clumeck, et al, reported on heterosexual promiscuity among African *male* patients with AIDS in a letter to the *New England Journal of Medicine*. They found that of fifty-eight men with AIDS or ARC, forty-seven (eighty-one percent) were regular customers of prostitutes (average thirty-two sexual partners per year), while of fifty-eight men without symptoms, only twenty (thirty-four percent) had regular contact with prostitutes, with an average of three partners per year. They also reported that ten out of forty-two (twenty-four percent) African women who had been diagnosed with AIDS in Brussels and Kigali, Rwanda were professional prostitutes, although they did not report the number of sexual contacts the women with AIDS/ARC had or compare prostitutes with nonprostitutes, or women with AIDS/ARC with a control group of women.[11]

There are a number of differences in the way prostitutes work and in the health care delivery systems in the United States and the countries in Central Africa that help explain the differences in seropositivity. In the United States, most street prostitutes routinely use condoms for all sexual contact with customers, including fellatio (the most commonly requested service). Since the advent of the AIDS epidemic, the use of condoms has increased, particularly in cities with large numbers of AIDS cases. Also since the epidemic, prostitutes who work off the street — in massage parlors and brothels, for escort services, and independently as call girls — have modified their business practices to protect themselves from the virus. In Central Africa, however, condoms are not available, partly because of their cost and partly for cultural reasons, not the least of which is the impact of the Catholic Church.

While most of the prostitutes in the United States who have been diagnosed with AIDS or who have tested positive for antibodies have a recent history of IV drug use, such IV drug use is reported to be rare among prostitutes in Central Africa. However, many clinics in Rwanda and other Central African countries are not able to sterilize needles between patients because of the prohibitive cost, and some researchers think that the virus may be transmitted via unsterilized needles in clinics, particularly urban veneral disease clinics, as well as through heterosexual contact. Finally, female genital circumcision and infibulation appear to be more common in Central Africa than it was previously thought. As a result, women often bleed during sexual intercourse, which greatly increases their infection rate, and which could account both for the high seropositivity rate among women and for the high incidence of actual AIDS.[12]

In the Central African studies, a lower percentage of male customers (nine to twenty-eight percent) than female prostitutes (fifty-four to ninety percent) are seropositive, suggesting that female-to-male transmission is not as efficient as the studies of male AIDS patients would imply, although it probably does occur. On the other hand, the figures suggest that male customers are infecting female prostitutes as much as the reverse, although there has been no concern expressed, except in the American feminist press, about the risk to prostitutes.

Some researchers have begun to speculate that, since the virus is relatively difficult to culture from vaginal secretions (in contrast to blood or semen), men may, in fact, be infecting each other through the prostitutes (i.e., that infected semen from one customer remains in the vagina and later infects another customer). Thus, it is possible that men who do not use condoms may infect both women and each other.

Prevention

It is now widely accepted that careful use of condoms, for vaginal and anal intercourse and for fellatio, will reduce the risk of transmitting the AIDS virus. Their usefulness in reducing the risk of other sexually transmitted diseases is well documented, and one study at the University of California/San Francisco found that both latex and natural condoms block the passage of the virus in the laboratory. However, condoms do break (and some users have reported that natural condoms are less flexible, causing them to slip off more easily). Therefore, many researchers recommend that spermicides containing nonoxynol-9, a detergent that has been shown to kill the AIDS virus in the laboratory, as a back-up to the condom, unless one or both partners is allergic to nonoxynol-9.

Because of our society's reluctance to openly discuss sexual issues (in spite of a fascination with pornography), education about safe sex is being stifled. The television networks all have formal policies against running condom commercials, although they have no such compunction about running ads for tampons and disposable douches. At the time of this writing (January 1987), all of the networks, including public television, have been running news stories on the refusal of the networks to carry ads for condoms, and so it is likely that this policy will change. Interestingly enough, the national head of Planned Parenthood, in a MacNeill-Lehrer report on this issue, appeared to have difficulty with the concept of promoting condoms to prevent sexually transmitted diseases, and appeared to blame prostitutes for any spread of AIDS to the heterosexual population.

Although the federal and state governments have granted funds to numerous grassroots and government agencies for education, these funds have been held up because of fears that the educational materials (including brochures and videotapes) will be "too explicit."

At the Second World Whores' Congress in Brussels, held in October 1986, AIDS prevention was a major topic of discussion. The prostitutes from West Germany, where prostitution is legal but the prostitutes are regulated, reported that because they were required to be tested for antibodies to the AIDS virus on a regular basis, customers were refusing to use condoms. The Congress sent a telegram to the West German public health department about this and, as a result, the department has launched campaigns to educate customers about the need for condoms. British television stations have begun not only to carry ads for condoms, but to broadcast instructions on their proper use to prevent AIDS. Meanwhile, American stations continue their blackout.

There is a similar resistance to explicit drug-related education to prevent the spread of AIDS among IV users who are forced to share needles. In many states, it is illegal to sell needles without a prescription (average price twenty cents each), and so they are sold in an illegal market (for two to three dollars each). California's State Department of Public Health has established a review committee to "evaluate" all printed materials to be published by agencies receiving state funds (whether or not state funds are to be used to print the brochures), because of this reluctance to "'condone" controversial sexual activity or drug use.

Policy Considerations

AIDS is a terrifying disease because it is virtually always fatal, infectious (meaning you can catch it from someone), and sexually transmitted, and sexually transmitted diseases always produce an anxiety that is intensified in a sex- negative society like ours. In addition, the incubation period for AIDS in adults is from two to five years (some estimate up to fourteen years), during which time most researchers believe the virus can be transmitted from one person to another even though the carrier may have no symptoms or any idea that he or she *is* a carrier. The high fear of AIDS underlies the obvious desire for easy "solutions," and could result in such things as mandatory testing, quarantines, employment discrimination, and possibly mandatory sterilization.

In 1986, several states considered legislation to require certain groups of criminal offenders — especially prostitutes and sex offenders — to be tested upon conviction and/or as a condition for probation. So far, such proposals have been defeated, but as the epidemic spreads, it is likely that additional proposals will be introduced. At the present time, California's laws requiring consent and confidentiality of results is binding even when the individual is convicted of an offense and/or incarcerated. However, in Nevada, which has no laws regarding either consent or confidentiality, the public health department has adopted regulations requiring all women who work in legal brothels to be tested every month. Moreover, when one woman tested positive, she was fired from her job and her name, photograph and description were published in the newspaper. Some conservative members of the Nevada legislature are beginning to talk about closing the brothels "to prevent AIDS," although other legislators have pointed out that closing the brothels merely means an increase in street prostitution.

There have also been a number of proposals introduced that would, in one way or another, make it a crime for someone who is antibody positive to engage in sex with anyone else (whether the sex is mutually voluntary or forced, without regard to the use of condoms). So far, such proposals have failed.

A number of states have proposed mandatory testing of all people who apply for marriage licenses. In California, this was changed to a requirement that all people who apply be given information about the transmission of the AIDS virus, but a new mandatory marriage license bill was introduced again in the 1987 session.

In November 1986, the federal Food and Drug Administration issued guidelines to blood banks recommending that anyone who has worked as a prostitute since 1977 be barred from giving blood. However, the FDA stipulated that customers of prostitutes merely wait six months before donating — six months being sufficient time for antibodies that would show in routine ELISA blood screenings to be produced. The FDA, as its reason for treating customers differently from prostitutes, said that barring all customers would mean not having enough blood donors. Both the Women's AIDS Network in San Francisco and COYOTE protested the recommendations; if blood banks continue to add *groups* of people to the list of those who should not donate, rather than barring people who engage in specific *practices*, there really won't be anyone left to donate blood (except maybe totally celibate nuns who have never experimented with IV drug use). Both COYOTE and the Women's AIDS Network recommended that the existing guidelines (which bar gay and bisexual men as well as anyone who has ever used IV drugs) be changed to exclude people who have engaged in the following practices: 1) sharing IV needles without thoroughly sterilizing them between users; 2) engaging in vaginal intercourse, anal intercourse or fellatio without a condom when the partner is antibody positive, or when the antibody status is unknown; 3) receiving a blood transfusion or blood products; 4) being tatooed, piercing one's ears or receiving acupuncture; or 5) being inseminated by a donor who is antibody positive or whose antibody status is unknown. Although a number of officials from blood banks and from the American Association of Blood Banks said that our proposals were reasonable, the blacklisting of prostitutes, regardless of their individual risk, still stands.

Although most public health officials believe quarantines would be useless for this disease because of its long incubation period, the subject keeps being discussed, particularly by conservative candidates for public office. California voters, in 1986, had to mount an expensive campaign to defeat a LaRouche-sponsored initiative that would have mandated testing and reporting, and which recommended internment/quarantine. The measure was defeated overwhelmingly in every county in the state; however, similar measures are still being discussed in other states.

As discussed above, in Seattle, Washington, all women arrested for prostitution were tested for antibodies for several months without their consent. Since prostitution is already illegal in all fifty states (with the exception of some rural counties in Nevada) and the District of Columbia, it is difficult to see what such mandatory testing will accomplish, unless it is decided to incarcerate antibody-positive prostitutes for the rest of their lives. At any one time, there are approximately one million women who work as prostitutes in this country, and as many as ten to fifteen percent of all women have done so at some time in their lives. Even if the police were able to quarantine all seropositive prostitutes, it would not prevent the spread of AIDS. It would only provide an illusion of protection; other women would take the place of those who had been arrested. Some would already be IV drug users, others would become IV users, some would contract the virus from infected customers who failed to use condoms — interestingly, no one has suggested that all men be tested for the AIDS antibody. And AIDS would still be transmitted by nonprostitute men and women who were not rounded up by police.

The California State Legislature, in 1986, considered a bill that would have required all people applying for marriage licenses to be tested for antibodies to the AIDS virus. The bill has tremendous implications because of the potential for discrimination against individuals identified by name as seropositive. Fortunately, the mandatory testing provision was replaced with a requirement that all people applying for a license be given information on how AIDS is transmitted. The supposed justification for marriage license testing is that a small number of seropositive women, with and without symptoms of AIDS or ARC, have given birth to children who later developed AIDS. Some doctors have recommended that seropositive women not get pregnant, an unspoken implication being that pregnant women who discover that they are seropositive should have abortions and/or that nonpregnant seropositive women should either stop having sex or be sterilized. And this in spite of the fact that not all babies born to women with the antibodies come down with AIDS or even remain seropositive after the first few months. The December 6, 1985 issue of *MMWR (Morbidity and Mortality Weekly Report)* contains extensive data on this aspect of the disease.

We must also recognize that AIDS is not just a disease of white men. Forty percent of men and sixty-nine percent of women diagnosed with AIDS are people of color. Because of the greater poverty of people of color in our society, they are less able to obtain good medical care or to seek medical attention early in the course of the disease. Patients of color die sooner after diagnosis than white patients.

Conclusion

An underlying assumption seems to have been that when women or gay/bisexual men get AIDS it is their fault, but if heterosexual men come down with the disease, it is the fault of women and gay/bisexual men. A related assumption may be that when a "chaste" woman gets AIDS from her husband, she is a victim; however, her husband does not appear to carry any blame. As this epidemic continues, it will be increasingly important for us, as feminists, to know the facts; we need to exert leadership in dealing with the disease without blaming its victims. Concern should be for *everyone's* welfare: gay men, IV users, prostitutes, and other stigmatized people unfortunate enough to be infected with the virus. Old prejudices about these groups cause facts to be distorted and even misrepresented, perhaps unconsciously, to the detriment of public health. It is up to those of us who are used to reading between the lines and looking for evidence of bias and prejudice to help keep the focus on AIDS and its prevention, not on punishment.

The solution to the AIDS crisis is accurate and explicit education about risk reduction, as well as adequate funding for research into the causes, treatment, and prevention of the disease. Scapegoating will solve nothing.

Notes:

1. Miami, FL: The women were voluntarily tested in an AIDS screening clinic, as reported in the Los Angeles Times, December 8, 1985. The results of this study are skewed in that AIDS screening clinics only test people who are symptomatic or are otherwise thought to have AIDS or ARC.

2. New York, NY: These figures are based on two studies, one of twenty female IV users in a drug treatment program, two-thirds of whom tested positive, and one of seventy-five prostitutes in jail, one-third to one-half of whom were IV users, although they were not tested for the AIDS virus antibodies. Two-thirds of one-third to one-half of seventy-five women is equivalent to seventeen to twenty-five women, for a seropositivity rate of twenty-two to thirty-three percent. Based on personal conversations with Don Des Jarlais, of the New York State Division of Substance Abuse Services in 1985 and 1986.

3. The initial results of the first Seattle study were reported in a number of publications, including the December 6, 1985 *MMWR*. Although Hunter Hansfield, M.D., the Director of Public Health, has been urged to publish the results of the more accurate Western Blot test, he has declined to do so. My source is personal conversations with Debra Boyer, a member of the Seattle AIDS Advisory Task Force, on September 27, 1986 and again on November 8, 1986, and Ann Collier, M.D., on December 20, 1986. According to Boyer, the seropositivity in the IV population of Seattle appears to be extremely low. Collier is the chief investigator of the second study of thirty-five women, in which all participants were seronegative. Collier hopes to expand her study to replicate Project AWARE's study comparing prostitutes with a control population of women with multiple male partners or one or more high risk partners.

4. The Orange County, CA study was done in jail. The women were invited, but not required, to participate, although "voluntary" participation in an institutional setting, particularly in a prison, is questionable. Based on personal conversations with Roseann Lowery, from the office of Tom Prendergast, PhD, of the Orange County Department of Public Health on October 25, 1985.

5. The San Francisco figures are from a study by Project AWARE that was reported at the National Public Health Association meeting in Washington, DC, November 20, 1985. The co-chief investigators are Judith Cohen, PhD and Constance Wofsy, M.D. This study is probably the least skewed, at least

as far as the prostitutes are concerned, because of the fact that a broad range of prostitutes have been involved, including women who work at all levels, women who use IV drugs and women who don't, etc. They have been recruited to participate in a wide variety of ways in order to ensure a representative sample. Some researchers feel that because participants volunteer in response to outreach (i.e., they are not randomly selected), they are therefore more likely to be seropositive. However, my impression is that the participants are not necessarily worried about themselves; rather they are interested in participating in order to help further the research.

6. The Los Angeles study was done in Sybil Brand Institute for Women, on a voluntary basis, as reported by Amy A. Ross, PhD, from the Department of Pathology, USC School of Medicine, at the California NOW Conference, May 17, 1986. In a private conversation in December 1986, Scott Aguilar, who is working on the USC study, told me that the women who participated in the study were not only in jail, they were the women who had not been bailed out. Thus, they were even more likely to be IV users than the women who got bailed out quickly. Aguilar noted that some of the women tested positive for other sexually transmitted diseases, such as Chlamydia, gonorrhea and syphilis. Although Aguilar stated that the report to the Centers for Disease Control would stress the skewed nature of the sample and the fact that the figures should not be considered indicative for all prostitutes, it was not clear at the time of this writing how this study will be reported by the CDC in the MMWR.

7. Walter Reed Army Hospital, Washington, DC: This study was reported on in an article by Robert R. Redfield, MD, et al, in the October 18, 1985 issue of the Journal of the American Medical Association, pp. 2094-2096. Letters disagreeing with Redfield's conclusions were published in the April 4, 1986 issue, pp. 1702-1706. The Honduras study was reported in the Miami Herald, April 11, 1986. Redfield's response was reported to me by Sharon Young, of ABC-TV News, in a personal conversation, on December 13, 1986.

8. Los Angeles, CA: As reported in an article by Miles Corwin in the Los Angeles Times, December 8, 1985, and confirmed in a personal conversation. Corwin told me that at least one of the men had had sexual contact only with prostitutes. Beth Bergman, in an article slated to be published in the Stanford Law Review, discusses her conversation on September 18, 1986 with Dr. Rand Stoneburner, Director of the AIDS Surveillance Unit in New York City, and a social worker who interviews people with AIDS, in which both report the difficulty in determining risk factors using the standard questionnaire. They reported that when they departed from the questionnaire, and discussed risk factor with the patients, most who had initially reported contact with prostitutes later admitted to homosexual activity or IV drug use and shared needles. Thus, out of one hundred fifty-six cases of heterosexual transmission, one hundred fifty-four were females.

9. The figures for Rwanda and Kenya are taken from an article in the New York Times, November 8, 1985.

10. Kreiss, et al, "AIDS Virus Infections in Nairobi Prostitutes," *New England Journal of Medicine*, February 13, 1986, pp. 414-418.

11. As reported in a letter, by N. Clumeck, et al, published in the July 18, 1985 issue of *The New England Journal of Medicine*.

12. Hornaday, Ann, "New Theory: AIDS and Women," reporting on the speculations of Uli Linke, a doctoral candidate in anthropology at the University of California at Berkeley. *Magazine*, November 1986, p. 28.

PART III:
UNITED WE STAND, DIVIDED WE DIE: SEX WORKERS ORGANIZED

Whisper: Women Hurt in Systems of Prostitution Engaged in Revolt

Sarah Wynter

There has been a deliberate attempt to validate men's perceived need, and self-proclaimed right, to buy and sell women's bodies for sexual use. This has been accomplished, in part, by euphemizing prostitution as an occupation. Men have promoted the cultural myth that women actively seek out prostitution as a pleasurable economic alternative to low-paying, low-skilled, monotonous labor, conveniently ignoring the conditions that insure women's inequality and the preconditions which make women vulnerable to prostitution. Men have been so successful in reinforcing this myth by controlling the culture that their central role in the commercial sexual exploitation of women has become invisible. The myth is so pervasive that when women come forward and expose the conditions they've endured, the injuries they've sustained through systems of prostitution, they are most often disbelieved or considered to be the exception rather than the rule.

Men's distortion about the realities of women's lives to serve their own self-interest is not new to feminists. Not long ago, we struggled to debunk the lie that women invited, and in fact enjoyed rape. That we "asked for it." Not that long ago, we struggled to expose the lie that battered wives provoked attacks, that they "must like it or they would leave." It was not that long ago that we unmasked the lie that children were complicit in incestuous abuse, that they "must have liked it or they would have told."

When rape victims failed to report their attacks, when battered wives remained in abusive relationships, when incest survivors kept childhood molestations a secret, we, as feminists, didn't interpret their silence as support for the culture's denial of their victimization.

Instead, we joined together to condemn rape, battery, and sexual abuse and to demand legislation that would empower the victims.

These women, the raped, the battered, the incest survivors, along with their poor and disadvantaged sisters, are the selfsame women who are actively recruited and coerced into systems of prostitution. And the male hierarchy is spreading the same lies about the same women again: "They want it. They like it. If they didn't they would leave."

Another way that men attempt to validate prostitution as a career for women is by proposing that because of women's economic subordination (which men have insured), it is unfair to deprive women of the opportunity to earn a living wage by selling a service that they are compelled (by men) to offer for free. As feminists, we are bound to not only criticize and attempt to rectify economic subordination and compulsory sexual submission (which we have defined as rape), but the institution of prostitution which is the commerce of sexual abuse and inequality.

In parts of Europe and South America, drug kingpins hire poor women to transport heroin and cocaine into the United States. These women are called "mules," and they smuggle the drugs past customs by swallowing huge and potentially fatal doses in latex balloons. If there are no delays in the woman's voyage, when she arrives at her destination, the balloons are passed through her stool intact. This is not always the case. Sometimes one of the balloons is eaten away by the acids in the woman's stomach and she dies in transit from a massive overdose.

Some people claim that drug smuggling is a lucrative industry. And it is, for the dealer safe at home in France, or Italy, or Bogata. But for the woman captured by customs officials, or lying on the coroner's table, it was an act of desperation. Shall we then say that because a woman coerced by poverty gambles with her life to secure an income that being a mule is a valid occupational alternative that she freely chooses? Every time a prostitute climbs into a car or walks into a hotel with a strange man, coerced by the circumstances of her existence, sexual abuse, rape, battery or just plain poverty, she risks her freedom and her very life. Can we then say that prostitution is a valid occupational alternative that she freely chooses?

Prostitution is taught in the home, socially validated by a sexual libertarian ideology, and enforced by both the church and the state. That is to say that both the conservative right and the liberal left male hierarchies collude to teach and keep women in prostitution. The right, by demanding that women be sexually and socially subordi-

267

nate to one man in marriage, and the left, by demanding that women be sexually and socially subordinate to all men through prostitution and pornography. Their common goal is to exercise their prerogative to control and own women in both the private and public spheres.

Prostitution is taught to women in the home when the courts uphold the moral imperatives of the church (that women be unconditionally sexually available to their husbands), by maintaining the marital rape exemption in the penal code of most states. Prostitution is taught to girls in the home through paternal sexual abuse. The fact that social scientists have reported that upwards of seventy-five percent of women in the sex industry were sexually abused as children suggests that the ramifications of incest and sexual assault in childhood are causal factors in prostitution. Prostitution is taught through the social sanctioning of the commercial sexual exploitation of pornographers which maintains women's second class status and yet is touted by the liberal left as women's sexual liberation.

Prostitution isn't like anything else. Rather everything else is like prostitution, because it is the model for women's condition, for gender stratification and its logical extension, sex discrimination. Prostitution is founded on enforced sexual abuse under a system of male supremacy that is itself built along a continuum of coercion — fear, force, racism and poverty. For every real difference between women, prostitution exists to erase our diversity, distinction, and accomplishment while reducing all of us to meat to be bought, sold, traded, used, discarded, degraded, ridiculed, humiliated, maimed, tortured, and all too often, murdered for sex.

Prostitution is the foundation upon which pornography is built. Pornography is the vehicle by which men sexualize women's chattel status. Pornography cannot exist without prostitution. They are interdependent and create a sexual ghetto that insures women's inequality. It is impossible to separate pornography from prostitution. The acts are identical except that in pornography there is a permanent record of the woman's abuse.

The emerging profile of women used in prostitution clearly does not reflect the lies promoted in pornography and the mainstream media. As these social science ethnologies document, these are women with few resources; most are poor and have been subjected to sexual assault, rape, and battery. The average age for women entering prostitution is sixteen, although the number of nine-, ten-, and eleven-year-old girls in the industry is on the rise. Over half of adult prostitutes were adolescent runaways; approximately seventy-five percent of these teenagers were victims of sexual abuse. Between half and seventy-five percent of prostitutes have pimps, and almost all of them have had pimps at one time in the past. Many are women of color. Many are substance abusers or drug addicts. Many have dependent children. Many were battered wives who have escaped from, or were abandoned by, abusive husbands and forced into prostitution in order to support themselves and their children.

We, the women of WHISPER, reject the lie that women freely choose prostitution from a whole array of economic alternatives that exist under civil equity. In the United States women have been unable to pass the Equal Rights Amendment. Eighty percent of the people in poverty in this country are women with dependent children. Women earn approximately sixty-seven cents for every dollar men earn. It is estimated that one out of every four girls will be sexually abused before the age of sixteen, that a woman is battered every eighteen seconds, raped every four minutes, that two thousand to four thousand women are beaten to death by their husbands annually, and most states still carry a marital exemption in their penal code. Clearly this does not reflect civil equality.

We reject the lie that turning tricks is sexual pleasure or agency for women. We reject the lie that women can and do become wealthy in systems of prostitution. We reject the lie that women control and are empowered in systems of prostitution. We reject the false divisions imposed by society which differentiate between pornography, peep shows, live sex shows, and prostitution as it is commonly defined. Each is a type of commercial sexual exploitation and abuse which reduces women to commodities for the pleasure and profit of men. Each is premised on inequality due to a condition of birth: gender. Because the only prerequisite necessary to be targeted for this abuse is to be born female, the commercial trafficking in women is by definition a form of sex discrimination.

We reject the false hierarchy imposed on women by men which claims that "call girls" are inherently better off than "street walkers," when the only real difference between the two is the private abuse of women juxtaposed to the public abuse of women. The equivalent of this would be stranger rape juxtaposed to marital rape.

We oppose current and proposed legislation (including *current* versions of criminalization, legalization, and decriminalization *with* zoning or regulatory provisions) which treat the institution of prostitution as an "urban blight" or an "eyesore" that needs to be hidden from view yet kept available to men. These "solutions" insure men's unconditional sexual access to women without consideration for the physical and psychological consequences to individual women and the overall damage to the civil and social status of all women (by defining us as genitals that can be bought, sold, or traded). We want the state to stop defining prostitution as a "victimless" crime or as a crime committed by women, and acknowledge it for what it is — a crime committed against women by men. We want the state to stop arresting prostitutes and to start enforcing laws against men who traffic in women's bodies for their own pleasure and profit.

WHISPER has been founded by women who have escaped systems of prostitution to create a forum for us to speak out about the realities of our lives and to explore ideas for change. We have chosen the acronym WHISPER because women in systems of prostitution do whisper among ourselves about the coercion, degradation, sexual abuse and battery in our lives, while the myths about prostitution are shouted out in pornography, in mainstream media, and by self-appointed "experts" who have admittedly never experienced prostitution. We expect WHISPER to be a tool for change in our lives, and in our lifetime. Our purpose is to make the sexual enslavement of women history.

Workers: Introducing the English Collective of Prostitutes

Nina Lopez-Jones

In 1975 the English Collective of Prostitutes came together as an autonomous organization within the International Wages for Housework Campaign. Since prostitute women are illegal workers who, most of the time, can't afford to come out publicly (and often not even to family and friends), its founding members called on a non-prostitute woman, Selma James, housewife, mother and founder of the Campaign, to be our first public spokeswoman. Not only was she willing to be trained by prostitute women, she also trained us: her experience as a long- standing organizer in the black and women's movements helped shape the Collective's connections and developed our skills and confidence. This built our autonomy and protected us from separatism: we needed our own independent power base so that we could work together with other women and men whose support we needed to win.

As more of us were able to speak for ourselves, we developed a policy of not revealing who was and who wasn't on the game. We wanted our members, illegal working women, to be able to speak out without having to come out. Also, we knew how the media manipulates the movement by creating "stars" who do not represent the constituency they are supposed to speak for. We were determined to choose our spokeswomen on the basis of their ability to represent the struggle of prostitute women, and keep them accountable to the women's movement for legal, civil, and economic rights.

The media is always looking for the "real" prostitute: the perfect victim — the street walker controlled by a pimp and preferably on drugs, who hates men and may be painfully inarticulate; or the professional whore — the high class call girl who is ready to defend

clients and declares how much she loves her job. These are the most
common examples of the many stereotypes which allow the media to
divide us from other women, to portray prostitute women as more
exploited and/or lower in consciousness than others. Social workers,
academics, politicians and even some prostitutes' organizations have
traded on these stereotypes, making a career or at least rising in
acceptance by agreeing to them. Behind these stereotypes is hidden
the most crucial truth: that prostitute women have poverty and
overwork in common with each other and with most others, especially women. They also share the increasing criminalization of
those who refuse this destiny.

For Prostitutes Against Prostitution

The title of our first statement in 1975 conveyed our starting
premise: for prostitutes against prostitution. By 1986, we had behind
us eleven years of practical organizing on that basis and we wrote:

> The 1980 United Nations figure, that women do two-thirds of
> the world's work and receive ten percent of the world's income
> (the International Labour Organization says five percent) and
> own one percent of the world's assets, spells out the basic truth
> about prostitution, both in the Third World and in Europe and
> other metropolitan countries. Women, who work at least twice
> as much as men, get much less income; therefore we are the
> sellers to men who are the buyers. It has been estimated that
> seventy percent of prostitute women in Britain are mothers,
> mostly single mothers, who go on the game to support them-
> selves and their families. To bypass economics and especially
> leave out women's poverty, as the political and moral right wing
> always does, hides the single biggest truth about women's lives.
> It undermines the basic case against the injustice of the
> prostitution laws. And it undermines the basis for prostitute
> and non-prostitute women working together against the sexism
> which dooms most of the women of the world to poverty and/or
> a twenty-four hour work day.
>
> Since 1975, we have been campaigning for the abolition of all
> laws against prostitutes, laws which punish women for refusing
> poverty; and for money, housing, legal defense and other
> resources to be made available to women and children on the
> game or who want to get off the game; for safe houses for
> runaway children where they could be anonymous to protect
> them from being picked up by the police and sent back home,
> sometimes to violence; and for higher wages and benefits so that

no woman or child is forced into prostitution by poverty, men, financial dependence or by lack of economic alternatives.

The workshop we held at the Forum for Non-Governmental Organizations at the United Nations End of Decade for Women Conference in Nairobi, Kenya, last July, attended by over three hundred women and a few men from all over the world, confirmed the importance of economics. Third World women present, and especially women from India, made it clear to reluctant social workers who didn't want to listen (as usual) that for many women and children the only alternative to prostitution is starvation. Rising unemployment and cuts in wages, benefits and social services have shown the poverty there is in metropolitan countries also (and this is increasing daily), where millions of women and children live below the so-called poverty line.*

No Bad Women Just Bad Laws

When we began, the fight for prostitute women to be acknowledged as part of the women's movement for financial independence and control over our own bodies, and part of the working class movement for more money and less work, was completely new. It is still controversial. Most of women's liberation was hostile to prostitute women on the grounds that exchanging sex for money was uniquely degrading. They said it encouraged rape by leading men to believe that all women are available, conveniently forgetting that men already thought that. The sex industry is not the only industry which is male-dominated and degrades women, but it is the industry where the workers are illegal and can least defend publicly our right to our jobs. We argued that for some women to get paid for what all women are expected to do for free is a source of power for all women to refuse *any* free sex.

The prostitution laws aim to divide women between those of us who are "respectable," "good" women and those of us who are "loose," "bad" women for refusing poverty by working in the sex industry. Money, in the eyes of the Establishment, makes good (working class) women bad. We recently protested against the way a murdered woman was put on trial by the media which implied that her parents were more distressed to find out their daughter was on the game than that she had been murdered. This is not unusual. In 1981

*Letter to Annemiek Onstenk, Women's Bureau of the Green-Alternative European Link in the Rainbow, European Parliament.

we picketed the High Court throughout the trial of the Yorkshire Ripper, a serial murderer who killed thirteen women and attacked many others. As in the similar cases of the Green River and Los Angeles murders, the police used the prostitution laws as an excuse to do nothing, labeling the victims as prostitutes, who were in any case black and/or too poor to matter. They only took the murders seriously after a relatively better off "respectable" woman was killed. Many more women died as a result, prostitute and non-prostitute alike.

The split in the women's movement on the issue of women working as prostitutes has always led to so-called feminists strengthening the hand of the police against everyone. A modern instance is the legislation against kerb crawling (men soliciting women for prostitution) introduced by the Thatcher government in 1985 with the support of anti-porn/pro-censorship feminists. The kerb crawling law was supposed to bring equality to prostitute women by arresting clients, and bring protection from harassment by kerb crawlers to other women. In fact, the law further increased police powers against prostitute women and black and other working class women and men. Prostitute women are always the first to be arrested, and now any man police choose can be arrested and convicted for kerb crawling on police evidence alone. This was one of the many moves to turn Britain into a police state. In January 1986, the new Police and Criminal Evidence Act came into operation, legalizing many acts of police violence. Within the same year, a new Public Order Act was passed to stop pickets, demonstrations and any other forms of public protest.

Determined not to allow the policing of prostitution to segregate prostitute women from other working class people, we launched the Campaign Against Kerb Crawling Legislation (CAKCL) which rallied many individuals and organizations concerned with civil rights. Although we were not able to defeat the coalition of right, left, feminist and "respectable" residents aiming for gentrification and a rise in property values, who together provided the Thatcher government with excuses for the kerb crawling law, CAKCL has so far prevented the police from making wider use of their new powers.

Grassroots Organizing Against Police Illegality and Racism

The network of the International Prostitutes Collective, which includes Canada, Trinidad and Tobago, and the United States, is autonomous from men, social workers, lawyers, academics, politicians, government agencies and other pimps and clients. Police violence, illegality and racism have of course been major focuses of our campaign.

All prostitute women are affected by the prostitution laws in varying degrees according to their country, race, nationality, age, place of work, whether they are mothers, etc. Our experience is that prostitutes' organizations which try to hide these differences make deals with the police to promote and protect one sector of prostitute women, usually the tiny minority of mostly white metropolitan women who can afford to be public, at the expense of the majority — black, Third World or immigrant, single mothers and other working class women and children, who can't afford to come out, who continue to be hounded by the police. Having attended the 1985 Whores Congress, organized by the ICPR, we boycotted the Second Congress. Our statement was published in the press:

> . . . Last year the police and media were invited. We protested: "Forcing women to identify themselves as prostitutes is to help the police to control prostitutes." We have fought to prevent non-prostitute professionals — police, media, academics, social workers, lawyers and politicians — from controlling the prostitutes' rights movement. The Whores Congress is planned with them . . .

We later learned that women attending were asked to surrender* their passports at the door. Only one woman from Belgium, where the Congress was held, attended — the rest were not about to come out to their local police.

We are not interested in legitimizing prostitution, but in legitimizing all prostitute women. We see prostitute women's interests in connection not with the police, the media, politicians, academics and clients, but with all others who share poverty and repression with us. And since black people are the first to suffer at the hands of the

---

*Ed. Note: At the European Parliament, it is the normal procedure to surrender one's passport upon entering. Because of the sensitive status of the women attending the 2nd World Whores' Congress, the International Committee for Prostitutes' Rights (ICPR) arranged for the European Parliament not to collect the passports. Participants in the Congress were issued special cards so that they would not have to go through the standard procedures. All list were turned over to the ICPR at the close of the congress.

police, ignoring, or even soft- pedaling, the role of police illegality in any of our lives, assists and supports every racist effort to segregate and muffle black self- defense and protest.

In *Money for Prostitutes Is Money for Black Women* (1975), Wilmette Brown, co-founder of International Black Women for Wages for Housework, spells it out:

> Who among us, as Black women is *above* prostitution? Racism — our being forced as Black women always to have the least money, the least possibility of getting a job, the least access to school, the worst housing, and the first "opportunity" to be fired, fined, or jailed — already means that all Black women are *suspected* of being or *expected* to be prostitutes anyway! In a sweep arrest — when women who are just walking down the street can be arrested as prostitutes — who gets swept up first? It's always open season on Black women.

The sex industry, like any other, keeps black women at the bottom of the hierarchy. Many madams, escort agencies, massage parlors and clubs do not employ black women and those who do keep a restrictive minimum quota. As a result, black prostitute women have less choice about where to work and are forced onto the street where working conditions are harder and more dangerous.

In April 1982, we initiated Legal Action for Women (LAW), a grassroots legal service for all women, in response to prostitute women's needs for advice and support. LAW, and our rights sheet, *Guide to the Rules of the Game — A-Z for Working Girls*, which was distributed in red-light areas all over the country, launched a movement of women pleading not guilty to prostitution offenses in court.

In November 1982, with the support of Black Women for Housework and Women Against Rape, we occupied the Church of the Holy Cross in King's Cross, London. Rephrasing our French sisters in 1975, we said, "Mothers need money. End police illegality and racism in King's Cross." The police had been arresting women who were not working, picking on black women in particular, refusing to catch pimps who were reported to them, arresting boyfriends of women who pleaded not guilty in court, and threatening to put their children in care. The twelve-day occupation was a major success:

1) It put prostitute women on the political agenda. We were on major national television news almost every day, and got an enormous amount of press coverage nationally and abroad. We all wore masks during the Occupation to prevent police and media from finding out which of us were on the game. Our masked faces have been an inspiration for prostitute women in several countries who have since

used the protection of masks during actions.

2) It started to break down the barriers between prostitute women and other working class people. We gathered support from a wide range of individuals and organizations, including members of Parliament, councilors, political activists, and especially from black women and gay men. In *Hookers in the House of the Lord* (1983), Selma James writes:

> One Black woman... spelled out that the prostitution laws are to young Black women what the "sus" laws are to young Black men.* This was a real breakthrough for us. After years of work, we could begin to see the illegality and racism of the police against hookers being lifted out of the exotic, even the erotic, where it could be dismissed and ridiculed; and onto the deadly serious terrain we share with others who are up against the law.

United We Stand, Divided We Die

The Occupation sent a message of support to Greenham Common Women's Peace Camp which was celebrating its first anniversary: the "military-industrial-complex" (President Eisenhower's phrase) that brought cruise missiles to Greenham is putting women and children on the game by robbing us of money and resources, and we are demanding back our share of the military budget. Some days later three Greenham women came to join *our* peace camp in the Church. Through our connections with Greenham we made visible how much prostitute women have in common with peace activists; some of us were the same women, but even when we were not, we shared a common experience of police brutality, arrest, illegality and prison.

The same "respectable" residents who attack us accuse Greenham women of being sexual deviants. Under the guise of "morality" and the defense of the nuclear family, monetarism is forcing women back into subservience through welfare cuts, higher unemployment, increased police powers and repressive legislation. Any woman struggling for an independent life, whether at Greenham, on the game, or by refusing marriage can be labeled loose or promiscuous. The latest attack has come through governments using AIDS to scapegoat gay communities, undermine prostitute women's livelihood, tighten immigration controls against Black and Third World people, and control everyone's sex lives. In a recent letter to the press

---

*Many young people, in particular young black people, were arrested on police evidence alone, under the "suspicion" that they were thinking of committing a crime. This law was repealed after many years of protest.

written jointly with Wages Due Lesbians, we protested against AIDS terrorism:

> In the climate of AIDS hysteria which the government is creating, the call for legalized brothels, isolation hospitals, etc., to "safeguard" the rest of the community is little short of demanding concentration camps to lock people away and keep us all isolated and divided from other people by the fear of "contamination" by association. . . Prostitution is one of the few ways for women to support themselves, their children and often whole families and communities. This is even more true in Third World countries where there is no "safety net" of the Welfare State. Women are caught between the danger of AIDS and the danger of starvation. The figures show that AIDS is not about attitudes — to sex or anything else — but about money, and about how poor people always pay most and are the most expendable. When AIDS or any other health crisis is disconnected from poverty, the way is opened for reinforcing racism — which can be deadly. (December 6, 1986)

Whether to defeat AIDS, to support women who want to get off the game, or to prevent women being forced onto the game by poverty, resources are the crucial question. Together with millions of other women all over the world, we are reclaiming the wealth that our unwaged and low waged work have helped produce. "Because," as Wilmette Brown says in *Black Women and the Peace Movement*, "together we can win."

U.S. PROStitutes Collective

Rachel West

The United States Prostitutes Collective (U.S. PROS) is a national network of women who work in the sex industry as well as other women who support our goals. We are part of the International Prostitutes Collective (IPC) and a sister organization of the English Collective of Prostitutes (ECP). U.S. PROS is an independent network that is part of the International Wages for Housework Campaign. Women in our network are working or have worked in all levels of the sex industry: women who work the streets, massage parlors, escort services, hotels, clubs, houses, strippers, dancers, mistresses, models, etc., full-time and part-time, black, Latino and white women.

We are campaigning for the abolition of the laws against prostitute women — not legalization or decriminalization — so that women can work as independent business women, controlling our own working conditions. Legalization in Nevada, in the United States, and in the Eros Centers of West Germany are basically the new sex assembly lines. The women have no control over working conditions, hours worked, the number of clients they see, tips they receive, etc. Women, when working, have to register with the police and therefore are registered as "known prostitute women." They are also subject to health checks and are restricted in their movements outside the brothels. Decriminalization in some countries has come to mean the same as legalization. Therefore the IPC is very careful to make the distinction between legalization/decriminalization and abolition of the laws. It is a dangerous game to go along with the "program" of some state planners for legalization that in no way would end the vulnerability that prostitute women face. We are not building a movement to carry out our oppression under the guise of legalization or decriminalization.

We are also campaigning for economic independence for women, so that none of us will be forced into prostitution for economic reasons: safe houses for juvenile runaways, increases in all income transfer payments such as welfare (a study in San Francisco has shown that when welfare is cut, the numbers of AFDC mothers picked up for prostitution increases) and against immigration controls so that women and children can move freely from one country to another.

How We Began

U.S. PROS is an expansion of the New York Prostitutes Collective (NYP) that began in 1979 as a group of black sex industry workers and other black women who supported our goals. From the start we were a sister group of the ECP and used the organizing experience of the ECP to help us start out and to help in our on-going organization. NYP organized pickets, public meetings, and helped to support other organizations working on behalf of prostitute women's rights, such as Prostitutes of New York (PONY), whose spokeswoman was Iris de la Cruz. PONY concentrated its efforts on working with street walkers and was an important part of the history of the movement for prostitute women's rights. Although PONY no longer exists, it is important that their work be recognized and recorded.

We also organized within the City University campus for increased student grants, the right to get both welfare and student grants and for campus childcare. By 1980 we had both become multi-racial and grown into U.S. PROS. Nineteen eighty was also the year of the Democratic Convention in New York City and Mayor Koch had gotten an additional sixty-nine thousand dollars to crack down on prostitute women during the convention. U.S. PROS organized our first police watch teams, consisting of volunteer lawyers, students, members of PONY and ourselves. Street walkers had a particularly hard time during the Convention. There was increased police harassment and police illegality; one woman was so desperate to get away from New York City police that when they pursued her she jumped into the East River.

U.N. Mid-Decade Conference on Women

Until 1980, the New York Prostitutes Collective had done quite a bit of support work for Margo St. James' COYOTE, including raising money to help bring her to New York City. We parted ways with

COYOTE in Copenhagen in 1980 at the U.N. Mid-Decade Conference on Women when we found ourselves opposing the feminist moralists and COYOTE. The latter were actively supporting a U.N. resolution on trafficking for the purposes of prostitution. The resolution, if passed as written, would have made it difficult, if not impossible, for a woman with a record of prostitution to cross an international border. Non-white women from Third World countries would have suffered the brunt of its implementation. U.S. PROS and other groups in the IPC opposed the resolution and made it clear that if we couldn't get rid of it altogether, we would organize to get it modified to include some protection for prostitute women and children. We wanted a clause that said prostitute women and children should not be treated as criminals.*

Much to our surprise, COYOTE not only did not support our efforts but publicly opposed us by issuing press releases stating that we were "dressed like whores but weren't really prostitute women," and by attacking the right of prostitute women to remain anonymous. This was especially dangerous at a conference crawling with Interpol officers. To expect prostitute women to come out in this environment, especially if they are black and/or immigrant women actively organizing against the establishment, amounts to nothing less than wanting to turn women over to the police. Despite efforts to undermine us, we did manage — through a consensus vote — to get the clause we wanted included in the official U.N. resolution. That experience, and others following, made it clear that the differences in the organized movement for prostitute women's rights were no different from those that have emerged in other movements with those with the least social power struggling not to be undermined by those with more power. We, however, were not to be deterred by the scabbing and continued our work minus a political relationship with COYOTE.

---

*Ed. Note: In Copenhagen, Margo St. James felt that it was important to recognize the concerns of the representatives of the countries of Latin America, Asia and Africa, as well as those from the North American and Western European countries. The resolution dealt primarily with the issue of forced prostitution. Although it was not perfect, St. James felt that it was more important to pass a resolution dealing with prostitution than to fight endlessly and end up with no resolution dealing with the issue at all. She and representatives of Wages for Housework Campaign disagreed rather violently about the proper approach to take in Copenhagen.

281

Who Are Prostitute Women?

In the United States women began to form support groups for the work of U.S. PROS in cities without active U.S. PROS chapters entitled No Bad Women, Just Bad Laws in Tulsa, Oklahoma; Boston, Massachusetts; New Haven, Connecticut and Portland, Oregon. They organized coalitions, pickets, press conferences, wrote letters, etc., on behalf of the rights of prostitute women. They stated clearly that the rights of prostitute women are the rights of all women. Both No Bad Women and the U.S. PROS networks are raising the public's awareness of who prostitutes are — in reality as diverse a group as any. We are mostly single mothers with children to support, women on welfare, women helping to support elderly relatives on fixed incomes, secretaries and other office workers supplementing low wages, students putting themselves through school, full-time housewives, nurses, teachers, juvenile runaways refusing to be raped and battered or emotionally abused at home, and other women refusing the low wages available to women in the straight job market. In other words, there is no real stereotype of who a prostitute woman is — she could be any of us. Prostitute women as drug addicts is one very common stereotype. Given how widespread the use of drugs in society is, we doubt there is much difference in the percentage of prostitute women on drugs and the percentage of others on drugs. AIDS is also misrepresented as being spread by prostitute women.

Another view we've had to challenge is that of feminists and anti-porn campaigners who like to blame sex industry workers for rape and violence against women. In Los Angeles we were instrumental, along with other women's groups, in overturning an anti-porn ordinance. We spoke out publicly about the devastating effects that greater censorship, and forcing sex industry workers underground, would have on working conditions and safety of women in the sex industry. The stereotype of prostitute women is promoted by the police, media and prostitute movement careerists whose funding and media access depends on putting forward the stereotype as the typical prostitute woman.

Racism and Police Illegality

Our day to day organizing includes fighting for the immediate civil rights of prostitute women and against the tremendous level of violence that prostitutes face because we are illegal. Our illegality makes us vulnerable to police brutality and racism, to extortion, kidnaping etc. by others who pimp off our vulnerability. The enforcement of the prostitution laws is both selective and racist. Although the majority

282

of prostitute women are white, the majority of those in jail for prostitution are black. Prostitute women are constantly subject to illegal arrests in street sweeps; they are beaten up and forced to have sex with police officers. U.S. PROS often organizes pickets outside the courthouse to protest these abuses and to bring to the public's attention just how much taxpayer money is wasted on harassing, prosecuting and jailing prostitute women. Money could be better spent on programs to assist women with childcare, housing, health care, academic scholarships, waged job training programs, increased welfare payments etc., all of which would reduce the reasons women go into prostitution in the first place. Prostitution is about money, not about sex. If women's basic economic situation does not change, then women will continue to work as prostitutes.

Given the economic status of women, how many of us are forced to rent our bodies, stay in marriages we want to get out of, make deals with the landlord, shop keeper, put up with sexual harassment on the job, smile when we don't want to, put out or get fired etc.? How many wives put in a greater effort at being sexy when they need extra money from their husbands? How many women choose the man who has better career prospects over the man who is a heartthrob? How much do we all have to prostitute ourselves because women internationally have so little to show for the tremendous amount of work we do? Perhaps in thinking over these things, non-prostitute women can see that they are really not so very far apart from the rest of us.

Street Sweeps

Street sweeps have never gotten rid of prostitution, just forced it into another neighborhood or further underground. The sweeps often result in women working under more isolated and dangerous conditions or in turning to a pimp for protection. Pimps and police have been known to have a close working relationship. During the Democratic Convention in 1984 in San Francisco, hundreds of women were threatened or arrested in street sweeps, brutalized and illegally jailed. U.S. PROS again organized police watch teams and went into the street every night with lawyers to monitor the police. In the areas we went to there was less police harassment, but we observed a number of illegal arrests and incidents of police brutality. We accompanied the women to court from the incidences we observed as witnesses during their cases and the charges against them were dropped.

New Entrapment Law

Recently in California a statewide law was passed making entrapment legal. This means that police officers can initiate a proposition and, if the woman accepts by going off with the officer or by undressing, she can be arrested. Under the old law, an officer could not do the soliciting. This new law will hit hardest the most vulnerable women. Given the selective and racist enforcement of the prostitution laws, black women will be hardest hit in its implementation.

We suspect this law can be challenged on the basis of its being unconstitutional. It remains to be seen whether civil liberties groups will take up the challenge.

Legal Action for Women (LAW)

U.S. PROS has also organized Legal Action for Women (LAW) in San Francisco, based on LAW in London (see ECP), a grassroots legal service for all women to challenge police and court practices. We've helped women plead not guilty to illegal arrests and win their cases. Since its formulation in 1984, LAW has helped hundreds of women, not only prostitute women, but any women who can't afford legal services. We have also set up a Prostitutes Complaint Bureau where we document cases of police and customer harassment or brutality.

Fighting Vigilantes

We have organized against vigilante harassment of prostitute women in Berkeley, Sacramento, Portland, Oregon and Tulsa, Oklahoma where vigilantes protected by the police patrolled the streets hunting down women they suspected of being prostitutes. We picketed City Hall protesting their support of the vigilantes, spoke at City Council meetings, met with local residents, spoke out to the public on television and radio. In a recent poll taken by a radio station in Berkeley in the neighborhood where the vigilantes patrolled, ninety-five percent of the residents interviewed were on our side.

The South Side Slayer and Other Serial Muders

Another immediate concern is prostitute women's vulnerability to violence, rape and murder. In Los Angeles, Margaret Prescod, who for a long time was public spokeswoman for U.S. PROS, founded the Black Coalition Fighting Black Serial Murders in response to police inaction and media inattention to the deaths of at least 17 women over a three-year period in South Central Los Angeles (a mainly black neighborhood). All but three of the victims were black. All the bodies were found in the same forty-mile radius. The police waited until ten women were already dead before notifying the public that a serial murderer was operating, and fourteen women were murdered before they ever formed a task force to investigate the murders.

Three days following the police announcement of the murders, International Black Women for Wages for Housework organized a multi-racial vigil outside the Central Police Station, met with police representatives and the press demanding action on the murders. The Black Coalition Fighting Black Serial Murders was founded in January 1986 to expand and continue the work already begun by International Black Women for Wages for Housework in consultation with U.S. PROS and the ECP. The membership of the Black Coalition includes women who live and work in South Central L.A. as well as others from various fields: ministers, lawyers and organizations ranging from the Southern Region NAACP to the Coalition Against Police Abuse. Some mothers of victims of the South Side slayer are also active supporters of the Coalition.

The Black Coalition has stated again and again that they are not convinced that all the women murdered were prostitutes and that the police have offered little evidence to support that claim. When the police could not dig up a prostitution arrest record on victim 17, they immediately said, "but she was a street woman." This statement reflects the attitude of the police towards poor women generally, especially if they are black.

We all know only too well that any of us at any time can be labeled a prostitute woman, if we dare step out of line in the way we speak and dress, in the hours we keep, the number of friends we have, or if we are "sexual outlaws" of any kind. When prostitute women are not safe, no woman is safe. Historically, serial murderers who begin with prostitute women inevitably go on to murder any woman (e.g., the Ripper case in England — see ECP), so when the LAPD claimed that non-prostitute women were safe, they were only giving women in L.A. a false sense of security, therefore placing all of us in greater danger.

From the start, the police, the media, elected officials and civic leaders were slow to respond to the murders, giving the impression that the deaths of these women were not important enough to cause much of a stir. When compared to other cases of serial murders in L.A., such as the Night Stalker and the Hillside Strangler, which received far greater attention and were treated as a general crisis, it is apparent that the lives of the murdered women did not seem to have

285

much value. This implies that the value of human life is determined by economic standing, racial background, and how one's living is earned.

If you're poor, black and they claim you're a prostitute, your life is worth nothing. The Hillside Strangler, who murdered prostitutes in a predominantly white neighborhood and killed mainly white women, received far greater attention from the start than the South Side Slayer. At the height of the investigation, there were one hundred fifty officers assigned to the case, compared to the original thirteen officers first assigned to the South Side Slayer investigation — and forty to fifty officers presently assigned to the case.

From the start, the Black Coalition Fighting Black Serial Murders protested vigorously the police handling of the case. The Coalition succeeded in getting the police to change the name of the task force from Prostitute Killer Task Force to South Side Slayer Task Force and from referring to the murders as prostitute slayings to calling them the South Side slayings. The Coalition lobbied, picketed, protested, called press conferences and pressured the police to take the murders seriously. They got the size of the task force increased, and there's been an increase in the numbers of women and blacks promoted in the LAPD as a result of their work and other community pressures. They also successfully lobbied to get local government officials to issue a reward which now stands at thirty-five thousand dollars.

The question of police accountability to the community they serve is a bottom line issue. The police initially refused to meet with the Coalition, but the Coalition did win a series of police community meetings on the issue. These meetings up to now have not been as productive as they could be, so more work has to be done to make them more effective. The police so far have refused the coalition's demand for special assistance from the FBI.

Another issue that has emerged in the South Side Slaying organizing is the right of a grassroots network to demand accountability of the police, elected officials and civic leaders without compromising their basic demands and goals. The Coalition has been faced with the political establishment, both black and white, attempting to compromise their efforts and to ignore demands made from the grassroots. The police have attempted to use the political establishment and community scabs to get them to "cool out" their demands, diffuse their activities and cause confusion and conflict internally. During the course of the organizing, threats have been made against Coalition founder and coordinator Margaret Prescod, including a dead bird hung outside her bedroom window.

Also, Michael Zinzun, a steering committee member and longtime activist of the Coalition Against Police Abuse, was so badly beaten by police that he is now blinded in one eye.

In spite of the physical dangers of organizing against police racism and illegality, the Black Coalition pressed ahead. They initiated a public information campaign on the South Side Slayer that was then taken up by police and public officials, and they won the demand for billboards and posters on buses. Another issue has been dealing with the media, who always take the word of the police at face value and are not doing their own independent investigation. How do they know, for example, that most of the women were working as prostitutes at the time they were killed? Although media coverage has improved as a result of community pressure, a lot more still needs to be done. The murders have received very little national media attention, and residents of Southern California are still not aware of the murders or familiar with the available composite sketch.

The Green River Murders

In the Seattle area, somewhere between forty-five and one hundred five women have been killed over a four-year period. Again, as in L.A., most of the women supposedly worked in the sex industry and many, if not most, were black. The same attitudes on the part of the police in L.A. existed in Seattle. The IPC has organized several vigils and pickets protesting the murders, including an action in Nairobi, Kenya in July 1985 at the UN End of Decade conference for Women. U.S. PROS in San Francisco has organized several pickets on behalf of the murdered women in Seattle. Despite efforts by the Women's Coalition to Stop the Green River Murders, and other groups, the crimes have not been solved and in fact the Green River Task force has been dismantled. Bodies of women have also turned up in Vancouver, Canada; Portland, Oregon; San Diego and Fresno, California. They probably amount to the largest specific population ever targeted by serial murders. Yet local and national outcry remains practically nonexistent and response from organized feminist groups has been minimal.

Take Back the Night

A major development in the South Side Slayers organizing was the setting up of the Take Back the Night Coalition, different from other TBTN groups nationally because their focus was not only the violence of individual men against individual women but also the violence of the state against women generally, and in particular against women of color. The Coalition is made up of thirty-two women's groups throughout the greater L.A. area. The Black Coalition — FBSM is a member of the Coalition which has organized weekly vigils outside Parker Center from June 1986 to December 1986. They have also organized a TBTN march to protest the South Side Slayings and the violence against immigrant and refugee women by the Immigration and Naturalization Service. There were approximately eight hundred participants in the March that many hail as the most multiracial demonstration they had ever attended in L.A.

International Action Protesting the South Side Slayings

In April 1986 at an international conference entitled "Implementing Nairobi: Counting All Women's Work in the GNP," organized by the International Wages for Housework Campaign and International Black Wages for Housework, women agreed to do a day on national and international action protesting the South Side Slayings. In July 1986 women in L.A., San Francisco, Tulsa, Oklahoma, Philadelphia, Vancouver, British Columbia, and London, England, held vigils and die-ins protesting the South Side Slayings. In London, English women wearing masks joined with the ECP and International Black Women for Wages for Housework outside the U.S. Embassy, where they made the connection with the mishandling of the South Side Slayings with the mishandling of the Atlanta child murders.

In San Francisco, U.S. PROS and our supporters took flowers and held a vigil outside the Federal Building. In Philadelphia, the Wages for Housework group organized a picket, demanded and won a letter from a congressman requesting a federal investigation in the way the murders were being handled by the joint task force of the LAPD and the Sheriff's Department. Over seventy women in Vancouver, Canada gathered in protest organized by Prostitutes and Other Women for Equal Rights (POWER). Meanwhile in Seattle in an independent action, the Women's Coalition to Stop the Green River Murders held a sit-in, one hour for the life of every woman taken in the Green River Murders. In Los Angeles, members of the Take Back the Night Coalition and the Black Coalition FBSM and others stood outside police headquarters with a mock coffin, flowers and women with sheets spread over them to symbolize the bodies of women. The international action was the first occasion for the South Side Slayings to get coverage on national television in the U.S.

U.S. PROS is frequently requested to turn up a "real" prostitute woman by the media or feminist groups. It seems that the word of an organized group of sex industry workers is not good enough. Again non-prostitute women are imposing on us the way they want us to organize without taking into consideration the risks involved for us and our families. Those of us who are presently working as prostitute women in U.S. PROS greatly resent this. Prostitute women are not an exotic side show. We are working women who need the money and are exploited like millions of women are every day. We can't ignore or hide the specific problems our illegality creates, but we know the only way to end our exploitation is to confront the differences between us and find common ground with other women on which we can organize together.

Thanks to women in the U.S. PROS network for contributing to this article.

Coyote/National Task Force on Prostitution

Purpose

The purpose of the National Task Force on Prostitution is to 1) repeal the existing prostitution laws; 2) empower prostitutes to bargain with their employers, when they work for agencies, in order to improve their working conditions; 3) inform the public about the reality, as opposed to the various myths, of prostitution; 4) educate to prevent the spread of AIDS and other sexually transmitted diseases; and 5) end the stigma associated with female sexuality and earning power (i.e., money).

The NTFP's goals include the repeal of all laws against soliciting, engaging, or agreeing to engage in sex in exchange for money or anything of value. In addition, we believe that no mutually voluntary aspects of prostitution should be criminal, including relationships between prostitutes and third-party managers (also known as pimps, panderers and procurers), renting a premises for the purposes of prostitution, residing in a place where prostitution occurs, or similar aspects of prostitution. Existing laws dealing with assault and battery, kidnapping, and sexual assault should be enforced in cases where violence, or the threat of violence, is used to force someone to engage in prostitution or to work in pornography. Immigration laws which prohibit anyone who has ever worked as a prostitute, whether legally or not, from entering the country should also be repealed, as should domestic legislation prohibiting prostitutes from crossing state lines to work within the United States or sending money earned through prostitution across state lines. Laws dealing with sexual abuse of juveniles should be enforced against those who profit from the sexuality of minors.

The NTFP makes a distinction between voluntary and forced prostitution. Voluntary prostitution is the mutually voluntary exchange of sexual services for money or other consideration; it is a form of work, and like most work in our capitalist society, it is often alienated (that is, the worker/prostitute has too little control over her/his working conditions and the way the work is organized). Forced prostitution is a form of aggravated sexual assault.

The NTFP supports the development of programs to assist adult and juvenile prostitutes in changing their occupation, as well as programs to provide shelter and support for any prostitutes who are victims of violence, whether the violence is ongoing or random.

The NTFP is working to prevent the scapegoating of prostitutes for AIDS and other sexually transmitted diseases, and to educate prostitutes, their clients, and the general public about prevention of these diseases.

The NTFP calls on local, state and national governments, as well as private foundations, to fund programs which provide services to prostitutes and ex-prostitutes.

History

COYOTE was founded in San Francisco in 1973 by Margo St. James, an ex-prostitute, because although there were many organizations working for women's rights, no organization was addressing prostitutes' issues. More importantly, no one was speaking about the issues from the perspective of the prostitutes themselves. Similar organizations sprang up in other parts of the country, including New York PONY, Massachusetts PUMA, Hawaii DOLPHIN, Detroit CUPIDS, Michigan PEP, Florida COYOTE, Kansas City KITTY, Los Angeles CAT, New Orleans PASSION, Sacramento COYOTE, San Diego OCELOT, Seattle ASP, and others. Most of the organizations consisted of a single activist who was able to come out of the closet and speak publicly on the issue of prostitution. Others consisted of small groups of activists. PUMA, in Massachusetts, eventually began to focus more and more on the issue of violence against prostitutes, and is now devoted to providing services for battered prostitutes. CUPIDS continues to meet in Detroit and to speak out against police harassment of prostitutes. CAT, in Los Angeles, began to work primarily with minors and is now Children of the Night, a service agency for juvenile prostitutes. Most of the other organizations eventually ceased operating as the active core members drifted on to other things. A major factor has always been the difficulty in obtaining funds, either from foundations or the government, to continue public education and/or service-oriented projects. A second and equally important factor is that speaking out about prostitutes' rights when you are a prostitute involves a good deal of personal risk; it is difficult to sustain the effort without financial and political support. For many people and organizations, prostitution is still an extremely controversial issue. For most legislators, it remains a joke except when it is used to gain prominence by attacking prostitutes.

The most politically active of all the chapters have been the San Francisco and the Atlanta chapters. In 1979, the National Task Force on Prostitution was formed with the idea of eventually developing a formalized national network of prostitutes' rights advocacy organizations. In 1984, the first national conference was held in San Francisco, at the same time as the Democratic National Convention. Conferences have been held every year since. There is a similar network in Canada, Canadians Organized for the Rights of Prostitutes (CORP), which has worked with the NTFP on some projects. The majority of the active chapter members are prostitutes and ex-prostitutes, although some non-prostitute advocates also participate.

In 1986, the NTFP organized a meeting of prostitutes' rights supporters, including many non-prostitute women, in New York, with the goal of establishing a network of solidarity organizations tentatively named the Feminist Alliance for Prostitutes' Rights. At the present time, FAPR groups meet in New York, Tampa, and Seattle. There are also many service agencies loosely affiliated with the Task Force, including the Mary Magdalene Project, in southern California, and Genesis House, in Chicago.

In 1985, Margo St. James and Gail Pheterson formed the International Committee for Prostitutes Rights (ICPR), based in The Netherlands. The National Task Force on Prostitution — and its affiliates — are members of the ICPR, which sponsored the World Whores' Congress in Amsterdam in 1985 and in Brussels in 1986. In 1987, participating organizations plan to hold regional meetings, including the Americas Regional Whores' Congress in San Francisco. The next World Whores' Congress in scheduled for 1988, probably in Italy.

Becoming an NTFP Affiliate

In order to be an affiliate of the National Task Force on Prostitution, a local organization must adhere to the policies developed at the annual San Francisco meeting. Any public statements (to the press, government agencies, college classes, organizations, etc.) made by anyone representing the local affiliate and the Task Force must be consistent with those policies.

To form an affiliate, look for other interested individuals and begin meeting. Ideally, a majority of the active members of the affiliate will be prostitutes and ex-prostitutes, who can speak and make decisions based on their own experiences. Some suggestions about what a local affiliate can do are listed below. Members of the Task Force are available for consultation (see list of affiliates at the end of this article).

After you have been meeting for several months and have developed some idea of what you would like to do, submit a formal proposal to the NTFP headquarters, in San Francisco, for approval. If possible, each affiliate should send at least one representative to the annual meeting of the National Task Force on Prostitution, held in San Francisco, California every summer.

SAMPLE PROJECTS

1. Find Out How Prostitutes Are Dealt with in Your Community

Police: Contact the local police department/vice squad to find out arrest statistics. Ask for the counts to be broken down into women and men, with each gender further broken down by race and by adult and juvenile. If they say they can't do it, ask for a copy of the statistical report they submit to the State Attorney General's Office and/or the U.S. Department of Justice.

Ask the police department how many prostitutes were raped the previous year, and how many were murdered. If they say they don't know, ask them why not. Ask them how they handle rape cases when the victim is a prostitute.

Find out if they confiscate condoms from individuals arrested for prostitution. If they do, try to work with your public health department to get the policy changed (condoms are essential to prevent AIDS; confiscating them during an arrest constitutes an increased AIDS risk).

Sheriff: Contact the sheriff's department to find out how prostitutes are processed in the county jail. Are they allowed to get out of jail post-arrest, on their own recognizance? Do bail bondspeople post bail for prostitutes? How about for pimps? How about for customers? Are prostitutes ever given a citation instead of being charged with prostitution? Are prostitutes eligible for work furlough programs?

Judges: Contact judges to find out how prostitutes are dealt with in the courts. Are first offenders granted pre-trial diversion? How are rape cases dealt with when the victim is a prostitute?

District Attorney/Public Defender: Contact the district attorney and the public defender to find out the policy regarding prosecuting people arrested for prostitution. Are customers and prostitutes dealt with in the same way? Are either or both urged to plead guilty to a lesser charge, such as disturbing the peace? Are they urged to plead not guilty? How does the district attorney handle complaints of rape or other abuse filed by prostitutes?

Pre-trial Diversion: Contact the pre-trial diversion project, if any, to find out if they accept prostitutes as clients. What kind of diversion do they set up for prostitutes? If they grant community service, see if they will place prostitutes to work with your affiliate.

ACLU: Contact the local chapter of the ACLU (American Civil Liberties Union) to find out if they have been handling any prostitution cases, or if they can refer you to ethical attorneys who do. If they have not done any work this issue, ask them if they would consider taking prostitution cases in an effort to get the laws repealed in the courts.

Battered Women's Shelter/Rape Crisis Center: Contact your local battered women's shelter to find out if they accept prostitutes as clients. Do they assume the problem is prostitution, or do they assume that prostitution is work and the problem is a relationship with a batterer? Ask if there are any prostitutes or ex-prostitutes on staff and, if not, whether they would consider hiring an ex-prostitute to work as a counselor with battered women. If not, why not?

Contact your local rape crisis program to find out if they get calls from prostitutes and, if so, are they able to help them? Ask if there are any prostitutes or ex-prostitutes on the staff and, if not, whether they would consider hiring ex-prostitutes to work as rape crisis counselors. If not, why not?

Health: Contact your local women's health center, public health unit, mental health program, and other medical agencies that offer services to women, to ask about their services for prostitutes. Find out what kind of AIDS prevention education is being offered to prostitutes and their customers.

Monitor the Media: Watch your local television news programs, and monitor your local newspaper, to see how they deal with prostitutes. If you find their coverage objectionable, see if you can get them to change their attitudes. In particular, watch how they treat the issue of prostitutes and AIDS. If they appear to blame prostitutes for heterosexual transmission of the disease, remind them that unsafe sex, not group labels, is what is responsible for transmission, and that prostitutes are significantly more likely to practice safe sex than non-prostitute women.

2. What Can You Do to Help Prostitutes?

Resource Guide: Put out a resource guide, including legal rights in your community, lists of agencies willing to work with prostitutes (health centers, shelters, mental health programs, lawyers, vocational counseling programs, displaced homemakers programs) as well as other women's programs. Include safe sex guidelines, as well as resources for further information about AIDS. If anonymous (not merely confidential) testing is available in your community, include that information in your resource guide.

Public Education: Hold community forums on prostitution. Possible speakers might include representatives of the ACLU, the National Lawyers Guild, the Public Defender's and District Attorney's Office, the Department of Public Health, your local AIDS education project, a staff person from the local pre-trial diversion program, as well as feminist attorneys, rape crisis counselors, counselors for battered women, and, of course, prostitutes.

Get Support Statements: Contact feminist and other women's organizations, gay and lesbian organizations, civil rights organizations, welfare rights organizations, criminal justice reform organizations, prisoners' rights organizations, and other progressive and/or civil liberties organizations in your area to find out if they have a formal position on prostitution. If so, try to obtain a copy of any resolutions they have adopted on the issue. If not, ask if they would be interested in having a speaker come to a meeting and/or if they would be willing to endorse a resolution calling for the decriminalization of prostitution.

Develop resolutions on specific police and criminal justice practices in your community, and invite other organizations to endorse/ co-sign the resolutions.

Jail Project: Investigate the possibility of developing a project inside the women's jail. Such projects can include providing tutoring or other services, bringing concerts and other entertainment into the jail, doing volunteer counseling, offering safe sex workshops, coming in to talk about the goals of the National Task Force on Prostitution, etc.

National Task Force on Prostitution Affiliates

National Task Force on Prostitution: P.O. Box 26354, San Francisco, CA 94126. Priscilla Alexander, Executive Director (415) 957-1292.
San Francisco COYOTE: P.O. Box 26354, San Francisco, CA 94126. Co-Directors: Priscilla Alexander (415) 957-1292; Gloria Lockett, (415) 232-7762.

Los Angeles COYOTE: Box 580, 1626 N. Wilcox, Hollywood, CA 90028. Norma Jean Almodovar, Director (213) 389-4495.

Georgia HIRE/COYOTE: P.O. Box 7781, Atlanta, GA 30309. Dolores French, President (404) 876-1212.

Massachusetts COYOTE: P.O. Box 621, Astor Station, Boston, MA 02123-0621. Helen McNamee, Coordinator (617) 445-7670.

Minnesota COYOTE: P.O. Box 4277, St. Paul, MN 55104. Rebecca Rand, Coordinator (612) 645-2230.

Rocky Mountain COYOTE: P.O. Box 4157, Boulder, CO 80306. Theodora Barychewsky (303) 440-9042.

COYOTE-New York: P.O. Box 1331, Old Chelsea Station, New York, NY 10011. Veronica Vera, Coordinator (212) 242-6449.

Shelters for Prostitutes

Mary Magdalene Project: P.O. Box 8396, Van Nuys, CA 91409. Rev. Ann Hayman, Director (818) 708-7234.

Genesis House: 911 W. Addison Street, Chicago, IL 60613. Edwina Gately, Director (312) 281-3917.

The Red Thread: Whores' Movement in Holland

Hansje Verbeek and Terry van der Zijden

Prostitution in Holland

Holland has the reputation of being rather liberal towards prostitution. Foreigners are often stupefied when they see the women sitting behind the windows, just like that, in the Red Light District. Consequently, in Amsterdam the District is a famous tourist attraction and is recognized as such by the municipality. Although the working conditions of the Dutch prostitutes contrast favorably with those of prostitutes abroad — and although most of them are able to work without being disturbed by the police — they are stigmatized. Women working as prostitutes are considered inferior and are treated as second-class citizens. A lot of them lead double lives because they want to keep their jobs secret. They continually fear discovery, have difficulty making contacts and become socially isolated. Other prostitute women completely withdraw into the prostitute scene which, because of its separation from the rest of society is also the place of other social outlaws.

In the beginning of the last century, Holland introduced abolitionism into the prostitution legislation. This means that prostitution is not prohibited, but to be a third party, to benefit from the prostitution of others *is* punishable. In practice, prostitution is tolerated within certain limits, and only in certain places, if the municipality determines that there is no "annoyance." Nowadays, when planning city renovations, many municipalities try to integrate prostitution, often settled in old quarters, into newly-built areas.

The average Dutch citizen feels indifferent towards prostitution, but people who are confronted with it daily in their own neighborhoods often protest it. Even in tolerant Amsterdam, people agitated to get rid of streetwalkers in their area. When the women moved to another place through a burgomaster's resolution, inhabitants of the new neighborhood tried everything — from lawsuits to physical intimidation — to chase the women away. Prostitution in Holland is not as accepted as is commonly believed.

Holland has about 15,000 prostitutes. They work in the streets, behind windows, in bars, brothels, clubs, at home or as escorts. Because prostitution policy is almost exclusively defined in terms of "annoyance" to society, a clear tendency to repel the most conspicuous forms of prostitution prevails. In a city like Amsterdam, expensive clubs can be in the limelight without being disturbed, but streetwalkers are driven away from their places.Even as streetwalkers are harassed, the conservative government, via the Department for Women's Emancipation Affairs, supports the Red Thread (the prostitutes' pressure group) by giving it a state grant.

The Red Thread started as a self-help group of prostitutes and ex-prostitutes, initiated by Jan Viseer of the A de Graaf Foundation in January 1984. The Foundation, which houses a unique library and documentation center on prostitution, also provides information on state and municipate policy concerning prostitution. By 1985, the Red Thread was an official foundation. Its aim: to promote the recognition of the occupation of prostitution and to serve the interests of prostitutes and ex-prostitutes. With this end in mind, the Red Thread pursues improvements in legislation, working conditions, social work and public opinion.

The Red Thread has boomed since the first International Whores' Congress, held in Holland in February 1985. The Congress was sparked by Gail Pheterson, an American social psychologist who had worked in Holland, and Margo St. James, founder of COYOTE.

Because of the overwhelming media interest in the Congresss, the Red Thread gained national and international attention. At the Congress, most of us came out publicly as prostitutes for the first time. But suddenly, the Red Thread members were regarded as experts representing *all* prostitutes. As such, we were asked to give our opinions about the most divergent matters. Our own and others' expectations put high pressure on us. At first we tried to meet all requests, because we finally had the chance to publicly champion our cause. Later, we felt we had been taken advantage of, especially in the feverish excitement at the time of the first Congress. Questions like: what do you think of seventeen-year-old prostitutes? Do you also stand up for heroin-whores? Is not the market spoiled by women —

especially foreign women — who work at a low price? Does it reassure you that you are registered by the police, or do you think your organization should be responsible for this registration in the future? What about whores who do not want an organization at all? We weren't prepared for these kinds of provoking, sometimes tendentious questions by journalists and others. Although we could often refer to the World Charter for Prostitutes' Rights, we hadn't had time to discuss ideological matters among ourselves.

One of the issues we eventually discussed was that the rights we were fighting for, to do our work freely, were rights denied *all* women. Therefore, we contacted feminists in the women's movement to make our own contribution. We exchanged thoughts and ideas and attacked the current opinion that whores help to maintain the subordination of women. The discussion of whether you can be both a whore and a feminist is still raging and has already provided us with a number of advocates. Public interest has been piqued; prostitution has become a hot item.

We have had organizational problems, mostly over unequal division of tasks. We especially felt a need for our own office to work from, to collect our knowledge and material, to meet, and to be accessible.

Today, the group is made up of an eighteen-member core, directly surrounded by a circle of interested women who appear at meetings now and then and want to keep informed but do not (yet) want to commit themselves. Of course, the Red Thread concerns itself with the interests of male prostitutes, too. For some time a few men were active within the Red Thread, but unfortunately not at the moment.

We are the negotiation partners in all kinds of deliberation with policy makers, social workers, and women's organizations. We are also regularly asked to give information or lectures. It strikes us that people are sometimes very eager to have a 'real' whore in their deliberations.

While we have the knowledge that only prostitutes possess, we do not have enough expertise in other fields to present our policy adequately. Therefore, we are now getting specific training to learn how to influence policy and handle publicity.

This year, we received a grant enabling us to hire a staff of three women. Of course we are making great plans now, but for the time being we are busy strengthening our organization, extending our activities and bringing new members.

Two subjects which receive most of our attention at the moment, AIDS and the working conditions of prostitutes, are discussed below.

AIDS

Even before AIDS was widely and openly being discussed in Holland, we realized that, after homosexual men and I.V. drug users, we would be the next scapegoats. When the research on AIDS transmission by heterosexual contact started and we were asked to serve as research subjects, we said that it was not us, but men and women who regularly have sexual intercourse without condoms who should be examined. We fight the idea that we should be considered sick and dangerous simply and solely because we ask money for sex. We do not shut our eyes, however, to the fact that some of us are not free to choose between working with or without condoms. Too little public attention is paid to the fact that women can be forced to work without protection. The same holds true for the question of how we can prevent becoming AIDS carriers. That is why we try to convince customers and proprietors that fucking without condoms is dangerous for everyone's health. People who have unsafe sex run the risk of getting infected — not whores who use condoms. We try to change the public's automatic connection between prostitution and AIDS by also focusing on other occupational diseases such as back problems, bladder and kidney infections, and stress. We emphasize that these ailments can be reduced by better working conditions.

Working Conditions

Improving the working conditions requires a number of legal changes which are imminent: abolishing the brothel prohibition and replacing it with a licensing system which should end compulsion, violence and exploitation, such as compulsory long working hours, being forced to do certain services, and playing the prostitutes off against one another. Aspects of safety — for instance, alarm- and fire-installation and good sanitary facilities — should be self-evident and not exceptions we should be 'grateful' for. Often, only matters like labor contracts and the payment of social premiums and other taxes are discussed. We think that these duties cannot be introduced until the rights of the prostitutes have been established. We do not want to be tied down in laws and rules made to control prostitution. We only wish for changes if they offer improvements.

The Pink Thread

Marjan Sax

The Pink Thread is the sister organization of the Red Thread. It came into being on the eve of the First International Congress of Whores in January 1985. The initiative to start Pink Thread came from two women who had helped found the Red Thread: Martine Groen, who directed the prostitute self-help group, and Gail Pheterson, who set up "alliance groups" of women in both the United States and in Holland. Their method was simple: they approached women whom they knew or thought were interested in the subject of prostitution, invited them for a pleasant evening, and the Pink Thread Amsterdam was a fact.

What is the Pink Thread?

The Pink Thread is a group for all women, whores and non-whores, forming a bridge between members of the women's movement and prostitutes.

The relationship between feminists and prostitutes has not always been good. Prejudices and a lack of information about one another's situation stand in the way of good cooperation. For instance, a lot of feminists regard whores as victims of male society. They are convinced that prostitution should be abolished and the prostitutes saved. Self-confident whores who say they need no pity are hardly understood. The opinion is that they let themselves be reduced to objects knowingly and willingly. Prostitutes, on their hand, look askance at feminists. They often find them "frustrated man-haters" who are not even capable of dressing attractively and who, in fact, "just need a good screw." The prejudices on both sides are fed by fables about the whores' trade and the often negative publicity about the women's movement. However, the misunderstanding is especially caused by the stigmatization of whores. We are played off against one another. As Gail Pheterson remarks: "Colored women, working-class women, lesbian women, Jewish women, divorced women, fat women, undisciplined women and in fact, *all* women can be called whores to justify ill-treatment in this way." Consequently women try to avoid this stigma and thus are made afraid of whores, for: "who associates with a whore will probably be one herself." Being labeled as a "whore" is exactly the thing women try to prevent at all costs.

The Pink Thread is a first step to narrow the gap between whores and non-whores. It is a non-threatening way for us to get to know and support one another.

Non-prostitutes show a growing interest in the lives and thoughts of prostitutes, and more and more feminists are becoming convinced that prostitutes have a right to independence and social recognition, just like all women.

The Pink Thread is a meeting place for women with very different backgrounds: some of them deal with prostitution through their jobs as social workers or doctors, but the greater part of the group consists of feminists who have come to feel connected with prostitutes in the struggle for women's liberation.

Activities

The Pink Thread is active in several fields:
  *giving practical and moral support to the Red Thread;
  *activating the discussion about prostitution in feminist circles;
  *developing ideas about the relationship between prostitution, sexuality and women's subordination.

In the initial stage of the Pink Thread the support to the Red Thread women was a priority. The Pink Thread gave the Red Thread administrative assistance, writing official letters and applications for subsidy, taking minutes for the Red Thread meetings and helping to organize. Pink Thread women are regularly invited to the Red Thread meetings to give information or to do odd jobs. As the Red Thread is getting better organized this supporting function is less necessary.

Women from the Pink Thread are involved with AIDS, by taking part in meetings and giving counter-information when the supposed connection between prostitution and AIDS comes up for discussion. The Pink Thread women also contributed a great deal to the preparations for the Second World Whores' Congress in Brussels in October 1986.

For some time the Pink Thread organized regular discussion and information evenings about prostitution during which the relationship between feminism and prostitution received the most attention. These evenings were chiefly attended by women who wanted to meet "real" prostitutes and know more about them. The atmosphere at these meetings was unrestrained because both parties were eager to know more about each other.

Approach

The Pink Thread meetings are open to women of both the Pink and the Red Thread and take place about once a month. The meetings are rather informal; there is a lot of chatting, information is exchanged and only a few matters are formally decided upon. There are about fifty members, but the number of participants varies. In Amsterdam there are usually ten to twenty women, with a few women who are very active. Others just come to give and receive information. After the Brussels Congress there appeared to be a need to work on feminism, health, and human rights (including racism and migrant women), so the Pink Thread divided into three groups, one for each area. Each group meets monthly now, and every three months Pink Thread holds a combined meeting.

National Growth

In the course of 1985, several Pink Thread organizations came into being. Besides the Amsterdam group, there are Pink Threads in Eindhoven, Nijmegen, and Utrecht. Their activities vary from town to town. In Eindhoven the emphasis is on the direct support of Red Thread women, while in Utrecht the members monitor the municipal prostitution policy and then try to exert influence by writing letters and articles in the newspapers and, if necessary, by carrying on campaigns. The national policy is also getting attention now that other legal arrangements concerning prostitution are being discussed. In November 1985 the Pink Thread- Utrecht organized a national day for both the Pink and Red Threads.

Sore Spots

Within the Pink Thread there is a clear difference in attitude between the women who deal with prostitution through their jobs and those who are interested from a feminist point of view. Those who work with prostitution hardly ask themselves how and to what degree prostitution affects them as women. They are criticized because they show their professional, not their personal, bearing. On the other hand, they themselves criticize the ideological discussions of the others and get irritated now and then. Moreover, the question of whether men could be members of the Pink Thread played an important role, especially in the initial stage, and brought division of opinion. At the moment, only in Utrecht have men joined the Pink Thread.

Apart from this there is of course tension between the whores and non-whores. The difference in education, social position and possibilities between women of the Pink Thread and the Red Thread can be reason for confrontation, and the non-whores occasionally are overwhelmed by the whores' old frustrations. We have to acknowledge that good intentions cannot always sufficiently bridge the worlds of whores and non-whores. Linguistic confusion and misunderstanding cannot always be prevented: this all is an inevitable process from which, after licking the wounds, both "parties" learn a lot. One thing is clear to everybody: the issue at stake is the collective struggle of whores and non-whores for the right of self-determination for *all* women. Financial independence, sexual self-determination, and protection against (sexual) abuse are the causes prostitutes as well as feminists are fighting for.

International Committee for Prostitutes' Rights World Charter and World Whores' Congress Statements

International Committee for Prostitutes' Rights

World Charter

Laws

Decriminalize all aspects of adult prostitution resulting from individual decision.

Decriminalize prostitution and regulate third parties according to standard business codes. It must be noted that existing standard business codes allow abuse of prostitutes. Therefore special clauses must be included to prevent the abuse and stigmatization of prostitutes (self employed and others).

Enforce criminal laws against fraud, coercion, violence, child sexual abuse, child labor, rape, racism everywhere and across national boundaries, whether or not in the context of prostitution.

Eradicate laws that can be interpreted to deny freedom of association, or freedom to travel, to prostitutes within and between countries. Prostitutes have rights to a private life.

Human Rights

Guarantee prostitutes all human rights and civil liberties, including the freedom of speech, travel, immigration, work, marriage, and motherhood and the right to unemployment insurance, health insurance and housing.

Grant asylum to anyone denied human rights on the basis of a "crime of status," be it prostitution or homosexuality.

Working Conditions

There should be no law which implies systematic zoning of prostitution. Prostitutes should have the freedom to choose their place of work and residence. It is essential that prostitutes can provide their services under the conditions that are absolutely determined by themselves and no one else.

There should be a committee to insure the protection of the rights of the prostitutes and to whom prostitutes can address their complaints. This committee must be comprised of prostitutes and other professionals like lawyers and supporters.

There should be no law discriminating against prostitutes associating and working collectively in order to acquire a high degree of personal security.

Health

All women and men should be educated to periodical health screening for sexually transmitted diseases. Since health checks have historically been used to control and stigmatize prostitutes, and since adult prostitutes are generally even more aware of sexual health than others, mandatory checks for prostitutes are unacceptable unless they are mandatory for all sexually active people.

Services

Employment, counseling, legal, and housing services for runaway children should be funded in order to prevent child prostitution and to promote child well-being and opportunity.

Prostitutes must have the same social benefits as all other citizens according to the different regulations in different countries.

Shelters and services for working prostitutes and re-training programs for prostitutes wishing to leave the life should be funded.

Taxes

No special taxes should be levied on prostitutes or prostitute businesses.

Prostitutes should pay regular taxes on the same basis as other independent contractors and employees, and should receive the same benefits.

Public Opinion

Support educational programs to change social attitudes which stigmatize and discriminate against prostitutes and ex-prostitutes of any race, gender or nationality.

Develop educational programs which help the public to understand that the customer plays a crucial role in the prostitution phenomenon, this role being generally ignored. The customer, like the prostitute, should not, however, be criminalized or condemned on a moral basis.

We are in solidarity with all workers in the sex industry.

Organization

Organizations of prostitutes and ex-prostitutes should be supported to further implementation of the above charter.

Draft Statements from the 2nd World Whores' Congress (1986)

Prostitution and Feminism

The International Committee for Prostitutes Rights (ICPR) realizes that up until now the women's movement in most countries has not, or has only marginally, included prostitutes as spokeswomen and theorists. Historically, women's movements (like socialist and communist movements) have opposed the institution of prostitution while claiming to support prostitute women. However, prostitutes reject support that requires them to leave prostitution; they object to being treated as symbols of oppression and demand recognition as workers. Due to feminist hesitation or refusal to accept prostitution as legitimate work and to accept prostitutes as working women, the majority of prostitutes have not identified as feminists; nonetheless, many prostitutes identify with feminist values such as independence, financial autonomy, sexual self-determination, personal strength, and female bonding.

During the last decade, some feminists have begun to re-evaluate the traditional anti-prostitution stance of their movement in light of the actual experiences, opinions, and needs of prostitute women. The ICPR can be considered a feminist organization in that it is committed to giving voice and respect to all women, including the most invisible, isolated, degraded, and/or idealized. The development of prostitution analyses and strategies within women's movements which link the condition of prostitutes to the condition of women in general and which do justice to the integrity of prostitute women is therefore an important goal of the committee.

1. Financial Autonomy

Financial autonomy is basic to female survival, self-determination, self-respect, and self-development. Unlike men, women are often scorned and/or pitied for making life choices primarily in the interest of earning money. True financial independence includes the means to earn money (or the position to have authority over money) and the freedom to spend it as one needs or desires. Such means are rarely available to women even with compromise and struggle. Financial dependency or despair is the condition of a majority of women, depending upon class, culture, race, education, and other differences and inequalities. Female compromises and struggles are traditionally considered reflections of immorality and misfortune rather than of responsibility, intelligence and courage. The financial initiative of prostitutes is stigmatized and/or criminalized as a warning to women in general against such sexually explicit strategies for financial independence. Nonetheless, "being sexually attractive" and "catching a good man" are traditional female strategies for survival, strategies which may provide financial sustenance but rarely financial independence. All women, including prostitutes, are entitled to the same commercial rights as other citizens in any given society. *The ICPR affirms the right of women to financial initiative and financial gain, including the right to commercialize sexual service or sexual illusion (such as erotic media), and to save and spend their earnings according to their own needs and priorities.*

2. Occupational Choice

The lack of educational and employment opportunities for women throughout the world has been well documented. Occupational choice for women (especially for women of color and working-class women), and also for men oppressed by class and race prejudice, is usually a choice between different subordinate positions. Once employed, women are often stigmatized and harassed. Furthermore, they are commonly paid according to their gender rather than their worth. Female access to jobs traditionally reserved for men, and adequate pay and respect to women in jobs traditionally reserved for women are necessary conditions of true occupational choice. Those conditions entail an elimination of the sexual division of labor. Prostitution is a traditional female occupation. Some prostitutes report job satisfaction, others job repulsion; some consciously chose prostitution as the best alternative open to them; others rolled into prostitution through male force or deceit. Many prostitutes abhor the conditions and social stigma attached to their work, but not the work itself. *The ICPR affirms the right of women to the full range of education and employment alternatives and to due respect and compensation in every occupation, including prostitution.*

3. Alliance Between Women

Women have been divided into social categories on the basis of their sexual labor and/or sexual identity. Within the sex industry, the prostitute is the most explicitly oppressed by legal and social controls. Pornography models, strip-tease dancers, sexual masseuses, and prostitutes euphemistically called escorts or sexual surrogates often avoid association with prostitution labels and workers in an effort to elevate their status. Also among self-defined prostitutes, a hierarchy exists with street workers on the bottom and call girls on the top. Efforts to distance oneself from explicit sex work reinforce prejudice against prostitutes and reinforce sexual shame among women. Outside the sex industry, women are likewise divided by status, history, identity, and appearance. Non-prostitutes are frequently pressured to deliver sexual services in the form of sex, smiles, dress or affection; those services are rarely compensated with pay and may even diminish female status. In general, a whore-madonna division is imposed upon women wherein those who are sexually assertive are considered whores and those who are sexually passive are considered madonnas. *The ICPR calls for alliance between all women within and outside the sex industry and especially affirms the dignity of street prostitutes and of women stigmatized for their color, class, ethnic difference, history of abuse, marital or motherhood status, sexual preference, disability, or weight. The ICPR is in solidarity with homosexual male, transvestite and transsexual prostitutes.*

4. Sexual Self-Determination

The right to sexual self-determination includes women's right to set the terms of their own sexuality, including the choice of partner(s), behaviors, and outcomes (such as pregnancy, pleasure, or financial gain). Sexual self-determination includes the right to refuse sex and to initiate sex as well as the right to use birth control (including abortion), the right to have lesbian sex, the right to have sex across lines of color or class, the right to engage in sado-masochistic sex, and the right to offer sex for money. Those possibly self-determining acts have been stigmatized and punished by law or custom. Necessarily, no one is entitled to act out a sexual desire that includes another party unless that party agrees under conditions of total free will. The feminist task is to nurture self-determination both by increasing women's sexual consciousness and courage and also by demanding conditions of safety and choice. *The ICPR affirms the right of all women to determine their own sexual behavior, including commercial exchange, without stigmatization or punishment.*

5. Healthy Childhood Development

Children are dependent upon adults for survival, love, and development. Pressure upon children, either with kindness or force, to work for money or to have sex for adult satisfaction, is a violation of rights to childhood development. Often the child who is abused at home runs away but can find no subsistence other than prostitution, which perpetuates the violation of childhood integrity. Some research suggests that a higher percentage of prostitutes were victims of childhood abuse than of non-prostitutes. Research also suggests that fifty percent of prostitutes were not abused and that twenty-five percent of non-prostitutes were abused. Child abuse in private and public spheres is a serious violation of human rights but it does not mean that the victims cannot survive and recover, especially given support and resources for development. A victim deserves no stigmatization either in childhood or adulthood. *The ICPR affirms the right of children to shelter, education, medical or psychological or legal services, safety, and sexual self-determination. Allocation of government funds to guarantee the above rights should be a priority in every country.*

6. Integrity of All Women

Violence against women and girls has been a major feminist preoccupation for the past decade. Specifically, rape, sexual harassment at work, battering, and denial of motherhood rights have been targeted as focal areas for concern, research, and activism. Within the context of prostitution, women are sometimes raped or sexually harassed by the police, by their clients, by their managers, and by strangers who know them to be whores. Prostitute women, like non-prostitute women, consider rape to be any sexual act forced upon them. The fact that prostitutes are available for sexual negotiation does not mean that they are available for sexual harassment or rape.

The ICPR demands that the prostitute be given the same protection from rape and the same legal recourse and social support following rape that should be the right of any woman or man.

Battering of prostitutes, like battering of non-prostitutes, reflects the subordination of women to men in personal relationships. Laws against such violence are often discriminately and/or arbitrarily enforced. Boyfriends and husbands of prostitutes, in addition to anyone else assumed to profit from prostitution earnings (such as family and roommates), are often fined or imprisoned in various countries on charges of "pimping" regardless of whether they commit a violent offense or not. Boyfriends and husbands of non-prostitute women are rarely punished for battering, even when the woman clearly presses charges against them. *The ICPR affirms the right of all women to relational choice and to recourse against violence within any personal or work setting.*

Women known to be prostitutes or sex workers, like women known to be lesbians, are regularly denied custody of their children in many countries. The assumption that prostitute women or lesbian women are less responsible, loving, or deserving than other women is a denial of human rights and human dignity. The laws and attitudes which punish sexually stigmatized women function to punish their children as well by stigmatizing them and by denying them their mothers. *The ICPR considers the denial of custodial rights to prostitutes and lesbians to be a violation of the social and psychological integrity of women.*

7. Pornography: "Writings of Harlots"

Sexually explicit material or pornography refers specifically in original Greek to the writing of harlots. Today, pornography has been taken over by a male-dominated production industry wherein the female models and actresses rarely determine the content of their products. Moreover, like prostitutes, pornography workers are stigmatized as whores, denied recourse after abuse, and are often blamed .or abuse committed against them. They are also denied adequate financial compensation for distribution of products in which they appear. *The ICPR claims the right of sex workers (as opposed to managers) to determine the content, production procedure, and distribution procedure of the pornography industry.* Such empowerment will require solidarity among sex workers, solidarity between women both within and outside the sex industry, and education of women in the production of sexually explicit material. In support of such a feminist self-determining movement, the ICPR calls for public education campaigns to change the demands of a market which eroticizes children and the abuse of women.

8. Migration of Women through Prostitution ("Trafficking")

Trafficking of women and children, an international issue among both feminists and non-feminists, usually refers to the transport of women and children from one country to another for purposes of prostitution under conditions of force or deceit. The ICPR has a clear stand against child prostitution under any circumstances. In the case of adult prostitution, it must be acknowledged that prostitution both within and across national borders can be an individual decision to which an adult woman has a right. Certainly, force or deceit are crimes which should be punished whether in the context of prostitution or not. Women who choose to migrate as prostitutes should not be punished or assumed to be victims of abuse. They should enjoy the same rights as other immigrants. For many women, female migration through prostitution is an escape from an economically and socially impossible situation in one country to hopes for a better situation in another. The fact that many women find themselves in another awful situation reflects the lack of opportunities for financial independence and employment satisfaction for women, especially for third world women, throughout the world. Given the increased internationalization of industry, including prostitution, the rights and specific needs of foreign women workers must be given special attention in all countries.

The ICPR objects to policies which give women the status of children and which assume migration through prostitution among women to be always the result of force or deceit. Migrant women, also those who work as prostitutes, deserve both worker rights and worker protections. Women who are transported under conditions of deceit or force should be granted choice of refuge status or return to their country of origin.

9. A Movement for All-Women's Rights

It is essential that feminist struggle include the rights of all women. Prostitutes (especially those also oppressed by racism and classism) are perhaps the most silenced and violated of all women; the inclusion of their rights and their own words in feminist platforms for change is necessary. *The ICPR urges existing feminist groups to invite whore-identified women into their leading ranks and to integrate a prostitution consciousness in their analyses and strategies.*

Prostitution and Health

Prostitute health and prostitute access to health care services are deeply affected by social stigma and legal discrimination. Those injustices function not only to deny healthy work conditions and effective services to prostitutes, but also to foster distorted beliefs about prostitutes among the general public. Historically, prostitutes have been blamed for sexually transmitted diseases and authorities have justified social and legal control of prostitutes as a public health measure. The assumptions that prostitutes are more responsible for disease transmission than other groups and that state control of prostitute behavior prevents such transmission are contrary to research findings. Presently, the assumption that prostitutes are carriers of AIDS and that forced AIDS testing will prevent the disease have been shown to be unfounded in the West. The situation in various third world countries is as yet unclear. Female prostitutes in the West are not a risk group for AIDS. The small minority of prostitutes who are needle-using drug addicts are at risk from shared needles, not from commercial sex.

The ICPR demands realistic portrayals of the health of diverse prostitutes and implementation of effective health education and treatment services. Those services must respect prostitute dignity and foster customer responsibility for disease prevention (i.e condom use) in sexual transactions. A list follows of injustices and rights which are crucial to prostitute health and public responsibility.

Human Rights Violations in Health Policy and Practice

I. *Discrimination* against women in public health laws and practices is a basic violation of human rights. The ICPR demands:

A. (1) Repeal of regulations which deny free choice of a doctor to prostitutes.

(2) Abolition of compulsory medical certificates.

(3) Repeal of laws to combat venereal disease which are invoked only against prostitutes.

(4) Prohibition of forced or incentive testing of prostitutes in prison for any purpose.

(5) Free, anonymous, and voluntary testing for venereal disease, including AIDS, at easily accessible health facilities available for all people, including prostitutes.

B. Widespread education and regular screening for sexually transmitted diseases among all sexually active people. Note that venereal disease is a risk for different groups of sexually active people, that condoms are the best known preventive measure against VD, and that prostitutes are more likely to be aware of sexual health care than other persons.

C. Health insurance and compensation benefits for all workers, including prostitutes. Note that the stigmas and regulations which prevent job mobility for prostitutes (such as the denial of required letters of good conduct to prostitutes) make it extremely difficult or impossible for prostitutes to change work when desired or when necessary for health reasons.

II. *Registration* of prostitutes with state and police authorities denies human rights to privacy and dignified employment. The ICPR demands:

A. Independent and confidential public health services for all people, including prostitutes. Collaboration between health providers and public authorities, such as police or researchers, should be illegal.

B. Abolition of mandatory registration of prostitutes and of unofficial pressure on prostitutes to register with the police.

III. *Criminalization* of prostitutes for purposes of public health is unrealistic and denies human rights to healthy work conditions. As outlaws, prostitutes are discouraged, if not forbidden, to determine and design a healthy setting and practice for their trade. The ICPR demands:

A. Decriminalization of all aspects of adult prostitution resulting from individual decision. Specifically, prostitutes must have the right to work indoors and the right to advertise; they must also have the right to solicit outdoors according to general zoning codes (i.e., active solicitation should be allowed in areas zoned for businesses). Denial of those rights forces prostitutes into medically unhygienic, physically unsafe, and psychologically stressful work situations.

B. Application of regular business codes to prostitution businesses, including codes for cleanliness, heating, and leave for sickness and vacation. Also, codes for mandatory condom use should be enacted. Regulations should be enforced by worker organizations and not by state authorities.

Medical and Counseling Services

I. *Education* of health workers about the realities of prostitution health issues is necessary to combat prejudice and misinformation within medical and counseling services. Prostitutes and ex-prostitutes should be employed to participate in such training.

II. *Integration* of prostitutes in the medical and counseling services is essential for effective policy-making and service delivery.

III. Vocational counselors must respect a woman's decision to *work as a prostitute or not*. Leaving prostitution must never be a prerequisite for counseling service.

IV. Health authorities should disseminate information about *safe sexual practices*. In particular, condom use should be recommended for all vaginal, oral, or anal sexual transactions.

Drugs and Alcohol

I. Those prostitutes who are addicts, a minority in most branches of prostitution, usually entered prostitution to support their habit. Inadequate drug policies are responsible for addicts practicing prostitution; *prostitution is not responsible for drug addiction.*
   Social alternatives to prostitution are needed for addicted women. Both drug laws and drug treatment programs need to be re-evaluated. A clinical and social rather than a criminal model should be considered for controlling addictive substances. Treatment programs should be given adequate funding and research support.

II. There are no inherent connections between drug addiction and prostitution. Laws which criminalize both and practices which utilize addicted prostitutes as police informants are largely responsible for the connection between drugs and sex work on the streets. *Prostitution must be decriminalized and police must stop using prostitutes for illicit criminal investigations.*

III. Addicted prostitutes who use needles, like other needle-using addicts, must have *access to legal, inexpensive needles* in order to prevent the spread of disease (specifically, hepatitis and AIDS).

IV. It should be *illegal* for any employer, including managers of sex businesses, *to force employees to drink alcohol.*

Prostitution and Human Rights

The European Convention on Human Rights was drafted within the Council of Europe in 1950 and came into force in 1953. All twenty-one of the member States have ratified it. Those States include: Austria, Belgium, Cyprus, Denmark, France, Federal Republic of Germany, Greece, Iceland, Ireland, Italy, Liechtenstein, Luxembourg, Malta, the Netherlands, Norway, Portugal, Spain, Sweden, Switzerland, Turkey, and the United Kingdom. A published summary of the Convention is reprinted at the end of this statement.

The International Committee for Prostitutes' Rights (ICPR) demands that prostitutes, ex-prostitutes, and all women regardless of their work, color, class, sexuality, history of abuse, or marital status be granted the same human rights as every other citizen. At present, prostitutes are officially and/or unofficially denied rights both by States within the Council of Europe and by States outside of it. No State in the world is held accountable by any international body for those infractions. To the contrary, denial of human rights to prostitutes is publicly justified as a protection of women, public order, health, morality, and the reputation of dominant persons or nations. Those arguments deny prostitutes the status of ordinary persons and blame them for disorder and/or disease and for male exploitation of and violence against women. Criminalization or state regulation of prostitution does not protect anyone, least of all prostitutes. Prostitutes are systematically robbed of liberty, security, fair administration of justice, respect for private and family life, freedom of expression, and freedom of association. In addition, they suffer from inhuman and degrading treatment and punishment and from discrimination in employment and housing. Prostitutes are effectively excluded from the Human Rights Convention.

The World Charter of Prostitutes' Rights which was adopted by the ICPR in 1985 demands that prostitution be redefined as legitimate work and that prostitutes be redefined as legitimate citizens. Any other stance functions to deny human status to a class of women (and to men who sexually service other men).

The European Parliament recently took a step toward decriminalizing prostitution and prostitute workers by adopting a resolution on violence against women which includes the following clauses (see Hedy d'Ancona resolution, June session of Parliament, 1986):

"In view of the existence of prostitution the European Parliament calls on the national authorities in the Member States to take the necessary legal steps:

(a) to decriminalize the exercise of this profession,

(b) to guarantee prostitutes the rights enjoyed by other citizens,

(c) to protect the independence, health and safety of those exercising this profession. . .

(d) to reinforce measures which may be taken against those responsible for duress or violence to prostitutes. . .

(e) to support prostitutes' self-help groups and to require police and judicial authorities to provide better protection for prostitutes who wish to lodge complaints. . "

Concrete implementation of those steps requires specifications of the violations in each State. One goal of the Second World Whores' Congress is for prostitutes from countries represented within the Council of Europe and outside of it to specify those violations. The summarized list stated here will be elaborated at the congress.

Violations of the Human Rights of Prostitutes

1. *The right to life*

Murder of prostitutes is a common occurrence throughout the world. And, those murders are commonly considered less offensive than other murders, as evidenced by the fact that prostitute murderers are often not sought, found, or prosecuted.

2. The right to liberty and security of person

The physical safety of prostitutes is threatened by the criminal sphere in which they are forced to work.

The physical liberty of prostitutes is restricted by state and city regulations which prohibit their presence in certain districts or at certain times. For example, a woman standing on the street "looking as if she is a prostitute" can be fined for passive solicitation in France even if she is not negotiating a sexual transaction. Or, a prostitute in Toronto, Canada can be given a curfew (21:00) by the court if she hasn't paid three or four solicitation tickets; if she disobeys the order, she can be sentenced to six months in prison for disobeying a court order.

The right to liberty and security of persons is totally denied to women who are deceitfully or forcefully made to practice prostitution. In particular, the common transport of third world women to the West under false pretenses denies both liberty and security to women. The right *not* to work as a prostitute is as essential as the right to work if one so decides. Sexist and racist denial of both rights is widespread.

Prostitutes usually do not enjoy the same police protection of their liberty and security as other citizens. Due to the criminalization of their profession, they risk fines or arrests so they avoid calling upon police for protection. Police are frequently known to grant immunity from criminal action in exchange for information and/or sex, i.e. rape by the state as the cost for liberty.

Forced medical testing which denies choice of one's own doctor and medical facility denies liberty to prostitutes. Denial of worker's compensation prevents prostitutes from liberty and health security in case of illness.

Forced or pressured registration with the police stigmatizes prostitutes and frequently violates their privacy and liberty to change professions if they so choose. Prostitutes are denied job mobility by requirements for letters of good conduct which are granted only to those who can prove that they have not engaged in commercial sex for at least three years (for example, in Switzerland).

3. The right to fair administration of justice

Application of laws and regulations against prostitution is usually arbitrary, discriminatory, corrupt, and hypocritical. In Paris, for example, street prostitutes are given an average of three tickets per week for passive or active solicitation; at the same time, they are heavily taxed for their prostitution earnings.

Prostitutes who are raped or physically battered are unlikely to succeed in bringing charges against the rapist or batterer. The prostitute is considered fair game for abuse even by state and judiciary authorities.

Foreign women who were deceitfully or forcefully transported for purposes of prostitution rarely succeed in bringing charges against the violating party.

Male law enforcement officials, like other men, are frequently customers and/or violators of prostitute women. Police, for example, in the United States, Canada, and Great Britain, regularly entrap women by posing as customers and arresting them as soon as they mention a price for sex. Even if the prostitute is careful not to mention a price (many have learned to expect police deceit), she may be convicted because a police officer's word carries more credit than a whore's word in court.

Prostitution laws are discriminately enforced against women, especially third world and poor women, and against third world male associates of those women.

4. *Respect for private and family life, home and correspondence*

Laws which criminalize those who profit from the earnings of prostitutes are frequently used against the family of prostitutes, for example in the United States and France. Such "anti-pimping" laws violate a prostitute's right to a private life by putting all of her personal associates, be they lovers or children or parents or roommates, under (even more) risk of arrest than exploiters and physical violators.

Confiscation of personal letters or literary work of prostitutes, for example in the United States, is a clear denial of respect for home and correspondence, not to mention a denial of freedom of expression.

5. *Freedom of expression and to hold opinions*

The word of prostitutes is generally assumed to be invalid in public, for example as evidence in court. The opinions of prostitutes are rarely given a hearing, even in relation to their own lives.

In private, prostitutes are often used as police informants and as counselors to male customers. In public, be it on the street or in court, their testimony and opinion are silenced.

6. *Freedom of peaceful assembly and association, including the right to join a trade union*

Prostitutes are prevented from working together for purposes of safety, cooperation, and/or commercial advantage by specific statutes which criminalize "keeping a house" or other necessarily cooperative work forms.

Until prostitutes are recognized as legitimate workers, rather than as outlaws or vagrants or bad girls, they cannot officially form trade unions.

7. *The right to marry and found a family*

Both the right to marry and the right not to marry are frequently denied to women, in particular to the prostitute woman. Marriage is impossible if husbands thereby become outlaws, i.e. pimps. The denial of rights and legitimacy to unmarried women, on the other hand, can force women to marry against their will. A prostitute may also be denied the privilege of motherhood when the courts declare ¬er unfit on the basis of her professsion.

9. *The right to veaceful enjoyment of possessions*

The possessions of prostitutes and their associates are confiscated on the ground that they were obtained with "illegal" money; they are also confiscated when a prostitute cannot pay the fines levied against her for the practice of her profession.

9. *The right to leave a country including one's own*

Prostitutes are denied the right to travel across national borders by signs or cuts on their passports (or identity cards) which indicate their profession. Also, police records registered on computers at certain borders will prevent prostitutes from leaving or entering the country.

10. *Prohibition of torture and inhuman or degrading treatment and punishment*

The above mentioned violations indicate inhuman treatment. Degradation of prostitutes is the norm both among official bodies, such as governmental and judiciary institutions, and among community bodies, such as neighborhood committees and social service agencies.

Forced prostitution should be recognized as a case of torture.

11. *Prohibition of slavery, servitude and forced labour*

Servitude exists both in cases of forced prostitution and in cases of voluntary prostitution under forced conditions. State regulated brothels such as found in Hamburg (Germany) and Nevada (United States) allow no choice in clientele, no right to refusal, no right to a fair share of the earnings, forced isolation, and forced overwork. Most brothels in the Netherlands force unhealthy practices such as no condoms (or less earnings for condom sex) and/or forced alcohol consumption.

Juvenile prostitution is a case of forced labour but the managers, be they managers of pornography or prostitution, are rarely prosecuted whereas the children are often stigmatized and punished.

12. *Prohibition of discrimination in the enjoyment of rights and freedoms guaranteed by the Convention*

Prostitutes are discriminated against in the enjoyment of every right and freedom. Prostitutes of color, foreign prostitutes, street prostitutes, drug addicted prostitutes, and juvenile prostitutes suffer extra and often extreme discrimination.

13. *Prohibition of the collective expulsion of aliens*

Expulsion of foreign women who entered the country under conditions of deceit or force and who often await persecution in their native country is a violation of human rights.

BIBLIOGRAPHY

This bibliography is divided into nine sections: The Voice of the Prostitute; Global History of Prostitution from the Ancient to the Modern Era; Modern History of Prostitution in Western Europe and the United States; Contemporary Prostitution in Non-Western Countries; Prostitution and the Law in the United States; Studies: Psychology, Sociology, Criminology; Feminist Analyses of Prostitution; The Pornography Debate; and Prostitutes in Fiction. There is no section specifically devoted to AIDS because not much has been published specifically about prostitutes other than the articles cited in the article on AIDS in this volume.

1. The Voice of the Prostitute

Adler, Polly, *A House is Not a Home*. New York: Popular Library, 1953. The memoirs of Polly Adler, born in Russia in 1900, emigrated to the United States when she was twelve years old, began running a "house of assignation," when she was twenty, becoming a more traditional madam after being arrested, and running a number of very successful brothels until she retired in 1945. The book is often available in used bookstores.

Barrows, Sydney and William Novak, *Mayflower Madam: The Secret Life of Sydney Biddle Barrows*. New York: Arbor House, 1986. First person account of the experiences of an upper middle class, privileged descendent from people who arrived here on the Mayflower, who ran an exclusive outcall service until she was arrested in 1984. The book tells, in extensive detail, how a modern outcall service is run; a good companion to Polly Adler and Nell Kimball's books.

Hollander, Xaviera, et al, *The Happy Hooker*. New York: Dell Publishing Co., Inc., 1972. Although the book tends to glamorize prostitution and is aimed more at tantalizing people than telling about reality, Hollander also discusses problems with violent tricks and corrupt and violent police.

Jaget, Claude, ed., *Prostitutes — Our Life*. Bristol, England: Falling Wall Press, 1980. A series of interviews with six of the prostitutes who occupied the cathedrals in Lyons, France, in 1975, to protest the treatment of prostitutes by police and to call attention to a series of murders of prostitutes. Includes an afterword by Margo St. James, founder of COYOTE.

Lederer, Laura, "An Interview with a Former Pornography Model," in *Take Back the Night: Women on Pornography*, Laura Lederer, ed. New York: William Morrow & Co., Inc., 1980.

Longstreet, Stephen (ed.), *Nell Kimball: Her Life as an American Madam*. New York: The Macmillan Company, 1970. Fascinating memoir of a woman born before the Civil War, who became a prostitute not very long after the war, and eventually became a successful madam in St. Louis and in New Orleans' famed Storyville district. She retired in 1917, when Storyville was closed on orders of the military, who wanted to "protect" the soldiers from venereal diseases. (See Allan Brandt's *No Magic Bullet*, below, for a thorough analysis of the failure of the closure of the brothels to reduce the incidence of venereal disease.)

Madeleine: An Autobiography. New York: Persea Books, 1986. A reprint of a memoir originally published in 1919, with an introduction by Marcia Carlisle, an historian who has been studying prostitution in Philadelphia around the turn of the century. Madeleine was born in the Midwest shortly after the Civil War, worked as a prostitute in Chicago and a number of frontier cities, and as a madam in the Northwest Territories, in Canada. Originally published with an introduction by Judge Ben B. Lindsey, as a partial antidote to the hysteria about "white slavery."

Millett, Kate, *The Prostitution Papers*. NY: Ballantine Books, 1973. Also, as "Prostitution: A Quartet for Female Voices," in Gornick, Vivian and Barbara K. Moran, eds., *Woman in Sexist Society*, NY: New American Library, 1971. Interviews with four women who worked as prostitutes in New York.

Perkins, Roberta and Garry Bennet, *Being a Prostitute*. Winchester, MA: Allen & Unwin, Inc., 1985. A series of interviews with both female and male prostitutes who work in Australia, as well as an excellent article about prostitution in Australia that includes a summary of the results of surveys of both female and male prostitutes in that country.

Roberts, Nickie, *The Front Line: Women in the Sex Industry Speak*. London: Grafton Books, 1986. Roberts writes about ner own life as a child and adolescent, and her decision to leave her hometown and move to London to get away from dreary, monotonous and sometimes unhealthy jobs. She chose to live in and around the Soho district, and eventually took a job in a strippers' club when she ran out of money. Among other things, she discusses the negative impact of pressure from police and others to "clean up" the area on working conditions in the clubs. She also includes interviews with other strippers and with male and female prostitutes.

Weene, Seph, "Venus," in *Sex Issue: Heresies* * 12, 1981. Essay by a former pornography actress. Among other things, she discusses her feelings of power when she is performing.

Zausner, Michael, *The Streets: A Factual Portrait of Six Prostitutes as Told in their Own Words*. New York: St. Martin's Press, 1986. Although the author's methods are questionable (for example, he snorted cocaine with the young women he interviewed), what comes through is the incredible strength of the young prostitutes as they attempt to cope with enormously difficult lives.

2. Global History of Prostitution from Ancient to Modern Era

Boswell, John, *Christianity, Homosexuality and Tolerance*. Chicago: University of Chicago Press, 1980. Includes a good deal of information on how prostitution functioned and was tolerated or repressed, from Ancient Greece through the Renaissance.

Bullough, Vern and Bonnie Bullough, *Prostitution: An Illustrated Social History*. NY: Crown Publishers, Inc., 1978. Extensive survey of the way various cultures have dealt with prostitution. Illustrated with pornography from the time and place, showing the change in the 19th century, at which time pornography became more hostile.

Lerner, Gerda, "The Origin of Prostitution in Ancient Mesopotamia," in *Signs*, Winter 1986, pp. 236-254. Also in *The Creation of Patriarchy*, New York: Oxford University Press, 1986. Discusses the development of secular prostitution in market districts, generally near the temples; suggests the shift from an early recognition and valuing of the prostitute as a sexually experienced woman to a forced separation of "good" and "bad" women through the use of the veil.

Murphy, Emmett, *Great Bordellos of the World: An Illustrated History*. London: Quartet Books, 1983. Although very much from a male, perhaps customer, perspective, this book provides a good deal of information about the way prostitution operated at various times and places, as well as the changing status of prostitutes. Filled with illustrations, some of them from the time and place described, some later reconstructions, showing the way prostitutes fit into their societies and/or were viewed by male painters.

Tannahill, Reay, *Sex in History*. New York: Stein and Day, 1980. Although not about prostitution, per se, because a significant part of the written records about sexuality deals with prostitution, this book includes a great deal of information about prostitution in Western and Asian history.

Wells, Jess, *A Herstory of Prostitution in Western Europe*. Berkeley: Shameless Hussy, 1982. Documents the structures imposed by the patriarchy on prostitution from Ancient Greece to Victorian England.

3. Modern History of Prostitution in Western Europe and the United States

Barnhart, Jacqueline Baker, *The Fair but Frail: Prostitution in San Francisco 1849-1900*. Reno: University of Nevada Press, 1986. For the first few years of the Gold Rush, prostitutes in San Francisco were respectable citizens, welcome in public society. However, when "good" women began to move to the City, and to marry some of the tradesmen, prostitutes' status began to decline. A good companion to the memoirs of Nell Kimball and Madeleine (see Voice of the Prostitute, above).

Brandt, Allan M., *No Magic Bullet: A Social History of Venereal Disease in the United States since 1880*. NY: Oxford University Press, 1985. Excellent and fascinating account of efforts to control venereal disease (particularly in the military) before and after both World Wars by controlling prostitution. Also documents the ambivalence of public health officials about how to prevent venereal disease: 1) control men's sexuality or 2) recommend prophylactic measures. Good lessons for us as we work to prevent the AIDS epidemic from getting worse.

Bristow, Edward J., *Prostitution and Prejudice: The Jewish Fight against White Slavery 1870-1939*. NY: Schocken Books, 1983. Excellent discussion of the extent of Jewish involvement in prostitution — both as prostitutes and as pimps and madams — during the period of intense Jewish immigration from Europe. At one time, prostitutes and pimps established their own synagogues and cemeteries because the mainstream Jewish religious organizations refused to allow them to participate.

Brown, Dee, *The Gentle Tamers: Women of the Old Wild West*. Lincoln, NE: University of Nebraska Press, 1958, reissued 1981. The role of prostitutes in the westward migration in North America is often ignored. This book includes two chapters, "Some Ladies of Easy Virtue" and "Pink Tights and Red Velvet Skirts" that include information about some of the more well-known women who for at least a time supported themselves through one form or another of prostitution.

Butler, Anne M., *Daughters of Joy, Sisters of Misery: Prostitutes in the American West 1865-90*, Urbana, IL: University of Illinois Press, 1985. Although Butler's work suffers from her bias, her judgments of women who work as prostitutes, the book contains a lot of information about frontier prostitution east of the Rockies, especially the relationship between prostitutes and the military. Unfortunately, Butler dismisses, out of hand, any evidence which contradicts Butler's assumption that prostitutes were uniformly depressed, impoverished, miserable, sick, or that they lived lives of chaos, degradation, and disorder. The book also could benefit from a listing of the laws regarding prostitution.

Coffin, Judy, "Artisans of the Sidewalk," *Radical History Review* 26, 1982, pp. 89-101. A review of Alain Corbin, *Les Filles de noce: Misere sexuelle et prostitution au 19e et 20e siecles*. Paris: Aubier Montaigne, 1978. Discusses the occupation of French churches by prostitutes in 1975 in the context of the history of reglementation of prostitution in France.

Connelly, Mark Thomas, *The Response to Prostitution in the Progressive Era*. Chapel Hill, NC: The University of North Carolina

Press, 1980. Shows how feminist concerns with violence against women and the sexual exploitation of women and children were manipulated by fundamentalist moralists in the late 19th and early 20th centuries, resulting in a "purity" crusade which, by making prostitution illegal, made things worse instead of better.

DuBois, Ellen Carol and Linda Gordon, "Seeking Ecstasy on the Battlefield: Danger and Pleasure in Nineteenth-century Feminist Sexual Thought," *Pleasure and Danger: Exploring Female Sexuality*, Carole S. Vance, ed. Boston: Routledge & Kegan Paul, 1984. Excellent discussion of the splits in the women's movement over sexuality, and prostitution, in the first wave of the feminist movement.

Finnegan, Frances, *Poverty and Prostitution: A Study of Victorian Prostitutes in York*. Cambridge: Cambridge University Press, 1979. A good companion to Walkowitz' study of the Contagious Diseases Acts in Victorian England.

Goldman, Marion S., *Gold Diggers and Silver Miners: Prostitution and Social Life on the Comstock Lode*. Ann Arbor: The University of Michigan Press, 1981. Excellent account of the way prostitution was organized in Nevada during the height of the silver mining days of the 19th century.

Jeffrey, Julie Roy, *Frontier Women: The Trans-Mississippi West 1840-1880*. New York: Hill and Wang, 1979. Fairly extensive discussion of prostitution in the chapter entitled, "The Rarest Commodity. . . Are Women."

Jeffreys, Sheila, *The Spinster and her Enemies: Feminism and Sexuality 1880-1930*. London: Pandora, 1985. Looks at the first wave of feminism's work on prostitution, which was viewed as sexual slavery, and on rape and child sexual abuse. Although the author is writing from a strong anti-pornography, and presumably anti-prostitution perspective, there is much useful information about the ambivalence of our foremothers in dealing with prostitution.

Kishtainy, Khalid, *The Prostitute in Progressive Literature*. London: Allison & Busby, 1982.

Otis, Leah Lydia, *Prostitution in Medieval Society: The History of an Urban Institution in Languedoc*. Chicago: The University of Chicago

Press, 1985. Traces the evolution of prostitution from its informal structure in the 14th century through its private organization in red-light districts in the early 15th century, the development of regulated and then municipal-owned brothels in the later 15th century, and prohibition in the 16th century. Otis has great sympathy and respect for the women who worked.

Perry, Mary Elizabeth, "'Lost Women' in Early Modern Seville: The Politics of Prostitution," in *Feminist Studies* 4:1, February 1978, 195-214.

-----, "Lost Women," in *Crime and Society in Early Modern Seville*. University Press of New England, 1980. An excellent essay in a fascinating book about "marginal" people in Spain from the time of the expulsion of the Moors and Jews through the late Renaissance. Until recently, Perry taught one of the only courses on the history of prostitution, at UCLA. After a decade of teaching as a "temporary" professor, she was denied tenure even though her classes were among the most popular in the History Department.

Rosen, Ruth, *The Lost Sisterhood: Prostitution in America, 1900-1918*. Baltimore, MD: Johns Hopkins University Press, 1982. One of the best discussions of the events leading up to and following the U.S. prohibition of prostitution in the second decade of this century. Includes an extensive discussion of the sociological data from surveys of prostitutes done at the time, and explodes the myth that all women who worked as prostitutes at that time were victims and/or forced into slavery.

-----, and Sue Davidson, eds., *The Mamie Papers*. Old Westbury, NY: The Feminist Press, 1977. The letters of Mamie Pinzer, a young Jewish former prostitute, to Boston Philanthropist Fanny Quincy Howe, from 1910 to 1922.

Walkowitz, Judith R., *Prostitution and Victorian Society: Women, Class, and the State*. Cambridge: Cambridge University Press, 1980. Extensive detail about the feminist movement to repeal the Contagious Diseases Acts in England in the 1860s and 70s, a movement led by Josephine Butler. England, the first to try to use medical-based legislation to control prostitutes in the 19th century, is now the first country to pass laws that would authorize quarantining people with AIDS.

----, "Male Vice and Female Virtue: Feminism and the Politics of Prostitution in Nineteenth-Century Britain," *Powers of Desire: The Politics of Sexuality*, Ann Snitow, et al, eds. NY: Monthly Review Press, 1983.

4. Contemporary Prostitution in Non- Western Countries

Bridel, Renee, "Traffic of Children," in *International Feminism: Networking Against Female Sexual Slavery*, Report of the Global Feminist Workshop to Organize Against Traffic in Women, held in Rotterdam, the Netherlands, April 6-15, 1983, edited by Kathleen Barry, Charlotte Bunch and Shirley Castley.

Eisen Bergman, Arlene, *Women of Viet Nam*. San Francisco: Peoples Press, 1974. Includes an extensive discussion of the development of large-scale, forced prostitution to provide for the "rest and rehabilitation" of American soldiers during the war in Viet Nam.

El Saadawi, Nawal, "The Illegitimate Child and the Prostitute," in *The Hidden Face of Eve: Women in the Arab World*. London: Zed Press, 1980. Written by the outspoken feminist who was jailed by Sadat shortly before his assassination.

Hariharan, A., et al, "The Sexual Revolution," in *Far Eastern Economic Review*, 91:21-32, January 9, 1976. Excellent description of prostitution systems in various countries in Southeast Asia, the area in which sex tourism (i.e., Kisaeng prostitution) is so prominent.

Mark, Mary Ellen, *Falkland Road*. New York: Alfred A. Knopf, 1981. A photoessay about prostitutes in a poor district of Bombay with a brief text based on the women's statements about themselves.

Matsui, Yayori, "Why I Oppose Kisaeng Tours," in *International Feminism: Networking Against Female Sexual Slavery*, Report of the Global Feminist Workshop to Organize Against Traffic in Women, held in Rotterdam, the Netherlands, April 6-15, 1983, edited by Kathleen Barry, Charlotte Bunch and Shirley Castley.

"Position Paper prepared by Movimiento El Pozo for the Peruvian Commission set up by Congress to study Prostitution, February 28,

1983," in *International Feminism: Networking Against Female Sexual Slavery*, Report of the Global Feminist Workshop to Organize Against Traffic in Women, held in Rotterdam, the Netherlands, April 6-15, 1983, edited by Kathleen Barry, Charlotte Bunch and Shirley Castley.

Ramesh, Asha and Philomena H.P., "The Devadasi Problem," in *International Feminism: Networking Against Female Sexual Slavery*, Report of the Global Feminist Workshop to Organize Against Traffic in Women, held in Rotterdam, the Netherlands, April 6-15, 1983, edited by Kathleen Barry, Charlotte Bunch and Shirley Castley.

White, Luise, "Prostitution, Identity, and Class Consciousness in Nairobi during World War II," in *Signs*, Winter 1986, pp. 255-273. Fascinating discussion of three forms of prostitution in Kenya under colonial rule prior to and during World War II, showing the impact of the forced segregation of women and men on the development of prostitution as both a way for women to earn money and for men, who were separated from their families, to have sex lives. Many of the prostitutes had lovers, as distinct from customers.

Yamazaki, Tomoko, *The Story of Yamada Waka: From Prostitute to Feminist Pioneer*. Tokyo: Kodansha International, 1985. A biography of Yamada Waka, sent from her village in Japan to America, where she was recruited into prostitution, escaped from a Seattle brothel, spent some time in San Francisco in Cameron House, a shelter for women leaving prostitution in the early part of this century, and returned to Japan where she became a feminist writer and devoted her energies to helping prostitutes change their occupation.

5. Prostitution and the Law in the United States

Berring, Robert, et al, "Representing the Unpopular Client," *Law Library Journal*, 72:674- 89, Fall 1979.

Boles, Jacqueline and Charlotte Tatro, "Legal and Extra-Legal Methods of Controlling Female Prostitution: A Cross-Cultural Comparison," *International Journal of Comparative and Applied Criminal Justice*, 2:71-85, Spring 1978. Suggests that the function of prostitution laws is primarily "symbolic" in that they define "good and evil" rather than effectively control or regulate prostitution. Also suggests that the less repressive the laws, the less likely prostitutes are to be dependent on pimps.

Decker, John F., *Prostitution: Regulation and Control*. Littleton, CO: Fred B. Rothman & Co., 1979. Comprehensive analysis of the history of the treatment of prostitutes under the law, including the development of the law, a survey of the approaches taken by several countries, methods and discriminatory enforcement of the laws, and proposals for a mildly regulated form of decriminalization.

Farmer, Mary K., et al, "A Proposal for the Legalization of Prostitution in Connecticut," *Connecticut Law Journal*, 49:163, 1975.

Haft, Marilyn G., "Hustling for Rights," *The Civil Liberties Review*, 8-26, Winter/Spring 1974.

----, "Legal Arguments: Prostitution Laws and the Constitution," in Jennifer James (ed.), *Perspectives on Prostitution*, Seattle: Social Research Associates, 1980.

Jennings, Anne, "The Victim as Criminal: A Consideration of California's Prostitution Law," *California Law Review*, 64:1235-84, Spring 1976.

Milman, Barbara, "New Rules for the Oldest Profession: Should we Change our Prostitution Laws?" *Harvard Women's Law Journal*, 3:1-82, Spring 1980.

Murray, Ellen F., "Anti-Prostitution Laws: New Conflicts in the Fight Against the World's Oldest Profession," *Albany Law Review*, 43:360-87, Winter 1979.

Parnas, Raymond I., "Legislative Reform of Prostitution Laws: Keeping Commercial Sex Out of Sight and Out of Mind," *Santa Clara Law Review*, 21:669-696, Summer 1981.

Rosenbleet, Charles and Barbara J. Pariente, "The Prostitution of the Criminal Law," *American Law Review*, 11:373, Winter 1973.

Wade, Daniel E., "Prostitution and the Law: Emerging Attacks on the

'Women's Crime,'"*University of Missouri/Kansas City*, 43:413-26, Spring 1975.

Wandling, Theresa M., "Decriminalization of Prostitution: The Limits of the Criminal Law," *Oregon Law Review*, 55:553-66, 1976.

Women Endorsing Decriminalization, "Prostitution: A Non-Victim Crime?" *Issues in Criminology*, 8:137, Fall 1973.

6. Studies: Psychology, Sociology, Criminology

Adler, Freda, "The Oldest and Newest Profession," *The Criminology of Deviant Women*, Freda Adler and Rita J. Simon, eds. Boston: Houghton-Mifflin Co., 1978.

Baizerman, Michael, et al, "Adolescent Prostitution," *Children Today*, September/ October 1979. Includes some discussion of who the customers are and why they look for juvenile prostitutes.

Bracy, Dorothy H., "Concurrent and Consecutive Abuse: The Juvenile Prostitute," in *The Criminal Justice System and Women*. NY: Clark Boardman Co., Ltd., 1982.

Cohen, Bernard, *Deviant Street Networks: Prostitution in New York City*. Lexington, MA: Lexington Books, 1980. Excellent study of thirteen "stroll" districts in lower and mid-Manhattan. Covers such questions as pimp/prostitute relationships (younger women have pimps, older women do not); racism in the enforcement of prostitution laws; police practices.

Conrad, Gary L., et al, "Sexually Transmitted Diseases Among Prostitutes and Other Sexual Offenders," in *Sexually Transmitted Diseases*, October-December 1981, pp. 241-244.

Crow, Ruth and Ginny McCarthy, eds., *Teenage Women in the Juvenile Justice System: Changing Values*. Tucson: New Directions for Young Women, Inc., 1979.

Darrow, William W., "Prostitution and Sexually Transmitted Diseases," in *Sexually Transmitted Diseases*, K. K. Holmes, et al, eds. New York: McGraw-Hill, 1984. pp. 109-116. Discusses the history of testing prostitutes for sexually transmitted diseases, treatment practices and their relationship to creating resistant strains of gonorrhea, the biases of existing studies, and the results of modern studies. Although he acknowledges the relationship between condom use, or non-use, and STD rates, his recommendations for preventing STDs include using police to "refer" prostitutes to medical attention. Given the history of quarantines and forced treatment with antibiotics in this country, even in the absence of known infections, his recommendations seem punitive, not effective. Darrow is the director of the prostitutes and AIDS studies funded by the Centers for Disease Control.

Davis, Nanette J., "Prostitution: Identity, Career, and Legal Economic Enterprise," in *Studies in the Sociology of Sex*, James M. Hanslin and Edward Sagarin (eds.) New York: Schocken Books, 1978.

Exner, John E., Jr., et al, "Some Psychological Characteristics of Prostitutes," *Journal of Personality Assessment*, 41:474-85, October 1975. Exner, et al found that the only measurable difference between prostitutes and controls, who were matched for education and economic background, was that the prostitutes earned more money.

Goldstein, Paul J., *Prostitution and Drugs*. Lexington, MA: Lexington Books, 1979. Detailed study of several different groups of prostitutes concerning their use of alcohol, heroin, methamphetamines, and other drugs. Documents strikingly different patterns of drug use depending on locus of prostitution. Important reading for anyone working on AIDS prevention.

Heyl, Barbara Sherman, "The Madam as Entrepreneur," *Sociological Symposium*, 11:61-82, 1974. Also, NJ: Transaction Books, 1979.

----, "The Madam as Teacher: The Training of House Prostitutes," *Social Problems*, 24:545-55, June 1977.

----, "Prostitution: An Extreme Case of Sex Stratification," in *The Criminology of Deviant Women*, Freda Adler and Rita J. Simon, eds. Boston: Houghton-Mifflin Co., 1978.

James, Jennifer, "Prostitutes and Prostitution," in *Deviants: Voluntary Actors in a Hostile World*, Edward Sagarin and Fred

Montanino, eds. General Learning Press, Scott, Foresman & Co., 1977. This is one of several articles based on Dr. James' research when she was with the Department of Psychiatry and Behavioral Sciences at the University of Washington/Seattle. James studied the history of sexual and physical abuse in prostitutes' childhood, motivations for entrance into prostitution, addiction, the treatment of women as sexual criminals and victims, etc. This particular article is the most comprehensive, but all are worth reading.

----, "Prostitute-Pimp Relationships," *Medical Aspects of Human Sexuality*, 7:146-60, 1973.

----, *Prostitution and Addiction: An Interdisciplinary Approach*. Unpublished paper, 1975.

----, "Motivations for Entrance into Prostitution," in *The Female Offender*, Laura Crites, ed. Lexington, MA: Lexington Books, 1976.

----, "Women as Sexual Criminals and Victims," in *Sexual Scripts: The Social Construction of Female Sexuality*, Judith Long Laws and Pepper Schwartz, eds. Hinsdale, IL: The Dryden Press, 1977.

----, "Self-Destructive Behavior and Adaptive Strategies in Female Prostitutes," in *The Many Faces of Suicide*, Norman L. Farberow, ed. New York: McGraw-Hill, 1980.

----, "The Prostitute as Victim," in *The Criminal Justice System and Women*, Barbara Raffel Price and Natalie J. Sokoloff, eds. NY: Clark Boardman Co., Ltd., 1982.

Janus, Sam, et al, *A Sexual Profile of Men in Power*. New York: Paperback Publishers, Warner, 1978. Although this book is flawed by its simplistic, pseudo-Freudian analysis of the behavior it documents, the information about the behavior of politicians and other powerful men with prostitutes is fascinating. The hypocrisy of legislators and judges is inescapable.

Lynch, Theresa and Marilyn Neckes, *Cost-Effectiveness of Enforcing Prostitution Laws*. Cambridge, MA: Unitarian Universalist Service Committee, 1978.

McLeod, Eileen, *Women Working: Prostitution Now*. London: Croom Helm, Ltd., 1982. The author, a founding member of PROS, a prostitutes' rights campaign organization in England, discusses the movement, and what the prostitutes feel about their work and want from the movement.

Plummer, Kenneth (ed.), *The Making of the Modern Homosexual*. London: Hutchinson & Co. (Publishers) Ltd., 1981. Although not about prostitution, per se, the discussion of the role of labels and stigma to create and maintain an outcast class is directly relevant to an understanding of prostitution.

Potterat, John J., et al, "On Becoming a Prostitute: An Exploratory Case-Comparison Study," in *Brief Reports*, March 20, 1984. Compared fourteen prostitutes and fifteen non-prostitute women who had tested positive for gonorrhea at a Colorado Springs VD clinic and had reported two or more male contacts. The only significant differences in their backgrounds and characteristics seemed to be that prostitutes were more likely to be first-born, had more education, were less discriminatory in their selection of lovers/ sex partners, and tended to have greater self-confidence and self-esteem. However, the authors view prostitution as a manifestation of illness or disorder.

Silbert, Mimi H., PhD, principal investigator, *Sexual Assault of Prostitutes*. San Francisco: Delancey Street Foundation, 1981. Dr. Silbert and her colleagues interviewed two hundred prostitutes, most of them street prostitutes, ranging in age from nine through the mid- to late thirties, about their experiences of sexual assault prior to and during their involvement in prostitution.

Velarde, Albert J., "Becoming Prostituted: The Decline of the Massage Parlor Profession and the Masseuse," *British Journal of Criminology*, 15:3, 251-63, July 1975. In spite of the title, this is an excellent description of the stigmatization process through which women recruited to work in supposedly legitimate massage parlors were subtly coerced into engaging in sexual activity so that by the end of the first day of work they had become prostitutes.

7. Feminist Analyses of Prostitution

Barry, Kathleen, *Female Sexual Slavery*. Englewood-Cliffs, NJ: Prentice-Hall, Inc., 1979. Paperback, NY: Avon Discus, 1981. One of the first books by a contemporary feminist to analyze prostitution, this book was important in that it helped to get the issue discussed. However, Barry's analysis suffers from her inability to understand that although some prostitution is a form of slavery, other prostitution is at least as voluntary as most other forms of wage labor, and that some women like the work and consider it their profession. Like Sarah Wynter, of WHISPER, Barry tends to view all prostitutes as helpless victims. Barry went on to write an essay for the *Report of the Global Feminist Workshop to Organize Against Traffic in Women*, in which she "reifies" (to use one of her favorite words) prostitutes, both viewing them as victims, and calling them to account for their alleged upholding of patriarchal abuse of women.

Carmen, Arlene and Howard Moody, *Working Women: The Subterranean World of Street Prostitution*. NY: Harper & Row, 1985. A loving report of the work done by the Judson Memorial Church, in New York City, to try to improve the conditions of the women who work as street prostitutes in Manhattan.

Enloe, Cynthia, "The Militarization of Prostitution," in her book, *Does Khaki Become You: The Militarization of Women's Lives*. Boston: South End Press, 1983.

ISIS: International Bulletin 13, November 1979. Special issue devoted to tourism and prostitution. Includes articles on the whore/Madonna dichotomy and the relationship between tourism and prostitution in a number of Asian countries. Also discusses the relationship between U.S. military bases and prostitution.

Macmillan, Jackie, "Prostitution as Sexual Politics," *Quest: A Feminist Quarterly*, 4:1, 41-50, Summer 1977. Feminist analysis, supports decriminalization as a necessary step in ending the problems associated with illegal prostitution.

Nestle, Joan, *A Restricted Country*. Ithaca, NY: Firebrand Books, 1987. Erotic writing and articles about lesbian life, including a section on lesbians who worked as prostitutes in the 1950s.

Pheterson, Gail, *The Whore Stigma: Female Dishonor and Male Unworthiness*. Amsterdam: Dutch Ministry of Social Affairs and Employment, Emancipation Policy Coordination, 1986. A work in progress, this study explores in depth the nature of the stigma associated with prostitution and its effect on prostitutes' lives, and compares it with the effect of stigmas on other oppressed groups.

Smart, Carol, "Prostitution, Rape and Sexual Politics," in her book, *Women, Crime and Criminology: A Feminist Critique*. London: Routledge and Kegan Paul, 1976.

----, and Barry Smart, eds., *Women, Sexuality and Social Control*, London: Routledge and Kegan Paul, 1978.

Snitow, Ann, et al, *Powers of Desire: The Politics of Sexuality*. NY: Monthly Review Press, 1983. Excellent anthology of articles dealing with a variety of aspects of women's sexuality, including prostitution and pornography.

Vance, Carole S., ed., *Pleasure and Danger: Exploring Female Sexuality*. Boston: Routledge & Kegan Paul, 1984. Anthology of papers presented at the conference on sexuality held at Barnard College in 1982.

"Women & Prostitution," a series of articles translated by the People's Translation Service, in the Spring 1984 issue (No. 12) of *Connexions: An International Women's Quarterly*.

8. The Pornography Debate

Alexander, Priscilla, "Response to Andrea Dworkin," in *Gay Community News*, (winter) 1986. Discusses the stigmatizing of women who work in the sex industry by the authors of the "model anti-pornography ordinance," and especially by Andrea Dworkin who tries to get around her use of the word "whore" as a stigmatizing label by comparing prostitutes, who work for money, with "village sluts."

---- and Margo St. James, "And Pornography Goes Free," *Sojourner*, February 1982. Discussion of the problems that resulted from the *de facto* decriminalization of pornography, in the 1960s and 1970s, while prostitution was left criminalized.

Bryant, Barbara, "Sexual Display of Women's Bodies—A Violation of Privacy," *Women's Law Forum*, X:3, Summer 1980.

Burstyn, Varda, ed., *Women Against Censorship.* Vancouver: Douglas & McIntyre, 1985. A series of articles, most of them written by Canadian feminists, looking at the pornography issue from the perspective that although there are problems with some pornography, censorship is not the solution to those problems. Especially interesting are Burstyn's essays, "Political Precedents and Moral Crusades: Women, Sex and the State," and "Beyond Despair: Positive Strategies."

Coop, David and Susan Wendell, eds., *Pornography and Censorship.* Buffalo, NY: Prometheus Books, 1983. Includes articles from a variety of perspectives.

Duggan, Lisa, "Censorship in the Name of Feminism," *Village Voice,* October 16, 1984.

Ellis, Kate, "I'm Black and Blue from the Rolling Stones and I'm Not Sure How I Feel About It: Pornography and the Feminist Imagination," in *Socialist Review,* 14:3/4 May-August 1984, pp. 103-125.

Elshtain, Jean Bethke, "The New Porn Wars," *The New Republic,* June 25, 1984, pp. 15-20.

Faust, Bernice, *Women, Sex and Pornography: A Controversial Study.* NY: Macmillan Co., 1980. Looks at the question of why there is so much pornography for men and virtually none for women. Posits the theory that one reason is that women are more affected by touch than by visual stimulation.

Jacobs, Caryn, "Patterns of Violence: A Feminist Perspective on the Regulation of Pornography," *Harvard Women's Law Journal,* Vol. 7, 1984, pp. 5-55.

Kensington Ladies' Erotica Society, *Ladies Home Erotica.* Berkeley: Ten Speed Press, 1984. A collection of erotic stories, poetry, and a few drawings by women, in an exploration of what female, or feminist, pornography might be like.

"Midsection: Sex & Censorship," *Film Comment, 20:6,* November-December 1984, pp. 29-49. Includes several articles for and against the MacKinnon ordinance.

"New FACT Group Battles Censorship Laws," *New Directions for Women*, January/February 1985. Includes several articles for and against the ordinance.

On Our Backs: Entertainment for the Adventurous Lesbian. Published by a group of lesbians in San Francisco, many of whom have worked in the sex industry, exploring what pornography produced by women, for women, could be like. P.O. Box 42196, San Francisco, CA 94142.

Philipson, Ilene, "Beyond the Virgin and the Whore," in *Socialist Review*, 14:3/4 May-August 1984, pp. 127-136.

Sheinfeld, Lois P., "Banning Porn: the New Censorship," *The Nation*, September 8, 1984, pp. 174-175.

"The Place of Pornography," a forum held at the New School for Social Research in New York, published in *Harper's*, November 1984, pp. 31-45.

Vance, Carole S., "The Meese Commission on the Road," *The Nation*, August 2/9, 1986, pp. 1, 76-82. Carole Vance, one of the founders of the New York Feminist Anti-Censorship Task Force, attended all of the hearings and business meetings of the Attorney General's Commission on Pornography, during 1985 and 1986. This article is a brief statement of her analysis of and reaction to the Commission. She is working on a book about the hearings and their implications.

Weir, Lorna and Leo Casey, "Subverting Power in Sexuality," in *Socialist Review*, 14:3/4 May-August 1985, pp. 139-157.

9. Prostitutes in Fiction

Brown, Rita Mae, *Southern Discomfort*. New York: Bantam Books, Inc. 1982. Set in the period from 1918-1928, this novel includes several prostitutes among its characters, reflecting careful research into the way prostitution worked prior to prohibition, the relationship between the anti-alcohol and anti-prostitution movements, and the discrepancy between how prostitutes viewed themselves and their work and how they were perceived by others.

El Saadawi, Nawal, *Women at Point Zero*. London: Zed Books, Ltd., 1983. Novel about a woman who leaves an arranged marriage in which she is brutalized, works as an independent prostitute, becomes involved with a brutal pimp, kills him and is sentenced to death. Based on her own experiences working as a psychiatrist in an Egyptian prison.

Hayes, Penny, *The Long Trail*. Tallahassee, FL: Naiad Press, 1986. Story of a woman in a frontier town, in the 19th century, who falls in love with a woman who works as a prostitute in a saloon, their developing relationship, and their travels to an eastern city.

McCunn, Ruthanne Lum, *Thousand Pieces of Gold*. New York: Dell Publishing Co., Inc., 1981. Biographical novel about Lalu Nathoy who was sold by her father when famine struck northern China in 1871 and was forced to work as a prostitute, first in Shanghai and then in a gold rush mining town in America. Eventually, marrying a man who won her in a poker game, she lived the rest of her life as a homesteader.

Shulman, Alix Kates, *On the Stroll*. New York: Alfred A. Knopf, Inc., 1981. Contrasts the life of a young girl who runs away from home and gets turned out by a would-be pimp with the life of an aging bag lady who, in her youth, was a kind of courtesan to military brass at the end of World War II.

Wilson, Barbara, *Sisters of the Road*. Seattle: The Seal Press, 1986. This mystery is about the murder of a young ex-prostitute and the attempts of the heroine, an amateur sleuth, to find the murdered girl's co-worker. Confronts and comes to terms with many of the feminist discomforts about prostitution.

***

CONTRIBUTORS' NOTES

Aline: lives off the northern coast of California with two cats. She has indulged in assorted passions for seventeen years. She cynically describes herself as a pansexual atheist feminist with Buddhist leanings. She is writing a book and hopes to reincarnate to a more loving planet in her next lifetime.

Carole: "I am a thirty-four year old lesbian feminist who has done sex work and plans never to do so again. I am a recently identified survivor of incest whose ground has been shaken since that tentative naming. Sex work for me was a means of survival, an extension of what I'd learned to do as a woman in a misogynist environment, and a liberation from 'nice-girl-smiling-in-offices.' I support the efforts of women to gain power and dignity in our work and sexuality, to be honest about where we have been and where we are today, so our tomorrows may be freer. Still, today, I need to be anonymous."

Sunny Carter: born in New Mexico in 1950 of Irish stock, Sunny has a firm belief that God invented whiskey so the Irish wouldn't take over the world. Changing locale as easily as her hair color, this (sometimes) redhead has lived in Dallas, Las Vegas, Baltimore, Atlanta, New York City and St. Croix, U.S. Virgin Islands. "I'm a Pisces. I can't stay still any more than the ocean can." Besides a five-year career as a call girl, she has been a writer, teacher, medical technician, mother, poet and gorilla. "I love being a gorilla. For twenty-five dollars I put on my gorilla suit and deliver flowers or whatever." Sunny is an advocate for prostitutes' rights and is currently writing a book on AIDS.

M. M. Chateauvert: lives in Washington, D.C. where she researches women and work issues. This story was written in 1982 while she was a student at the University of Iowa.

Judith Edelstein: "I'm Jewish, a feminist, and a lesbian. My hometown is Chicago, but I've lived in Portland, Oregon for fourteen years. The massage parlor experiences I draw from in my story occurred about nine years ago. Currently, I teach English at two community colleges and write both fiction and nonfiction."

Kellie Everts: The first and only "stripper for God," Kellie Everts has given more than one thousand sermons on the stages of burlesque theatres and nightclubs. She has appeared on Real People and Good Morning America, among other television programs. She believes in the natural superiority of women, that matriarchy is the will of God, and that the patriarchal system is a "demonic perversion" that has caused the downfall of mankind.

Scarlot Harlot/Carol Leigh: "I have been working as a prostitute for ten years and as an artist for most of my life. When I was a small child I was committed to becoming an actress. When I was introduced to feminism at the age of nineteen, I realized that I would have more power and influence as a writer.

After a lengthy 'career' as an undergraduate, I attended Boston University's master's program in creative writing. I had hoped to study with Anne Sexton, but she committed suicide the semester I arrived. I studied fiction with John Cheever. My major influences have been Margo St. James, Phyllis Chesler and Kate Millett.

In 1976 I founded and taught in The Hampshire Street Women's Poetry and Fiction Cooperative, where we learned to develop more positive images of women for the media. When I moved to San Francisco in 1978, I began working and writing as a prostitute. As a skilled writer, I was pleased to find this life/art mission. For the next several years I chronicled my life in various media. I produced, created and performed a one-woman, multi-media performance piece, directed by Joya Cory, *The Adventures of Scarlot Harlot*, called 'a fascinating act of vaudeville and self-revelation.' I published three booklets, a monthly newsletter called *The Harlot Herald*, and I've worked as a columnist for *Appeal to Reason*, edited by John Bryan, where most of this material first appeared.

From 1984 to 1986, frightened by the AIDS crisis, I left the city for a tour of the Northwest and Southwest where I lectured and performed. I settled in Tucson, Arizona and produced, edited and starred in a six-episode situation comedy with T.W.I.T. (Tucson Western International Television) while I did political work under the auspices of T.W.A.T. (Tucson Whores and Tricks).

In late 1986 I returned to San Francisco. I am currently engaged in safe sex education and finding ways to reach as broad an audience as possible, performing as a political comedian and writing a column for a women's newspaper, *Bay Area Women's News*.

I'm always very busy and I enjoy devoting as many hours as possible to various modes of expression. I study performance modes, acting, singing, dancing, writing and technical/production skills

342

including video editing. I spend most of my money on classes and production. Prostitution has been my solution to owning the means of production.

I've lived alone and with lovers. For the last few years I have traveled and lived with friends. I've worked as a prostitute by running ads in sex papers and personal columns in weeklies. I am looking forward to earning most of my money as an artist. I am most anxious to organize a national tour and address a national television audience."

Nina Hartley: "I am a third generation feminist who graduated from San Francisco State *Magna Cum Laude* with a bachelor's degree in Nursing. My maternal grandparents were communist professors in Alabama in the thirties and worked hard for the civil rights of blacks and political prisoners. My parents, also communists, were active in the civil rights movements of the fifties and sixties, even after my father was blacklisted in 1957. I was introduced to radical feminism in the early seventies by my mother. The most enduring concept from that body of philosophy, one that motivates me today, is the conviction that women deserve to define their individual sexuality for themselves, including the right to depict women's powerful, multi-faceted sexuality from a woman's point of view. The seeds of my acting career were planted at Berkeley High School, where most of my intellectual energies were directed toward involvement in its drama department, at the time one of the best in the country. It was in this environment that I learned respect for the power of dramatic expression."

Judy Helfand: "Here, in alphabetical order, are some of the labels which apply to me: farmer, feminist, forty-one, Jewish, lesbian, middle class, mother of two, white. I'm working for the day when combination of the terms 'sex' and 'industry' will be inconceivable."

Jean Johnston: was born February 2, 1954 in New York. "I'm an ex-hooker learning to live and love one day at a time. I began writing three years ago, and my poetry has recently been published in *Conditions*."

Karen: lives and works in the Bay Area.

Sharon Kaiser: "I am a lesbian, have an MSW, and live in Berkeley. I'm an ex-porno actress and ex-prostitute. I currently do business development with small businesses, and I work with COYOTE and the California Prostitutes Education Project. For years, I've been doing workshops on unlearning anti-Semitism, and more recently have begun doing lectures, workshops and radio talks on prostitution."

Tracy Lea Landis: Worked. Her story is a real one about the women who work in the pseudo-legal end of the business, massage parlors. Tracy worked for seven years in massage parlors on the west coast. She was a high school drop-out who has now acquired her high school equivalency and is pursuing a bachelor's degree in the midwest.

Mistress Lilith Lash: "I was born in Oakland in 1944. I grew up in San Francisco, so I didn't need to run away from home to have the North Beach and Haight Ashbury experiences. I got into B&D about ten years ago accidentally through answering *Berkeley Barb* ads. The ads were direct and regarded all sex, a favorite of mine from an early age. The people I met were creative and I discovered I liked the power games, though I don't consider myself a sadist.

About ten years ago, I combined business and pleasure by getting a job, as a dominant. It was a B&D club. Wanting more freedom and hours to write, I went into partnership with girlfriends. I have been writing since grade school and I've been published many times in the last ten years."

Gloria Lockett: "I was born in San Francisco, but raised in Vallejo, a small city to the north of San Francisco. I became pregnant for the first time at sixteen, had a boy and later, a girl. I moved back to San Francisco with my two children when I was eighteen, and got a job as a file clerk at City Hall. After a couple of years, I needed more money and began to work as a food clerk in a supermarket and as a part-time prostitute. Eventually, I became a full-time prostitute, working from 1968 until 1982, first on the street and later in bars, hotels and doing outcalls. More recently, I was hired as an interviewer and outcall coordinator for Project AWARE, an AIDS research project, and as a community health outreach worker for Mid-City Consortium, an AIDS prevention project working with IV users in the Mission District. My experience as a prostitute was an asset in my getting both jobs, as it obviously is in my role as co-director of COYOTE."

Nina Lopez-Jones: is a spokeswoman for the E.C.P. and coordinator of Legal Action for Woman (London), a grassroots legal service for all women. An immigrant to Britain, she lives and works in London.

344

Emma Marcus: "In 1983, I moved to Eugene, Oregon, where I live with my teenage daughter. I work at a straight job, producing educational videotapes. Sometimes I travel to San Francisco to visit my old girlfriends and make money."

Phyllis Luman Metal: "I grew up on one of my grandfather's ranches in western Wyoming. Starting when I was six, I went to Rowland Hall, an Episcopal girls' boarding school in Salt Lake City. I spent my school years there and my summers on the ranch until I graduated when I was seventeen. Shortly afterwards I married a sheep rancher from southern Wyoming. When I was twenty-five, I went to the University of Wyoming and met a soldier who was from New York. We were married and our daughter was born in Santa Barbara, California. Four years later he came back from the war and we moved to Los Angeles where he rejoined his friends in the film industry. I decided to finish my education and graduated with a BA in Social Welfare when I was thirty-six. I married an architectural sculptor from the San Francisco Bay Area and had three daughters by him when I was thirty-seven, thirty-eight and thirty-nine. I worked with him on his art projects and did my own art projects. My life centered around my children and my art until I fell in love with the jazz musician and went to Paris with him. I am now sixty-nine and in graduate school working toward a master's degree."

Peggy Morgan: "I am a writer living in Boston. My work has been published in *bad attitude*, and other publications, under my real name. I am a recovering alcoholic and am still dancing in the Combat Zone. Besides writing and staying sober, I'm kept going by my love for women, motorcycles and travel."

Nell: lives and works in the Bay Area.

Joan Nestle: teaches in the SEEK Program at Queens College/CUNY. She is co-founder of the Lesbian Herstory Archives.

Donna Marie Niles: "When asked to name my article for this anthology, two ideas flashed almost simultaneously before my eyes. The first was: 'I wanted to be a priestess, but in this world, that job description was a prostitute.' The second was from the title of a book: *The women who slept with men to take the war out of them.*

My article was originally written as a speech for a Take Back the Night march in Washington, D.C., in 1984.

I have always experienced feelings of kinship with ex-nuns, and was moved beyond my conscious comprehension when Sonia Johnson transformed from Mormon housewife to Amazon Warrior during my years of similar transition. The powerful connections between my sexual and spiritual, creative and emotional selves emerged from the murky depths. Since acknowledging an identification as both a covert incest survivor and adult child of an alcoholic, two huge pieces of what seemed at age nineteen to be an entirely chosen decision to be a hooker have become clearer.

I am now thirty-one years old. I live with my cats, Betty and Natalie, and work as a bookbuyer for a feminist bookstore. Challenging our dysfunctional, patriarchal, sado-masochistic relationships with a fierce love for ourselves and each other is my idea of a very political act. My lesbian life is precious."

Gail Pheterson: Raised and educated in the United States, Gail Pheterson has lived in the Netherlands since 1975 where she has been an associate professor of Women's Studies and Psychology. Her theoretical and activist work is focused upon building alliances between women (see *Signs*, Vol. 12, No. 1, Autumn 1986). Co-founder of the International Committee for Prostitutes' Rights, she is especially committed to de-isolating, de-stigmatizing, and decriminalizing whore-identified women.

Samara: A veteran of live sex shows in New York City, Samara is twenty-six years old.

Sapphire: A black, lesbian ex-prostitute, Sapphire lives in New York city where she is working on her second novel, *The Last Day of Winter/First Day of Spring*, and a performance piece, *Unknown Female Voices*. She is a Leo with a Taurus moon and Sagittarius rising.

Marjan Sax: born 1947, lives in Amsterdam, Holland. She has been a feminist-activist since the beginning of the women's movement in the early seventies. After majoring in Political Science, she worked in the field of adult education, social research and as a trainer of organizational/strategic skills in women's groups.

Ever since the struggle for free abortion, her main activist activities have been in the realm of the politics of sexuality. 'Sex' and 'money' are the subjects she is interest in most.

Jane Smith: is the pen name of a writer and poet who puts bread on the table by working part-time for a local newspaper. "Writing this piece was one step toward being proud of what I am. Someday, maybe I will feel secure enough to republish it under my own name." Jane lives with her husband of eighteen years and three teenage children in a handmade house on a remote hillside in upstate New York. She has published poems and nonfiction articles in small press and women's periodicals.

Rosie Summers: was one of the most unpopular girls in her high school in her suburban town. She was dressed in cheaper clothes, and she was nervous and shy with other teenagers. At fifteen she left home, went to reform school and then to several foster homes. Two weeks after her eighteenth birthday, she moved to New York City, where she had many brief, heartbreaking affairs with men, and where she often went hungry and even sometimes homeless. She became a prostitute in 1973 and did this work partly because she believed she was receiving love from the men. Now, Rosie is a healthy and self-determined woman. She has attended college for several years, and she plans to go back. She is a writer and a practitioner of the Earth religions.

Debi Sundahl: is publisher of *On Our Backs* and producer of Fatale Video and BurLEZk, a weekly lesbian strip show in San Francisco for women only since 1984.

Terry van der Zijden: born in 1943. Switched from industrial circles to the world of sex work and worked for fifteen years as a prostitute. She has been active in the women's movement since 1976, and in the Red Thread since its founding. She is currently policy manager of the Red Thread.

Hansje Verbeek: born in 1949. After an adventurous life, and a dozen different jobs, Hansje Verbeek decided to study sociology. She became involved in the Pink Thread, and offered to assist the Red Thread. Her interest was not purely academic, but had grown out of earlier experiences as a club manager. She is now coordinator of the Red Thread.

Cecelia Wardlaw: "After my walk on the wild side, and three years without chemicals, I am now more productive than at any other period of my life. I am employed in the drug and alcohol field as a registered nurse. I organized the Women United in Recovery — a group of women recovering from a gamut of addictions, including drugs, alochol, gambling and food — which conducts an annual conference in the Pittsburgh area. I am hard at work finding funding sources for a women's halfway house."

Sarah Wynter: is the founder and editor of *WHISPER*, the only national newsletter written by and for women who have survived systems of prostitution and those who are trying to escape. She has presented her analysis of the conditions that make all women potentially vulnerable to commercial sexual exploitation (and maintain the oppressive status of already prostituted women) at the Seventeenth National Conference on Women and the Law, the Third National NCADV Conference, and the 1986 National NOW Conference, as well as before many university and community groups. In addition to her activism and national organizing efforts, she is currently collecting oral histories of women used in the sex industry. Her findings, which challenge the existing social science paradigms, will be published in a forthcoming book.

Rachel West: is a spokeswoman for U.S. PROS and coordinator of Legal Action for Women (San Francisco). She lives in San Francisco.

ABOUT THE EDITORS

Frédérique Delacoste was born in post-war France. She grew up in Paris, and lived as adventurous a childhood as possible, given the high walls of several boarding schools. She came to the United States in the mid-seventies and finally reached San Francisco in 1983. She has worked as a switchboard operator, a short order cook, a teaching assistant in Ohio; an import manager and bagel delivery person in New York City; a printer's apprentice and bookstore worker in Minnesota; a marketing consultant, a flower merchant and gardener in San Francisco. In 1980, she founded Cleis Press with Felice Newman and Mary Winfrey Trautmann. She co-edited *Fight Back! Feminist Resistance to Male Violence* (Cleis Press, 1981). Currently, she is co-publisher and co-editor at Cleis Press. This book is the most interesting and rewarding feminist work she has ever done.

Priscilla Alexander: "I was born in Boston, raised in New York City. My mother died when I was nine, a couple of years after she almost died in the waiting room of a hospital because we were poor. I had a good education — High School of Music and Art, Bennington College, Bank St. College of Education, San Francisco State University (yes, I moved west) — but I did not become a painter or set designer, my first loves, because no women successfully did either (unless they were lesbians, which I was sure I was not). After years of working as a 'girl Friday' for no money, and hungering to do work with meaning, I became a teacher. Eight years later, I was out of a teaching job, fumbling to find something beyond secretarial work, and, in 1976, found Margo St. James, who taught me to think about prostitution, and about the whore stigma that had paralyzed me in many ways. I am Jewish, a lesbian, a writer, a political activist — I am still poor, but the work fills me up. Oh, identification labels: I am co-director of COYOTE and executive director of the National Task Force on Prostitution. And I listen to prostitutes to whom I am accountable."

CLEIS PRESS

Cleis Press is a nine year old women's publishing company committed to publishing progressive books by women. Order from the office nearest you: *Cleis East,* PO Box 8933, Pittsburgh PA 15221 or *Cleis West,* PO Box 14684, San Francisco CA 94114. Individual orders must be prepaid. Please add 15% shipping/handling. PA and CA residents add sales tax. MasterCard and Visa orders welcome—include account number, exp. date, and signature.

Books from Cleis Press

You Can't Drown the Fire: Latin American Women Writing in Exile edited by Alicia Partnoy. ISBN: 0-939416-16-6 24.95 cloth; ISBN: 0-939416-17-4 9.95 paper.

Unholy Alliances: New Fiction by Women edited by Louise Rafkin. ISBN: 0-939416-14-X 21.95 cloth; ISBN: 0-939416-15-8 9.95 paper.

Sex Work: Writings by Women in the Sex Industry edited by Frédérique Delacoste and Priscilla Alexander. ISBN: 0-939416-10-7 24.95 cloth; ISBN: 0-939416-11-5 9.95 paper.

Different Daughters: A Book by Mothers of Lesbians edited by Louise Rafkin. ISBN: 0-939416-12-3 21.95 cloth; ISBN: 0-939416-13-1 8.95 paper.

The Little School: Tales of Disappearance & Survival in Argentina by Alicia Partnoy. ISBN: 0-939416-08-5 21.95 cloth; ISBN: 0-939416-07-7 8.95 paper.

With the Power of Each Breath: A Disabled Women's Anthology edited by Susan Browne, Debra Connors & Nanci Stern. ISBN: 0-939416-09-3 24.95 cloth; ISBN: 0-939416-06-9 9.95 paper.

Voices in the Night: Women Speaking About Incest edited by Toni A.H. McNaron & Yarrow Morgan. ISBN: 0-939416-02-6 9.95 paper.

Long Way Home: The Odyssey of a Lesbian Mother & Her Children by Jeanne Jullion. ISBN: 0-939416-05-0 8.95 paper.

The Absence of the Dead Is Their Way of Appearing by Mary Winfrey Trautmann. ISBN: 0-939416-04-2 8.95 paper.

Woman-Centered Pregnancy & Birth by the Federation of Feminist Women's Health Centers. ISBN: 0-939416-03-4 11.95 paper.

Fight Back! Feminist Resistance to Male Violence edited by Frédérique Delacoste & Felice Newman. ISBN: 0-939416-01-8 13.95 paper.

On Women Artists: Poems 1975-1980 by Alexandra Grilikhes. ISBN: 0-939416-00-X 4.95 paper.